AF557847

All in One, One in All

Oriental Institute of Chicago, USA, September 11, 2018

Dr. Hari Prasad Kanoria's objective is to ignite in all, the righteousness, harmony and peace of religions, humanity, inner power and balance the other power through spirituality.

All in One, One in All

Dr. Hari Prasad Kanoria

HAR-ANAND PUBLICATIONS PVT LTD
E-49/3, Okhla Industrial Area, Phase-II, New Delhi-110020
Tel.: 41603490
E-mail: info@haranandbooks.com/haranand@rediffmail.com
Shop online at: www.haranandbooks.com

Published by Ashok Gosain and Ashish Gosain for
Har-Anand Publications Pvt Ltd

Printed in India at Aarya Press

THE RAMAKRISHANA MISSION INSTITUTE OF CULTURE

(A Branch Centre of Ramakrishna Mission, P.O. Belur Math, dist. Howrah, West Bengal – 711 202)
GOLPARK KOLKATA – 700 029, WEST BENGAL, INDIA
Phone: 033-4030-1200, 2464-1303/04/05, 2466-1235/36/37
Fax: 033-2464-1307;E-Mail: golpark.rmic@rkmm.org, rmic.golpark@gmail.com, rmic.secretary@gmail.com;
Website : www.sriramakrishna.org

December 14, 2019

FOREWORD

I have the occasion to see the book titled "All in One, One in All" written by Dr. H. P. Kanoria. The book is based on values and his concept on spirituality. Prior to this book his other widely circulated book Enlightenment was well appreciated by all section of readers.

Dr. H. P. Kanoria is a business tycoon with a difference. Himself a Presidencian of the Economics Department, Dr. Kanoria could have been a great Economist of repute. But he chose to be an industrialist not because he wanted to build a huge fortune for himself but because he wanted to serve his country, indeed his Mother, by providing shelter to as many of her children as possible. By the grace of the Mother that happened much to his satisfaction.

His business net-work got spread all over the country now and is being looked after successfully by his able children. Dr. Kanoria is now supremely happy involving himself in exploring the mystery of the Inner life. I am happy for my association with this ardent devotee of the Divine who is now least bothered about his business but very much concerned, instead, with the future of Humanity. He is receiving unstinting support from his family to carry out his charity, to hold seminars, programmes of immense proportions, publish books on values and so on.

From his articles and books and devotional service it is obvious that his only desire is to infuse among the people the lofty ideal of seeking the dignity of man and thus build a Civil Society everywhere. The Mother will surely bless him in fulfilling his pious endeavour.

I wish all success for this book.

Swami Suparnananda

(From L-R) Dr. Hari Prasad Kanoria, Chairman, World Confluence of Humanity, Power and Spirituality, Shri Tathagata Roy, Governor of Meghalaya, Dr. Subramanian Swamy, Member of Parliament (Rajya Sabha) and Dr. Sanjeev Kanoria at the 12th World Confluence of Humanity, Power & Spirituality at Kolkata, on December 28, 2019.

Contents

Message by Sri Sri Ravi Shankarji

All in One, One in All

SACH BHARAT - SACH VISVA

ॐ सर्वे भवन्तु सुखिनः
सर्वे सन्तु निरामयाः ।
सर्वे भद्राणि पश्यन्तु
मां कश्चिद् दुःख भाग्भवेत् ।
ॐ शान्तिः शान्तिः शान्तिः ॥

oum sarve bhavantu sukhinah
sarve santu niramayah|
sarve bhadrani pasyantu
mam kascid duhkha bhagbhavet|
oum santih santih santih ||

May all be happy (sukhinah);
May all be healthy (niraamayaa)!
May all look (pasyatu) to the good of others;
May none suffer from sorrow (dukkha).
Om Peace, Peace, Peace.

Universal Prayer

O God! Thou art our Father, Mother, Friend,
We, thy children, love thee and our parents.
Thou art in our hearts and minds,
Make us fearless.

Thou art in Temple, Church, Mosque, everywhere
Thou art in Vedas, Bible, Koran, Gurugranth, all scriptures,
O God! Thou infinite's reflection in all living beings,
Love reflects as love

Thou art alone the truth.
In motherly way thou forbear us,
Life is a joyous journey,
Love and service that matter, all worship to Thee.

Joy, sorrow, censure, fame,
We bear all equally with thy blessed strength.
What we sow, we must reap,
No one but us to blame.

We have Eternal faith in the self in all,
O God! Grant us a mutual intimacy with Thee,
Bless us with love, wisdom, intellect, virtues,
Lead us through paths of trouble to perfection.

Thou art our Master, Thou art our soul's real friend,
Guide us in our daily activities and lead us,
Fearless, we are marching ahead to make Bharat- World
O God! never turn away from us, thy children.

We surrender our will at the altar of Thy will.
We love Thee, Thou love us
Thou love our complete surrender.
We aspire for work, knowledge and devotion

Work, work, for the world.
Love, love, love
Peace, peace and peace
Om, Amen, Amin, Ek Onkar, Ahura Mazda
God, God, God.

Dr. H. P. Kanoria

सार्वभौमिक प्रार्थना

तुम्ही हो माता पिता, तुम्हीं हो बंधु सखा हितकारी
हम हैं बालक तेरे, करते हैं प्रेम तुझ से, माता पिता से।
तुम्हीं हो हमारे हृदय और मन में
हे प्रभु बनाओ हमें निडर और निर्भय।

तू ही मंदिर, मस्जिद गिरजा में
वेद, बाइबिल, कुरान, गुरुग्रंथ, सभी ग्रंथों में
हे प्रभु! है तेरा अनंत प्रतिबिंब सभी प्राणियों में
प्रेम ही प्रेम के रूप में झलकता है।

तुम्हीं हो एकमात्र सत्य अनंत
माँ की तरह रखते हो हमारा ध्यान
जीवन है एक आनन्द, अनंत यात्रा
तुम्हें अर्पण कर्म, तन, मन, प्राण
दुख में, सुख में, मान अपमान में
तेरी कृपा से, हम करते हैं सहन
जो बीज हम बोते वही फसल पाते हैं।
निज कर्म का फल स्वयं ही भोगते हैं।

सभी जीवों का अंतरात्मा में है, अटूट विश्वास
हे प्रभु! स्नेह-प्रेग का संबंध है तुम्ही से।
हमें दो प्यार, आशीष, ज्ञान, बुद्धि और गुण,
मुसीबतों के पथ पर हाथ थामें ले चलो हमें अग्रिम।

तुम्हीं हो हमारे स्वामी, तुम्ही हो आत्मा के परम प्रिय बंधु
दैनिक कर्मों में मार्ग दर्शन करते रहे हमारा
निर्भय बढ़ते रहे निरंतर, बनाने को भारत-विश्व
हे प्रभु! हमसे दूर न होना, हम बच्चे तेरे ही।
समर्पण है हमारा आपकी सभी इच्छाओं पर
हमें हैं प्यार आपसे, आपको है प्यार हमसे
करते हैं संपूर्ण समर्पण आपके ही प्यार में
कर्म, ज्ञान, और भक्ति की लग्न रहे हमें

प्रियवर यही प्रार्थना हमारी
विश्व हित में निस्वार्थ करें कर्म
रहें निरंतर कर्मलीन, बिन फल आशा के
विश्व शांति, प्रगति है लक्ष्य हमारा
ॐ एक ओंकार, अहुरा मज्दा, आमीन, अमीन
हम आपके, आप हमारे
प्रभु! प्रभु! प्रभु!
शांति, शांति, शांति!

Dr. H.P. Kanoria

सार्वत्रिक प्रार्थना

हे प्रभो! हे ईश्वर! त्वमेव मे माता पिता मित्राणि च
तवैवाप्त्यानि वयं त्वयि पित्रोश्च च स्निहयाम्:
त्वञ्चास्ति अस्न्मनः प्राणसु
मा भैरिति मन्त्रेण आशीश्चकार अस्मान् निर्भयं निर्दु:खंच झिवनम्।
मन्दिरमस्जिदगीर्जादिभेदेन सर्वत्र ते वास:
गुरुग्रन्थवेदवाइवेलकोरानाइभेदाच्च सर्वत्र ते दिव्य मास्थानम्।
हे प्रभो! विराट! सर्वजीवेषु त एव प्रकाश:
तवैव प्रेम्ना प्रेममयेन सता सर्वजीवेषु ते बास:।

त्वमेवानन्त: सत्यसारश्च
मात्रिस्नेहेन च सहसे न:।
कृपया ते वयमानन्दिता:
जीवसेवया जीवप्रेम्ना च त्वमेवपुज्यते।
क्रुपया ते शक्त्या ते निर्वहामो वयं
सकलसुखदु:खमानापमानानि जीवितेषु।
कर्मबीजानि अस्माभिरेवोप्तानि, तत्फलानि चास्माभिरेव भोक्तव्यानि
नान्येषां दोषा: केषाञ्चित, अस्माभिरेव वहिष्यन्ते भारा:।

हे प्रभो! सर्वजीवानामान्त: स्थलेषु विद्यमाने देवत्वे एवास्ति मे विश्वास:
येनानीयते त्वय प्रेमबन्धनं, तदेवास्तु मे जीवितावलम्बनम्।
भजनप्रेमसद्भद्ध्या पुरयतु नो जीवनानि
संग्राममयेऽस्मिन् जीवने आनय महती सा पूर्णता।
हे ईश्वर! त्वमेवास्माकं शाश्वत: प्रभु:
नश्वरेऽस्मिन् जीविते चेतसोऽमरो मित्रम्।
संसार नित्यकर्मभ्यो वियोजय हे प्रभो!

निर्भयेन चेतसा पूरयिष्यामो महल्लक्ष्यानि भारतनिर्माण विश्वनिर्माण्योः।
हे प्रभो! मा विमुंचास्मान्! वयं तवैवापत्यानि
इच्चास्माकं सर्वा अर्पिताः त्वय्येव।
त्वैव प्रेम्ना वयमभिसिञ्चिता विश्वप्रेम्ना
समर्पितानि नो जीवितानि चरणयोस्ते।
हे महाप्राणा! नियोजयस्वास्मान् सेवनभजनभक्तिसु ते।

सेवस्व, सेवस्व, सेवस्व, प्रेम्ना विश्वप्रेम्ना च पुरयस्व नो जीवितानि।
शान्तिः शान्तिः शान्तिः
ओम् आमेन इति आमिन् इति एक एव ओंकारः आहरा इति माजदा इति
हे ईश्वर! रभुरस्माकम् ।।

Dr. H. P. Kanoria

Reverence to the Supreme Lord

To Him, the most exalted Lord offer reverence.
To Him, who rules the past, the present and the future.
Who presides over the entire universe.
Who is the overall sovereign of the world and the cosmos.
Who is above the reach at the time of death.
Who is immutable and absolute Bliss.
Who is immense in vastness.
Whose glory is unparalleled.
Around whom all the planets of the universe move.
Who commands all the world, existent or non-existent.
To Him in most reverence, we bow again and again.
To His glory we sing the songs of love of soul.

Dr. H. P. Kanoria
- Based on the Holy Vedas

Prayer to Mother Saraswati

O Mother Saraswati! Thou art the embodiment of knowledge
Thou art the embodiment of wisdom
Thou art the embodiment of intelligence
Thou art the embodiment of intellect
Thou art the embodiment of intuition and conscience
Thou art the embodiment of the discrimination
Between good and the bad
Thou art the embodiment of music, art and culture
Thou art the embodiment of all Goddesses.
Thou art the essence of the great Vedanta
Thou art like the swan, separating the milk and water
Thou art full of perfection
Thou art the symbol of purity in white apparel
Thou art sitting on a white lotus
Thou art holding a veena in thy hand
Thou have the white rosary in thy hand
Thou play the veena for the message of
Love, peace and Harmony.
Thou art the instrumental fall of egoistic beings.
Thou art being adored by Lord Brahma,
Lord Vishnu, Lord Shankara and all the Devas,
Thou radiate the joy of divine bliss
Thou art the giver of boons.
Mother! Lead us to perfection in
Thy motherly way
Mother, never turn thy radiant, gracious face from Thy children.
Maa Veena Pani we contemplate on Thee,
We meditate on thee.
Mother keep us free from ego
Mother grant us knowledge, wisdom
Intelligence, intellect, conscience and indiscrimination
Mother bless us to hear thy voice within our heart
We children bow at Thy lotus feet again and again.

Dr. H. P. Kanoria

माँ शारदा की प्रार्थना

हे माँ शारदा! तुम ज्ञान का अवतार हो,
मनीषा का अवतार हो,
प्रज्ञा का अवतार हो,
बुद्धि का अवतार हो,
अत: प्रज्ञा और विवेक का अवतार हो,
अच्छाई और बुराई में विभेद का अवतार हो,
कला, संगीत और संस्कृति का अवतार हो,
संपूर्ण देवियों का अवतार हो,
महान वेदान्त के सारांश का अवतार हो,
हंस की भाँति नीर-क्षीर विवेकवान
तुम पूर्णता का अवतार हो।
श्वेत कमल-आसीन,
श्वेत वस्त्रधारिणी,
एक हाथ में थामे वीणा,
दूसरे में श्वेत सुमरिनी,
वीणावादन से प्रेम, शान्ति
और सौहार्द्र का संदेश देती
अहंकार विनाशिनी
ब्रह्मा, विष्णु, महेश, देवाधिगण
करते जिसका वंदन
माँ! अपनी ममता से हमें
पूर्णता की ओर बढ़ाओ,
माँ! अपने बालकों से अपना
गरिमामय मुख न छिपाओ,
माँ वीणापाणि हम तुम्हारा मनन करते,
निरन्तर तुम्हारा ध्यान धरते,
माँ! अहं से हमें मुक्ति दो,
माँ! हमें ज्ञान, प्रज्ञा, विवेक-बुद्धि दो।
आशीष दो कि अंतर्मन का स्वर सुन पाएँ,
हम बालक तुम्हारे चरण कमलों पर
शीश झुकाते हैं बारम्बार।

Dr. H. P. Kanoria
Translation from English

सरस्वतै क्रियमाना प्रार्थना

हे मातः सरस्वती! तव
कलाते ज्ञान प्रतिबिम्विका।
शिल्पकर्म ते पाण्डित्य प्रतिबिम्विम् ।।
कलाते बुद्धि प्रतिबिम्बिका।
शिल्पकर्म ते स्वतःस्फुर्तज्ञान च विवेक प्रतिबिम्बिम् ।।
कलाते शुभाशुभविभाजक प्रतिबिम्विका।
शिल्पकर्म ते गीतकलासंस्कृति प्रतिबिम्विम् ।।
कलाते सकलदेवीनाम् प्रतिबिम्बिका।
शिल्मकर्म ते वेदान्तस्वरूपकम् ।।
शिल्मकर्म ते क्षिराम्वुनीः राजहंसवत् भेदकारिणि।
कलाते पूर्णात्मिका।
कलाते शुभ्रवस्त्ररूपपूतप्रतीकमयी ।।
शिल्पकर्म ते श्वेतपद्मासनास्थितम्।
कलाते स्वहस्तयोः वीणाधृति ।।
शिल्पकर्म ते स्वहस्तेजपमालाधृतम्।
वीणा वादनम् ते प्रेमशान्ति सौभ्रातृत्वख्यापनाय।
मोहग्रस्तजनानां मोहाप सारयितृ ते वीणावादम्।
कलाते ब्रह्मणा विष्णुणा शङ्ग्करेम शिष्टैश्च देवैः संस्तुता।
मातः, त्वम् दिव्याशीष प्रदानेन हर्षम् व्त्तनुषै।
शिल्पकर्म ते वरप्रदायितृ ।।
मातः! स्नेहमयेनपथा नः पूर्णतां प्रापय।
मातः! स्वापत्यभ्य आशीर्वादादिकम् न निराकुरु।
मातः वीणापाणि वयम् त्वां ध्यायामः।
त्वयि मनंसिनिवेशयामः।
मातः प्रदद ज्ञानबुद्धि पाण्डित्यभेदबुद्धिः।
मातः अशीः प्रदद यथा स्वहृदयेषु नादम् श्रतुमर्हाः स्त्राम।
वयम् ते अपत्यानि चरणकमलयोः भूयोः नमामः ।।

Dr. H. P. Kanoria
Translation from English

All in One, One in All

All in One, One in All
God calls! O Children.
Realise, All in One, One in All.
Behave with others as you would with yourself.
Look upon all the livings as your bosom friends.
Know that in all of them resides one soul.
All are but parts of that universal soul.
Believe all are your soul mates, love all alike.
Awaken the divine qualities of forgiveness,
compassion and service.
That will make you lovable in the eyes of all.
Withdraw from all strife and struggles of life.
Harbor no enmity for anyone in your heart.
Fear no one, have sublime peace.
Experience intense joy.
Feel secure under God's infinite shelter

– Based on the Holy Vedas-'

God Calls O Leader!

O Leader! Realise that the people have elected you.
Be just and merciful; Be just and firm.
Be strong, just, wise, honest, spiritual
Like a lion drive away all evil forces by being strengthened by people.
Be formidable and firm like a rock;
Follow the path of duty.
Be trusty of wealth and nature of the Nation.
Engage the people in hard work with honesty and righteousness.
Be not engaged in popularist measures squandering the wealth of Nation

Do not tax the people heavily.
Do not create the army of idle people.
Trust in the children of Nation, Help them to create wealth.
Never create conflict among minority and majority.
Promote unity in diversity.
Protect merchants, warriors, artisans and all who build Nation.
Protect women, children and senior citizens.
Live like a saint, not only appear like a saint.
Work hard, be fearless, be spiritual, believe in essence of all religions.
Have uniform laws for all the people.

Dr. H. P. Kanoria

सच भारत - गीत

ले आए...सच भारत
दिखायें... सच भारत...
आओ समझे और समझाएं
सारी दुनियां को दिखायें, बतायें
कर्म करो, सेवा करो.. फल की आशा मत करो
प्रेम करो करुणा करो... द्वेष की भाषा मत करो
बनाओ विश्व को सच... सच भारत
बता दो विश्व को ये सच... सच भारत

बाल जो चलो थी
हिमालय के उस पार से
बात जो बही थी
कभी गंगा की धार से
सेहरा की रेत से, बागों से खेत से
कि बस इंसान मान ये धरम है।

बात जो छुपी है कबीर के राम में
बाल जो लिखी है...
इकबाल के कलाम में
बुद्ध के पैगाम में... नानक सतनाम में
सारे संसार का ये सार प्यार एवं कर्म
बता दो विश्व को ये सच... सच भारत
प्रांत धर्म बाली है अलग पर एक चाह है
नेक है इरादे और अपनी नेक राह है
गिरे कोई तो उठायें हम
नयी रोशनी की ओर जा रहा सच भारत

मानवता धर्म है... और प्रार्थना... सच भारत
सत्य के मार्ग की... संकल्पना... सच भारत
बंध्यता अखंडता... न्याय है विश्वास है
जल की हर बूंद में... किसानों की आस है
गीता कुरान... महान... मन्त्र भी... सच भारत।

Dr. H. P. Kanoria

An Enlightened Being

All human beings are children of God.
All living beings are manifestation of God.
Love all intensely conceiving a part of Universal soul.
Do not look down on anyone.
No one is lower or higher.
Never hate anyone.
Never fall victim of hatred, grief or sorrow.
Too much wealth makes one greedy.
Feel and affirm that of being trustee of wealth.
Create and generate wealth for welfare of God's creation.
Flow with the stream of love for all and happiness.
Be enriched by love of all.
Perform all acts with devotion and full wisdom.
With submission and glorious vision of God.
Pray for God's love and release of all bondages.
With meditating mind and heart full of love.
Be noblest of all.
Have glorious success and humble fame.

Dr. H. P. Kanoria
- Based on the Holy Vedas

Ganesh Stotra

वक्रतुण्ड महाकाय सूर्यकोटि समप्रभः ।
निर्विघ्नं कुरु मे देव सर्वकार्येषु सर्वदा ।।

Vakratunda maaakaaya suryakoti samaprabha |
Nirvighnam kuru me deva sarva kaaryesu sarvadaa ||

(I meditate on Sri Ganesha)
Who has a Curved Trunk, Large Body,
Who has the Brilliance of a Million Suns,
O Lord, Please make all my Works, free of Obstacles, always.

Ganesh Vandanaa

गजाननं भूतगणादि सेवितं, कपित्थ जम्बूफलसार भक्षितम् ।
उमासुतं शोक बिनाशकारणं, नमामि विघ्नेश्वर पादपंकजम् ।।

Gajaananam bhuutaganaadi sevitam,
kapittha jambuuphalasaara bhaksitam |
Umasutam shoka binaashakaaranam,
namaami vighneshvara paadapamkajam ||

I bow to Gajaanana, who is having an elephant face; who is served by the bhuta gana means celestial attendance or followers, and others, who eats the core of kapittha and jambu fruits. Who is the son of Devi Uma and who destructs all sorrows from life. I prostrate at the lotus-feet of Vigneswara means the God who removes all obstacles of life.

Mahalakshmi Stuti

आदिलक्ष्मि नमस्तेऽस्तु परब्रह्मस्वरुपिणि ।
यशो देहि धनं देहि सर्वकामांश्च देहि मे ।। 1 ।।

adilakshmi namaste&stu parabrahmasvarupini |
yaso dehi dhanam dehi sarvakamamsca dehi me ||1||

Salutations to the AdilakShmi, who is the embodiment of the Absolute, give me fame, give me wealth, fulfill all my desires. 1

सन्तानलक्ष्मि नमस्तेऽस्तु पुत्रपौत्रप्रदायिनि ।
सन्तानलक्ष्मि वन्देऽहं पुत्रान् देहि धनं देहि सर्वकामांश्च देहि मे ।। 2 ।।

santanalakshmi namaste&stu putrapautrapradayini |
santanalakshmi vande&ham putran dehi dhanam dehi sarvakamamsca dehi me ||2||

Salutations to SanthanalakShmi, who is the giver of sons and grandsons give me sons, give me wealth, fulfill all my desires. 2

विद्यालक्ष्मि नमस्तेऽस्तु ब्रह्मविद्यास्वरुपिणि ।
विद्यां देहि कलां देहि सर्वकामांश्च देहि मे ।। 3 ।।

vidyalakshmi namaste&stu brahmavidyasvarupini |
vidyam dehi kalam dehi sarvakamamsca dehi me ||3||

Salutations to VidyalakShmi, who is the embodiment of the Highest Knowledge of the Absolute
give me knowledge, give me the arts, fulfill all my desires. 3

धनलक्ष्मि नमस्तेऽस्तु सर्वदारिंद्र्यनाशिनि ।
धनं देहि श्रियं देहि सर्वकामांश्च देहि मे ।। 4 ।।

dhanalakshmi namaste&stu sarvadaridrayanasini |
dhanam dehi sriyam dehi sarvakamamsca dehi me ||4||

Salutations to DhanalakShmi, who is the destroyer of all forms of poverty give me wealth, give me prosperity, fulfill all my desires. 4

धान्यलक्ष्मि नमस्तेऽस्तु सर्वाभरणभूषिते ।
धान्यं देहि धनं देहि सर्वकामांश्च देहि मे ॥ 5 ॥

dhanyalakshmi namaste&stu sarvabharanabhushite |
dhanyam dehi dhanam dehi sarvakamamsca dehi me ||5||

Salutations to DhanyalakShmi, who is decorated with all ornaments give me food grains, give me wealth, fulfill all my desires. 5

मेधालक्ष्मि नमस्तेऽस्तु कलिकल्मषनाशिनि ।
प्रज्ञां देहि श्रियं देहि सर्वकामांश्च देहि मे ॥ 6 ॥

medhalakshmi namaste&stu kalikalmashanasini |
praj~jam dehi sriyam dehi sarvakamamsca dehi me ||6||

Salutations to medhAlakShmi, who is the destroyer of the evil effects of Kali Yuga give me wisdom or awareness, give me prosperity, fulfill all my desires. 6

गजलक्ष्मि नमस्तेऽस्तु सर्वदेवस्वरुपिणि ।
अश्वांश्च गोकुलं देहि सर्वकामांश्च देहि मे ॥ 7 ॥

gajalakshmi namaste&stu sarvadevasvarupini |
asvamsca gokulam dehi sarvakamamsca dehi me ||7||

Salutations to GajalakShmi, who is the embodiment of all the Gods give me horses and cows, fulfill all my desires. 7

धीरलक्ष्मि नमस्तेऽस्तु पराशक्तिस्वारुपिणि ।
वीर्यं देहि बलं देहि सर्वकामांश्च देहि मे ॥ 8 ॥

dhiralakshmi namaste&stu parasaktisvarupini |
viryam dehi balam dehi sarvakamamsca dehi me ||8||

Salutations to DhiralakShmi, who is the embodiment of Absolute Energy give me valour, give me strength, fulfill all my desires. 8

जयलक्ष्मि नमस्तेऽस्तु सर्वकार्यजयप्रदे ।
जयं देहि शुभं देहि सर्वकामांश्च देहि मे ॥ 9 ॥

jayalakshmi namaste&stu sarvakaryajayaprade |
jayam dehi subham dehi sarvakamamsca dehi me ||9||

Salutations to JayalakShmi, the giver of success in all endeavours give me victory or success, give me auspicousness, fulfill all my desires. 9

भाग्यलक्ष्मि नमस्तेऽस्तु सौमंगल्यविवर्धिनि ।
भाग्यं देहि श्रियं देहि सर्वकामांश्च देहि मे ॥ 10 ॥

bhagyalakshmi namaste&stu saumamgalyavivardhini |
bhagyam dehi sriyam dehi sarvakamamsca dehi me ||10||

Salutations to bhagyalakShmi, who fosters auspiciousness give me good fortune, give me prosperity, fulfill all my desires. 10

कीर्तिलक्ष्मि नमस्तेऽस्तु विष्णुवक्षस्थलस्थिते ।
कीर्ति देहि श्रियं देहि सर्वकामांश्च देहि मे ॥ 11 ॥

kirtilakshmi namaste&stu vishnuvakshasthalasthite |
kirtim dehi sriyam dehi sarvakamamsca dehi me ||11||

Salutations to KirtilakShmi, who abodes in the chest of Vishnu give me success or attainment, give me prosperity, fulfill all my desires.

आरोग्यलक्ष्मि नमस्तोऽस्तु सर्वरोगनिवारणि ।
आरोग्यलक्ष्मि वन्देऽहं आयुर्देहि श्रियं देहि सर्वकामांश्च देहि मे ॥ 12 ॥

arogyalakshmi namaste&stu sarvaroganivarani |
arogyalakshmi vande&ham ayurdehi sriyam dehi sarvakamamsca dehi me ||12||

Salutations to Arogyalaksmi, who destroys all diseases and illnesses
give me long life, give me prosperity,
fulfill all my desires. 12

सिद्धलक्ष्मि नमस्तेऽस्तु सर्वसिद्धि प्रदायिनि ।
सिद्धिं देहि श्रियं देहि सर्वकामांश्च देहि मे ।। 13 ।।

siddhalakshmi namaste&stu sarvasiddhipradayini |
siddhim dehi sriyam dehi sarvakamasca dehi me ||13||

Salutations to SiddhalakShmi, the giver of all siddhis
(attainments or spiritual powers)
give me siddhis, give me prosperity, fulfill all my desires. 13

सौन्दर्यलक्ष्मि नमस्तेऽस्तु सर्वालंकारशोभिते ।
सौन्दर्यलक्ष्मि वन्देऽहं रुपं देहि श्रियं देहि सर्वकामांश्च देहि मे ।। 14 ।।

saundaryalakshmi namaste&stusarvalamkarasobhite |
saundaryalakshmi vande&ham rupam dehi sriyam dehi
sarvakamasca dehi me ||14||

Salutations to SaundaryalakShmi, one who shines with all
decorations give me beauty, give me prosperity, fulfill
all my desires. 14

साम्राज्यलक्ष्मि नमस्तेऽस्तु भुक्तिमुक्ति प्रदायिनि ।
साम्राज्यलक्ष्मि वन्देऽहं मोक्षं देहि श्रियं देहि सर्वकामांश्च देहि मे ।। 15 ।।

samrajyalakshmi namaste&stu bhuktimuktipradayini |
samrajyalakshmi vande&ham moksham dehi sriyam dehi
sarvakamasca dehi me ||15||

Salutations to SamrajyalakShmi, who gives enjoyment and
liberation give me liberation, give me prosperity,
fulfill all my desires. 15

मंगले मंगलाधारे मांगल्ये मंगलप्रदे ।
मंगलार्थं मंगलेशि मांगल्यं देहि मे ।। 16 ।।

mamgale mamgaladhare mamgalye mamgalaprade |
mamgalartham mamgalesi mamgalyam dehi me sada ||16||

Oh Auspicious one, giver of all forms of auspiciousness such as the mangalyam for the sake of auspiciousness, oh auspicious one, always give me mAngalayam. 16

सर्वमंगलमांगल्ये शिवे सर्वार्थसाधिके ।
शरण्ये त्रयम्बके देवि नारायणि नमोऽस्तु ते ।। 17 ।।

sarvamamgalamamgalye sive sarvarthasadhike |
saranye trayambake devi narayani namo&stu te ||17||

I salute and take refuge in Narayani, the three-eyed one, who gives all auspiciousness, who is herself auspicuous and who fulfils all desires. 17

शुभं भवतु कल्याणी आयुरारोग्यसम्पदाम्! ।
मम शत्रु विनाशाय दीपज्योति नमोऽस्तु ते ।। 18 ।।

subham bhavatu kalyani ayurarogyasampadam |
mama satruvinasaya dipajyoti namo&stu te ||18||

Salutations to the flame of the lamp, which gives auspiciousness and prosperity, gives long and disease free life and destroys all my enemies .18

Work hard with devotion righteously and selflessly for the welfare of humanity

Dr. Hari Prasad Kanoria at World Congress on Vedic Foundations of Management Science – Commemorating 125th year of Chicago Lecture of Swami Vivekananda at Oriental Institute of Chicago, USA on September 11, 2018

Sisters and Brothers.

I am privileged, honoured and blessed to present my understanding on the message and teachings of Swami Vivekananda who was an Enlightened Monk, a great reformer, a preaching Nationalist, a great humanist and an illuminated soul. His master Sri Ramakrishna Paramhansa said in spiritual love with tears of joy and in a sobbing voice, "You are Nar Rupi Narayan- incarnation of Narayan (God). You are Gyan - Siddha (Enlightened) Puratan Sanyasi. You have come for reform, awakening, removing the miseries of people and for service to humanity". Later Thakur denied him Nirivakal Samadhi — Liberation - Union with God. He told him to serve humanity which is worship of God.

In Chicago, USA Swami Vivekananda said with the voice of a lion, "I am proud to belong to a religion- Hinduism, which has taught

the world both Universal tolerance and acceptance. We accept all religions as True. The Hindu religion is the oldest surviving religion without a beginning and an end. It is perpetual and eternal (sanatana). It is based on divine revelation and realisation. It was the communication with cosmic entity (God) by the several enlightened rishis, saints and sages.

He addressed , "Hear, Ye children of Immortal bliss". It is sin to call a man a sinner. It is a standing label on human nature. Come up, O Lionsshake off the delusion that you are sheep, you are soul, immortal, spirit free, blessed and eternal. Ye are not matter, ye are not bodies. Matter is your servant, not you the servant of matter.

God is everywhere – the Almighty and the all merciful. He is our father, mother and friend. He is the source of all strength. Love Him for love's sake. Live in this world like a lotus leaf. Soul is divine. When the soul becomes perfect and enlightened it is freed from the bondage of body matter. Bondage can fall off through the mercy of God. Mercy comes on the pure. God reveals Himself to the pure heart. On attaining perfection, one lives a life of bliss infinite. The ultimate happiness is reached with universal consciousness.

Science is in finding unity. Its goal is to reach perfect unity. Chemistry's goal is to discover one element out of which all others could be made. Physics discovers one energy of which all others are but manifestations. So, science has proved that physical individuality is a delusion. Advaita said that Unity is the necessary conclusion of the other counterpart of the soul. There is one universal soul. All other souls are delusive manifestation of that universal soul. Lord Krishna said in Gita that the entire Universe has been manifested from my form. All beings are dependent upon me, but I am not dependent on them.

मया ततम् इदम्स र्वम् । जगद् अव्यक्त-मूर्तिना ।
मत्-स्थानि सर्व-भूतानि । न चाहम् तैष्व् अवस्थितः ।।

mayā tatam idam sarvam | jagad avyakta-mūrtinā |
mat-sthāni sarva-bhūtāni | na cāhaḿ teṣv avasthitaḥ | |

He is retaining this universe by a single fragment of Himself. Manifestation and not creation is the word of science.

Every religion is evolving a God out of material man. It is the same light coming through the glasses of different colours. The pictures of all bodies and all things are only rays of light streaming out of that one sacred light. Behold everywhere the pure spirit. We are children of the Almighty. We are sparks of the infinite divine force. Losing faith in one's self means losing faith in God. Work for union with whole humanity and God. Perform selfless action for the welfare of all – His manifestation. Be free from attachment, fear and anger and fully absorbed in God. Be purified by knowledge and devotion. Meditation may help to attain union with Him. Have unwavering faith in God. Love parents. Have balanced and healthy food. Food contains all the energies that build the body and mind. Avoid indigestible meal, meat and alcohol. It is hard to control body and mind with these foods.

Every youth must develop his personality with the characteristics of individuality. Play the role efficiently with perfection. Be self-motivated. Do hard work with devotion. Have integrity and discipline. Have faith in self and love for all and the Supreme Lord.

Have muscles of iron and nerves of steel. Be courageous and fearless. Face the brutes. Face the Maya. Face the Death. Cowards can never be victorious.

God is pleased where women are held in esteem. There is no chance for the welfare of the world unless the condition of women is improved. It is not possible for a bird to fly on one wing. Do work for the freedom and equality of women. Realise her importance for the functioning of home and society. Women are coming forward with a combination of a mother's heart and hero's will.

Swami Vivekananda said, "I believe in God, I believe in Man. I believe in helping the miserable. I believe in going even to hell to save others. I may have to be born again because I have fallen in love with man."

Love and service will make our every word sound like thunderbolt.

After his father's death, he was in dire calamities of having no food for days together for the family and himself. He could not even get job though was a graduate. His master told him to go to Mother Kali and ask her. He could not ask for himself though he went thrice to the goddess. He asked, "Beloved Ma, give me wisdom, conscience, intelligence, love for all and Ma and service to humanity." He was blessed by his Master for having the simple essentials of life.

Brothers and Sisters let us awake, arise and work hard with devotion righteously and selflessly for the welfare of humanity listening to the call given by Swami Vivekananda and Lord Krishna in Mahabharata. Let us serve the Living God who is in all and outside all.

Love is religion. Love is God. Service to humanity is worship of God.

The purpose of religion is spirituality. It is for assimilation, not for destruction

Dr. Hari Prasad Kanoria at the International Conference on Spiritual-Based Management organised on October 12-13, 2018 in Athens, Greece.

Brothers and sisters of Greece and the world. I am honoured and humbled by this invitation to speak on spirituality and humanity at this august conclave. My sincere thanks to the organisers for kindly giving me this opportunity to be amidst all of you today. Unfortunately, I could not be present in person due to my recent long stay in the US and London. Also, during these days, we have to worship Goddess Durga, the Mother of the Universe, who is the protector of humanity. She is omnipresent, omniscient, and omnipotent. Her heart is flowing with the ocean of motherly love and bliss. She is the destroyer of evil and protector of the righteous. She works for the welfare of humanity and is the giver of prosperity, health, and happiness.

Spirituality fosters morality, character, values, ethics. It makes one work hard with devotion, selflessness, the spirit of brotherhood and sisterhood, growth, empathy, sympathy, humility, kindness, fraternity, cooperative spirit, fearlessness, and divinity with love. It sharpens the intellect to distinguish between right and wrong. The spiritual light within unfolds the truth. It awakens the inner power and balances the outer power. It guides to develop super-consciousness. It enables us to develop our body, mind and soul to ward off allure and dive into the ocean of success. It develops the perception of oneness. It includes the entire humanity. It guides us through all stages of life. It unfolds our infinity. It helps our magnetic personality to blossom. It teaches us to balance in life for hard work, health, emotion, family and service to humanity. Religion means realisation and experience. It is not just ritual, rites, etc. All these methods are to synchronize body and mind to concentrate on some physical activities. After realisation, experiencing and seeing the light within, and then hearing the cosmic voices, enlightened men have established different religions.

All religions lead to Cosmic Entity. The purpose of religion is spirituality. It is for assimilation, not for destruction. Spirituality ignites the fire of love and service to Humanity.

God is the universal Father. There is one universal soul. We are manifested souls of One Universal soul. He is our Father, Mother and Friend. The essence of all religions is harmony, peace, humanity, love and unity in diversity. Science has proved that physical individuality is a delusion. Science is in finding unity. Its goal is to reach perfect unity. Chemistry's goal is to discover one element from which all others could be made. Physics discovers one element out of which, all are created/expanded/subdued. Hindu scriptures in the Bhagwad Gita spoke about the incarnation of Lord Krishna. Lord Krishna said, "The entire universe has been manifested from my form. All beings are dependent upon me but I am not dependent on them."

God is all-pervading, all-seeing and all-powerful. God calls, "O Children! Realise all in one and one in all. Behave with others as you would with yourself. Know that in all, one universe resides. We are the enjoyers of immortal Bliss. The architect of the universe is the overseer of truth, internal order, austerity and simplicity. Live in harmony and peace. Be in the consciousness of God's presence in all righteous activities. Consciousness of His presence will make one hardworking with devotion, righteously, fearlessly, selflessly, for the welfare of family, community, nation and the world. Humanity is the essence of all religions; service to the manifestation of God is worship of God. Hinduism's message is Sarvata Sukhaani Bhavatah.

All be happy, all be healthy, all be prosperous.

Prophet Mohammed: "Recompense evil, conquer it with good."

Bahai: "All humanity is one family", men and women are equal.

Sufism: "Thy light is in all forms. Thy love is in all beings. Love all beings as manifestation of God and serve them".

Jesus Christ: "Love thy neighbour, as thy love thyself." "Blessed are the pure in heart." "Seek first kingdom of God and his righteousness."

Guru Nanak: "Bear no hate to anyone. God dwells in every heart."

Lord Buddha: "Look equally with a kind heart to all the living beings."

Selflessness is the governing principle in the law of prosperity. Each one of us must live for others. Create and generate wealth virtuously for self and others. Commune with God and God's unlimited power.

Let us march ahead with the banner of inclusive and sustainable growth for the welfare of all and the preservation of the universe. Let us have the cosmic cooperative spirit. Let the youth be ignited with divinity and infinity. Let our mission and vision be assimilation and not destruction. Let us consider ourselves members of the human family. Let us unite our isolated consciousness with God. Let our heart throb with, "All in one, One in all." May God bless us to live in consciousness of Him and in service of His manifestation.

Om! Amen! Amin! Ek Onkar! Ahura Mazda.

Speech by Dr. H.P. Kanoria, Global Man of the Year at the GOD Awards, New York

Revered religious leaders, divine brothers and sisters, children of God.

It is a great privilege for me to be honoured with "Global Man of the Year 2015" at the (3rd Annual global Official of Dignity Awards) the 3rd G.O.D awards organized by "We care for Humanity" under the leadership of H.H Princess Maria Amor D.D.

I bow to all women whom the Princess Maria represents. God has created us in his own image with his love and virtues. He is the universal father, mother, brother, sister and friend. We are all his children. We are infinite, perfect and divine. God is beyond duality. He is both in men and women. Men and women have different gender, yes, but bodies die. Souls are immortal.

During the Vedic age in India, women were respected and honoured. They were great scholars, saints, enlightened souls and great warriors. They were symbols of purity and love.

Women have infinite 'shakti' or strength. Today, they are rising to the top positions as leaders, scholars, writers, millionaires, billionaires and professionals in all areas. They have become astronauts. They have moved to serve humanity. They are more spiritual. Women have created gigantic intellectuals. They can work out their own destiny.

Today at the United Nations let us take a vow. Let there be no difference from soul to soul on account of gender. All Nations have given women equal rights. They have awakened. They have arisen. They are not fearing. Princess Maria has been doing a great work. Her organization is We care for Humanity.

We have been working on the theme of Humanity, Power & Spirituality. We have written a book named "Enlightenment" which was inaugurated at 4th World Confluence of Humanity, Power & Spirituality by Dr. A.P.J Abdul Kalam, former President of India. As Managing Trustee of Srei Foundation, Calcutta, India, we have undertaken several social projects in different areas supporting free education of students; medical aid; supporting marriages;, housing; higher education; environment etc.

We have founded Acid Survivors Foundation India, which works for awareness of the heinous crime through acid, and its prevention, treatment and rehabilitation. The holistic approach to victims promotes the best recovery.

Paramhansa Sri Ramakrishna said to his disciple Swami Vivekananda that service to humanity is worship of God. Do not be selfish. Go; serve Humanity and all God's creation.

Vivekananda, said "Ye fool! Who neglect the living God and His infinite reflections with which the world is full. Him worship- the only visible, omnipresent God. Why do you run after imaginary shadows that lead alone to fights and quarrels".

All the enlightened saints take the suffering of humanity on themselves like Jesus Christ, Buddha and Paramhansa Shri Ramakrishna who had afflicted their own bodies to relieve others of their suffering. They have brought the harvest to happiness and illumination for all living beings.

As different streams having their sources in different places mingle with the sea, different paths to God which men follow owing to their respective tendencies/natures, various and different lead to one Cosmic God. Unity in variety is the plan of nature. Science is nothing but finding of this unity. Unity will not come by the triumph of any one of religion and destruction of others. The focus; should be on harmony and peace, not dissension. Each Soul is potentially divine. The goal of life is to manifest the divinity within each soul.

According to the World Health Organization (WHO), alcohol and drug addiction affects more than 10% of the world population. Situation is becoming worse in rural areas. There are other injurious products on sale. Food is adulterated. Injurious foods are sold under brand names with sophisticated advertisements and false health building information. All religions promote earning by righteous means. Swami Yogananda says, “Liquor increases man’s desire for money and sex, and it is, therefore the worst evil”. Humanity needs action on this front.

The global slowdown will increase poverty. The US and the Euro zone are drowning under the sea of debts. Some countries like Greece are on the brink of sovereign default. Austerity measures are yet to be taken. Let us Awaken Humanity. Awaken Humanity.”Be rich by righteous ways/ means be simple with austerity, We should not to waste, not to allow waste, We should create wealth to generate wealth, and be honest in money, making thoughts and action; Let us work hard and fearlessly.

Global employment of population had reduced from 62.3% in 1991 to 61.2% in 2011.Humanity is affected by poverty, terrorism, destruction, tortures, wars, power struggles, food crisis, global warming, religious fanaticism and the global financial crisis. Weakness is exploited. Nature is excessively exploited to create class imbalance, Majority have been suffering from stress, anxiety, depression, and other bad habits like excessive food intake, alcoholism, smoking and so on.

Service to humanity brings strength and new life. God - the infinite love, peace, happiness is the very self in all beings. Let us sprout his new humanity in mind, heart, and action.

O God! Bless us to be more humane and live in peace and harmony with all mankind.

Speech by Dr. H.P. Kanoria, at first Annual Commemoration of WARP Summit in Seoul, Korea

My salutation to all! I bow to all. Victory to peace and humanity! It is a great honour to grace the World Alliance of Religion for Peace. I greatly appreciate the work undertaken by HWPL under the leadership of Chairman, Mr. Man Hee Lee for the Harmony & Peace of Religions. It is true that various religions are flowers of different colours to be tied with the chord of love into a beautiful bouquet to be offered at the altar of humanity, love & peace.

Fundamentals of all religions are - righteousness, love, service, austerity, simplicity, faith in self and Divine Lord. I organise the World Confluence of Humanity, Power and Spirituality every year with this mission & vision. It is my privilege to inform you that the World Confluence of Humanity, Power & Spirituality is being held on 22nd & 23rd December' 2015 in New Delhi, India. Spirituality inspires and aspires us to develop divinity and humanity, ignite infinite inner power, and balance the power ofauthority and money to live an enlightened life. Children are inspired to be alchemists in order to develop virtues of spirituality and humanity. Women are the source of inspiration and selfless service. World is one family. Mother earth shelters all humanity.

I heartily invite all present here to grace our World Confluence on 22nd & 23rd December' 2015 in New Delhi, India. This will strengthen our resolve to spread the message of peace and humanity in this world.

Addressing people assembled in World Parliament of Religions, in Chicago (U.S), Swami Vivekananda, a true monk and a great reformer said with a voice of a lion, "Sisters and brothers, I am proud to belong to a religion, Hinduism which has taught the world both universal tolerance and acceptance". We accept that all religions are true. Hinduism is the oldest surviving religion. It is considered perpetual and eternal (Sanatan). It is based on divine revelation and realisation of the God within us. It was formed through the direct realisation of the cosmic entity (God) by several saints, sages and seers. They had taken their journey of enlightenment through service to merge with God.

As the law of gravity existed before its discovery by Newton, the spiritual treasury and spiritual laws existed and was realised by the enlightened souls. This would exist even if all humanity forgot. The moral, spiritual and spiritual connection between two souls and the relation between the individual spirit and the universal spirits would remain forever. Scriptures of Hindus (Vedas) teach us that creation is without a beginning or an end. Science has proved that the sum total of cosmic energy is always the same. Science is in finding of unity. Its goal is to reach perfect unity. Scientists have proved that physical individuality is a delusion. Chemistry's goal is to discover one element out of which all others could be made. Physics discovers energy of which all others are but manifestations.

God is the only soul of which all souls are but delusive manifestations. The entire universe has been manifested from Him (God). All beings are dependent upon him.

In his address, Swami Vivekananda said, "Hear, Ye, Children of immortal bliss! Even Ye reside in higher spheres. Allow me to call you, brethren by sweet name-heirs of immortal bliss-ye Hindu refuses to call you sinners.

It is sin to call a man sinner. You are a divine soul so Ye are not matter, ye are not bodies. Matter is your servant, not you the servant of matter. When the soul becomes perfect and enlightened, it frees us from the bondage of body-matter. God reveals Himself to the pure heart".

A Hindu uses an external symbol when he worships. It helps him to keep his mind fixed on the being (God) to whom he prays as he applies all attributes of God to the images. A Hindu during worship uses all sorts of rituals, flowers, incense sticks and so on. It is all love for God.

It is to engage the mind to whom one loves. It is not polytheism. He finds attributes of one to manifestations of many. He associates the ideas of holiness, purity, truth, virtues, omnipresence and such ideas with different images. Hindu religion is centred in realisation. Man is to become divine by realising the divine within Idols are only the support. External worship is the lowest stage. Mental prayer is the next stage. The highest is the realisation of God within us. Hindu travels from lower to higher truth and from truth to truth, not from error to truth. Sri Krishna, an incarnation of God said, "I am in every religion as the thread through a string of pearls. Every religion is evolving a God out of material man. It is the same light coming through glasses of different colour". A realised person works for the welfare of all beings. His love is selfless, no expectation, no attachment to world except God. He sees God.

He talks to God. He lives with God. The words of love alone will come out of his heart. It is union of man; humanity and God I Moses, Jesus Christ, Prophet Muhammad, Ahura Mazda, Chaitanya Mahaprabhu, Swami Vivekananda, Sri Ramakrishna Paramahansa, Paramhansa Sri Yogananda are only different faces of the same prophets of all ages. Lord Krishna taught his disciple Arjuna, four paths for union (Yogas) with God. Karma Yoga (the Yoga of selfless action without attachment and expectation of fruits); Jnana Yoga (union through knowledge) - God is his own self, God is the life of his life; Raja Yoga (union through concentration) - It is controlling the mind and Bhakti Yoga (union through devotion). Love, love, love alone with faith in man's divinity.

Swami Vivekananda said, "The Hindu is universal religion, it so happens will have no location in place or time. It will be infinite like God. The Sun of universal religion will shine on all followers of all preachers and religions. It will have no place for persecution or for tolerance in its polity."

Hindu religious recognises divinity in every man and woman. Its whole force is central, making humanity realise its own true which is divine nature. Love your religion; be humble and respectful to other religions also. You are infinite. The body is the manifestation of the spirit which is within you.

Have faith in yourself and God. Affirm that you are not a sinner. You are a perfect and infinite soul. Come out of the bondage of habit. Be a master of body-matterhabit. March on the path of perfection, realisation and unity with the ultimate cosmic infinite God.

Be one with universal unity, unity in the variety is the plan of creator. Love all people but face brutes. Be not fanatic, but face fanatics. If you are a Christian, be a better Christian. If you are a Zoroastrian, be a better Zoroastrian. If you are a Hindu, be a better Hindu. If you are a Muslim, be a better Muslim. Keep harmony and peace with all.

Hindus believes in Vasudhaiva Kutumbakam, that means "World is one Family"

Hindus pray:

ॐ सर्वे भवन्तु सुखिनः	Om Sarve Bhavantu Sukhinah
सर्वे सन्तु निरामयाः ।	Sarve Santu Nir-Aamayaah I
सर्वे भद्राणि पश्यन्तु	Sarve Bhadraanni Pashyantu
मा कश्चिद् दुःखभाग भवेत् ।	Maa Kashcid-Duhkha-Bhaag-Bhavet I
ॐ शांतिः शांतिः शांतिः ।	Om Shaantih Shaantih Shaantih 11

1: Om, May All become Happy,

2: May All be Free from Illness.

3: May All See what is Auspicious,

4: May no one Suffer.

5: Om Peace, Peace, Peace.

Let us march ahead with the flag of humanity and spirituality, and unity in order to serve the purpose of peace and unity of mankind.

Om, Amen, Amin , Ek Onkar, Ahura Mazda

Om Shanti! Om Shanti! Om Shanti!

World peace! National peace! Family with peace!

Victory to Humanity & Peace to all.

Dr. H. P. Kanoria

The Truth of Hinduism

Hinduism is Sanatana Dharma. It means eternal law.

Philosophy of Dharma is – Righteousness, Love, Service, Austerity, Simplicity and Faith in the Divine Lord.

Artha (money) is the means of living. It is not the aim. Dharma precedes Artha. To earn money in righteous way without hurting others, without cheating others, without grabbing others' means of livelihood and possession. Kama denotes love and lust. Love for all and is righteous ways of love, satisfies natural instinct of Kama (lust) for ongoing creation. Lust is to be limited. Indulgence is bad. To be lion, it is to be limited. So, Righteousness (dharma) precedes artha (money) and kama (lust & love).

Moksha means liberation. Human body is manifestation of infinite parambrahma. In duality, as human being, we enjoy Brahma (Supreme Lord) like one enjoys sugar. In non-duality a person is merged with the Lord. Liberation means to realise this ultimate truth and merge in the Lord while following the path of Dharma, Love and Service.

Scriptures of Hinduism are based on Sruti (revealed) and Smriti (remembered). Main scriptures are four Vedas, Upanishads, Puranas, Mahabharata, Ramayana, The Bhagwat Gita a treatise from the Mahabharata spoken by Lord Krishna to Arjuna is the essence of the teaching of the Vedas, finally Hinduism. Hinduism believes in "creation, sustenance and destruction of world by Divine Lord". Reincarnation based on Karma Yoga, Rajas Yoga, Bhakti Yoga and Gyan Yoga is the teaching of Lord Krishna.

The syllable Om represents Parambrahma. Om is the divine sound at the time of creation of the world when the world was void. Scriptures give insight and philosophical teaching to the living world and how to realise the ultimate truth and reality with all happiness in austerity and simplicity.

Max Muller and Josh Woodroffe translated Vedas & Upanishads in English for the knowledge of the world. Enlightended teachers like

Sri Tulsidas, Sant Kabir, Sri Sri Aurobindo, Paramhansa Ramkrishna, Paramhansa Sri Yoganandji, Swami Vivekanandji, Swami Rama have been awakening the true meaning of existence and love, the magnetic force balance the cosmic creation. Epic Ramayana sways the common masses, influences their devotion to God and establishes the righteous living and destruction of person/ persons who follow the path of unrighteousness.

Hindu believes that there is a spirit – Him the sword cannot pierce – Him the fire cannot burn – Him the water cannot melt – Him the air cannot dry. Human should be eternal and immortal, perfect and infinite and death means only a change of centre from one body to another.

Vedic sage proclaimed "Hear you children of immortal bliss, come out of darkness, delusion, and know him. You are not sinner. Like all rivers flowing to sea, all various paths of religion lead to one cosmic / divine power / God. It is oneness. It is universal oneness.

Dr. H. P. Kanoria

O Man!

O Wedded Man! Be virtuous. Be master of habits not slave.

Be free from vices of addiction.

With the courage and conviction follow the path of Dharma.

Remain respectful and dutiful to parents and seniors.

Be serviceable, lovable, humble and gentle to all.

Perform marital duties with love, strength, humour and valour.

Obey God - assigned duties and be happy.

Pray to Lord for a happy family life, wedded bliss and joy to all.

Dr. H. P. Kanoria

- Based on the Holy Vedas

Hinduism

Dr. H.P. Kanoria

Root Cause of Good and Evil

Human being is manifested by God in his own image. He says, 'I am alone, let there be many'. Fundamentally human being is divine and he is so perfect. God has also manifested good and evil. Illusion leads to evil. It leads to imperfection. God tests us. We all have to pass through the illusion that causes evil and imperfection. We have to overcome these evils through our intellect i.e. reasoning through our conscience. There is a constant war between good and evil. Good becomes victim of evil easily. It is difficult to be on path of goodness. People choose evil like violence, greed, fulfillment of sensuous desires, violence against women, religious fanatism, own supremacy over God, feeling of himself as God, possession of others wealth as his own. As per Hinduism, when evil over rulesand good people suffer, God incarnates as a human being to finish all evil minded people indulging in evil activities. Hindu epics, Ramayana and Mahabharata have the story of God's incarnations. In the war between good and bad people, good people won the war with the leadership of God to establish righteousness and goodness. God protects good people.

Everyman and woman has to bear the fruits of his action. It is a theory of science, for every action there is an equal and opposite reaction. As you sow, so you reap. This is the law of nature. Reaction of every action accumulates. Reaction of this life is carried over to the next life (birth). Good action (Karma) has a good reaction. Bad action (Karma) has a bad reaction. After finishing reaction of previous life, one can enjoy the reaction of his present good action. Present good action builds the future good life. Such persons are born in good families with good health and engage in service and love to humanity. He promotes peace and harmony.

Solution to the Problem of Evil

Solution to the problem of evil - Scriptures have provided solution to be away from evil. Human being is divine. He is sharer of immortal bliss. He has to listen to the inner voice of his soul. He has to practice austerity i.e. self-control. He has to supervise and regulate the sense organs which naturally flow to the gratification of sensual desires. The respective sense organs take the mind away violently. It has to be pulled back by intellect. So, exercise the intellect to control and regulate the senses. One has to strengthen the mind. One must not allow the mind to split him. Action must be done for good of the community and humanity. Strengthen the mind by diverting the mind by focusing the mind on God. Remember and feel the presence of God every moment.

Engage in good thoughts, speech and action. He should always think that he is not the doer. God is the doer for good. He is just an instrument in the hands of God. Study the scriptures daily. Assimilate and then practice the learning in consciousness, sub consciousness and super consciousness. Always think of God and serving and loving the children of God.

Lord Krishna (God incarnated) said to his disciples in the battlefield of war between evil minded people and good people. God was on the side of good people. The best way to resolve the problem of evil is surrender to God, love to Him spontaneously without asking for anything in return. See divinity in Nature – sun rising and sun set, flowers blossoming, streams flowing and so on.

"Fix mind on me, be devoted to me and bow down to me. Thus uniting yourself with me and seating me, as the Supreme goal and soul refuge, you shall certainly realize me (or come to me)". Bhagvat Gita 9.34, a great scripture of Hinduism. People called Gita as "Mother Gita". It has condensed knowledge of all scriptures of Hinduism.

Who am I?

According to Hindu Scriptures – Veda – Upanishad, Bhagvad Gita, Ramayana, Lord Vishnu (Principal God) has manifested Himself in human beings (men-women), all inanimate and animate with His Cosmic Power. Ekoham Bahusyami (GIVE SANSKRIT ALSO), I am alone let there be many. Human beings are His children. Every human being has soul which is immortal, being a fragment of His Cosmic Energy. Soul is in body which is mortal. When body dies, soul moves to a new body. It takes birth again & again till it reaches perfection i.e. divinity which is enshrined in each soul, but it is covered and influenced by Illusion (deceptive image of Reality). Illusion (Maya) is the kinetic energy, the force of action of Brahma (God). Kinetic energy is greed, pride, lust, anger and ego. These energies lead to fall of human beings. These engulf the divinity of the soul. It is very invisible potential energy. These energies can be conquered by the giant force of Will and God's grace. Divine qualities are the milestones. Divine qualities are forbearance, patience, renunciation, restrain and control the senses i.e. lust, anger, greed etc. The five senses are the five horses of a chariot i.e. a human being. Senses are controlled by the mind and intellect.Mind is superior to senses. Intellect is superior to mind. Control the mind by intellect to control worldly desires. For this do meditation, prayers and read scriptures. Seek God with childlike faith and love. Duty and renunciation are the two wheels of the chariot i.e. human being and love for God is its axle. Service is the road. The scriptures are guiding lights to dispel the ignorance – illusion and sensual desires and free one from anger, greed, lust etc. Purify the intellect with self-knowledge and discrimination.

Every human being is playing his role in Cosmic movie (world). Environment produces illusion. Rise above temporal illusion. Realise God within. Hold Him. Fill the mind with ideas and not ambitions. God incarnates Himself for protecting the good, for transforming the wicked and establishing righteousness. Hell and Heaven are in the world. Good work with motive of righteousness and service to humanity results in happy living in the world. Otherwise one suffers which is like living in hell.So, we are spirit. We are perfect. We are divine. Brahmasmi - I am Brahma (God), "Hung Sun" – "I am He", "Shivoham" - I am Shiva (God). We are manifested children of God. We are playing our roles on the stage of drama of the world.

Bad people are engaged in harming others, destruction of creation, killing, cheating, adultery and kidnapping women. They are cast to hell where they are punished in different methods.

Therefore, live rightly now and grieve for your sins. Righteous persons stand with great boldness before those who have afflicted and oppressed them. Jesus Christ was being crucified and tortured. As he was a good son (Godlike) of God, he was not having any pain. He said, "Father, forgive them as they don't know what they are doing". Job was stripped of all his wealth. All His children had died on being tested by Angel. His house was gutted in fire. He was lying naked on the road. But, he remained faithful to God. He continued to love God. He did not challenge the judgement of God. He said, 'who am I to judge the judgement of God'. At last God returned everything to Him and blessed Him with His choicest Blessings.

Peace of mind, purity of mind and simplicity of purpose are essential to be a good man and enjoy heaven on this earth itself. God never deserts one who loves Him and His creation.

The eight noble paths are Right view or understanding belonging to wisdom, Right thought or intention, Right speech, Right action, Right livelihood, Right effort, Right mindfulness and Right concentration.

Notion of Heaven and Hell were created by wise men-women/ enlightened men-women. Notion of heaven was created to motivate good persons to remain good and bad persons to become good by promising so many comforts, happiness, joy etc. in heaven. There will be neither pain nor suffering. Joy, joy and joy alone. Notion of Hell was created to restrain good persons to become bad and bad persons to become good. Fear psycho was introduced. Punishment/tortures in all unthinkable/undreamable will be only given. Making to lay on hot rolls, no food, little bad smell food or rotten food for sustaining alive etc. will only be given. Hell and heaven are on earth. One has to bear and enjoy their respective action. Every action has a reaction and retribution as proved in both physics and chemistry. No family will share your sins. You have to bear it alone.

Even saintly person (Godly person) falls in the grip of Saitan (bad person) if he doesn't follow the messages of God through study of scriptures acquiring right knowledge and utmost 'self – realisation' and renunciation of attachment, but remaining in the service of God and His creation.

Heaven and Hell

Notion of Heaven and Hell were created by wise men-women/ enlightened men-women. Notion of heaven was created to motivate good persons to remain good and bad persons to become good by promising so many comforts, happiness, joy etc. in heaven. There will be neither pain nor suffering. Joy, joy and joy alone. Notion of Hell was created to restrain good persons to become bad and bad persons to become good. Fear psycho was introduced. Punishment/tortures in all unthinkable/undreamable will be only given. Making to lay on hot rolls, no food, little bad smell food or rotten food for sustaining alive etc. will only be given. Hell and heaven are on earth. One has to bear and enjoy their respective action. Every action has a reaction and retribution as proved in both physics and chemistry. No family will share your sins. You have to bear it alone.

Even saintly person (Godly person) falls in the grip of Saitan (bad person) if he doesn't follow the messages of God through study of scriptures acquiring right knowledge and utmost 'self – realisation' and renunciation of attachment, but remaining in the service of God and His creation.

Life Span

Yes, God has manifested the soul which is embodied in the body. Soul (Atman) is immortal, indestructible, eternal and self-luminous. It is the cause of all causes, all pervading, unaffected, immutable and inexplicable. No one can destroy the indestructible soul (Atman). Body is mortal. After death, the soul goes to another body i.e. reborn in new entity. Soul reborn again and again till perfection is not achieved and the purpose of God is not achieved.

Look at the nature - everything animate and again inanimate, born of and then perished. Look at the tree - it dies and again new plant comes. So, the life span given by God is for 100 years to fulfil the purpose of God.

Hindu scriptures had divided human life in four periods or Asramas which are Brahmacharya (Student), Grihastha (Householder), Vanaprastha (Semi – Retired i.e Service) and Sannyasa (renunciation and living in remembrance of God).

Student life or Brahmacharya - upto 24 years – This period gave importance to study different subjects including scriptures, acquire knowledge and learn art of living including yoga, meditation and martial art.

Household: 24-48 years – This period put emphasis on marriage and family life, happiness, satisfaction of lust with celibacy, nurture the children, adapting profession, agriculture, business and work to the best of ability.

Semi Household: 48+ Semi Retired i.e Service for own self and train the children in all respectincluding profession, love and service to humanity and God.

Retired life: 48-72 years. Renunciation and living in remembrance of God.

Renunciation: Meditation - Concentration on God

1. Dharma -Righteousness
2. Artha - Earning money -Profession
3. Kama -Happiness in limited way

Renounced Life: 72 + above- This period put emphasis to achieve the seed and the principal of life i.e Moksha – Liberation These goals of life with different stages are viewed for living for the higher ideal in Hindu Philosophy, service, love, harmony and peace.

Increasing Lifespan by Spiritual Awakening

Yes! Paramhansa Sri Yogananda said that if a person were able to draw his required energy from cosmic sources he should eliminate the toxic fallout. If he lives a life as prescribed by scriptures and nature, meditation, consecration in presence of God and also practiced Yoga postures (Stimulating his endocrine system and live in consciousness of God), his lifestyle would be prolonged. It will be possible to have full span of life of 100 years or more.

An Indian saint Yogi Devraha baba who passed away in 1989 lived this lifestyle. He never ate food only and drank water from the Yamuna river. He lived for more than 250 years. Lalan Fakir lived more than 150 years.

As more people begin meditation practices and learn to tap their inner cosmic energies, people life span is increasing now-a-days. The body has a natural healing power too. Added with medical science, life span can also be prolonged to a certain extent if it abides the science of nature and living.

Yes, practice the principle of life – health and celibacy. By power of spirit, longer they live. Concentrate the whole life on God.

Reason of Sickness

Time has changed and it is our perception which has changed also.

In the Hindu scriptures, Bhagwad Gita, Lord Krishna (God) said, "Not to eat less and more – balance food; sleep not much and more. Be righteous, work hard to the cut of ability, fix your mind on me, surrender to me, love me."

Every human being is born with past karma or past actions – (both good or bad /evil) which one has to work out along with the present good and evil done. It multiplies and/or diminishes. So, sickness and disability depends according to work done during the lifetime and the way of living following the science of health and nature.

Heaven and Hell

Heaven

From the viewpoint of Hinduism, heaven and hell are merely different worlds, bound by time, space, and causality. According to Hinduism, desires are responsible for a person's embodiment. Some of these desires can best be fulfilled in a human body, and some in an animal or a celestial body. Accordingly, a soul assumes a body determined by its unfulfilled desires and the results of its past actions. An animal or a celestial body is for reaping the results of past karma, not for performing actions to acquire a new body. Performance of karma to effect any change of life is possible only in a human body, because only human beings do good or evil consciously. Human birth is therefore a great privilege, for in a human body alone can one attain the supreme goal of life. Thus, in search of eternal happiness and immortality, the apparent soul is born again and again in different bodies, only to discover in the end that immortality can never be attained through fulfillment of desires. The soul then practices discrimination between the real and the unreal, attains desirelessness, and finally realizes its immortal nature.

Affirming this fact, the Katha Upanishad says: "When all the desires that dwell in the heart fall away, then the mortal becomes immortal and here attains Brahman."

Hinduism - Salvation - Liberation

Salvation (or moksha) is reached when the worshiper is freed from the cycle of reincarnation, and his spirit becomes one with god. One becomes free by ridding oneself of bad karma—the effect of evil action or evil intent. This can be done in three different ways: through selfless devotion to and service of a particular god, through understanding the nature of the universe, or by mastering the actions needed to fully appease the gods.

In Hinduism, with over a million different gods, there are differences of opinion regarding the nature of salvation. The Advaita school teaches salvation occurs when one can strip away the false self and make the soul indistinguishable from that of god. The dualist insists that one's soul always retains its own identity even as it is joined with god.

Hindu Scriptures

Hindu's scriptures, "God is abiding as soul in all beings. All beings are like sun and sunlight different as well as non-different.

Concept of Afterlife

The concept of Heaven and Hell is described in Hinduism. Heaven is ruled by semi-God deputed by Lord Vishnu, the Supreme God. Heaven is beautiful. It is full of fragrance. Flowers blossom in heaven. Good and loving beings and beautiful women with purity are all around. Good food is given. Prayers and songs of God with sweet music are sung. All beings live in divine bliss of love for God.

Hell

Hell is ruled by the Lord of Death. He is called Yama. The environment is very fearful. All sorts of fearsome people move around. Punishments/tortures in all unthinkable and undreamable are also given. According to their actions/work in this world they are punished and tortured in different degrees. One is made to lay on hot plates. No food or little food with bad smell or rotten food is given. After passing through all tortures, one is reborn again and again till he reaches perfection by the process of purification, self-realization, good works, maintenance of peace, harmony and engaging in the service of humanity and the creation of God.

There is a third Loka i.e. A world other than heaven and hell; it is called Vishnu Loka (Supreme God named Vishnu-Narayan-Krishna). There is no pain and suffering. One is in unison with God's love. Bliss, Bliss and Bliss are all around. Joy, Joy, Joy.

Heaven

We are the manifested children of God. We are Spirit. We are perfect. We are divine. Brahmasmi – I am Brahma (God). Shivoham – I am Shiva (God). We are playing our roles on the stage of the world. We have illusions. We have intellect. Our mind and intellect are driven by senses pleasures. Every person has a soul which is immortal. Soul is in the body which is mortal. Our life is governed by cosmic rule of birth and death. It is cosmic cycle. One is born again and again till he does not have perfection and divinity, which is enshrined in every human being. Soul is the fragment of His Cosmic Energy. A human being goes to heaven when he has divine qualities. He conquers the kinetic energy of greed, pride, lust, anger, hatred, jealousy and ego by gigantic force of will and God's grace. He has the forbearance, patience, renunciation, restrain and control of senses i.e. lust, anger, greed, killing, harming another being and God's creation.

Way to get to heaven is to be a good human being by controlling the senses by mind and intellect; be righteous, not harming any person and Creation of God, work to the best of ability with selfless motive for the creation and generation of wealth for the welfare of humanity; engage in the welfare of all creatures. Sarvabhutahite Ratah; and remain truthful.

A person goes to hell, when he becomes the servant of bad habits i.e. alcohol, adultery etc. and becomes victim of kinetic energy i.e. greed, pride, lust, anger and ego, cheating, injustice, untruthfulness, destruction, jealousy, harming others; not protecting animates and inanimate; indulging in sensual desires; not performing his duties to the best of his ability; working for selfish motives, disrespect to women and lethargy. He is engaged in unjust activities, unnecessary killing of creatures and unjust war.

A person who loves God, not His gifts; he has presence of God in His consciousness. He loves God as a miser loves money, as an ardent man loves his sweetheart and as a drowning person loves breath. He yearns for God. He gives his love to God spontaneously without asking for His gift – pleasures, riches, glory, fame etc. This person goes to Vishnu Loka (world of Lord Vishnu-Supreme God). He lives in Love and Bliss of God with all comforts. He just enjoys God's love. He does not take birth again. He reaches perfection and divinity. He is not subject to born again. Because, death is certain for the one who is born, and birth is certain for the one who dies. Therefore, you should not lament over the inevitable.

(Bhagavad Gita -2.27)

Fix your mind on me, be devoted to Me, worship Me, and bow down to Me. Thus uniting yourself with Me and setting Me, as the supreme goal and soul refuge, you shall certainly realise (or come to) Me. (Bhagavad Gita - 9.34)

Will of the Creator (GOD)

Hinduism (Sanatan Dharma) is eternal without beginning and end. Human beings were manifested in the image of God (Lord Vishnu). Lord Vishnu was alone. He said "I am alone. Let there be many." All are His manifestations by His Supreme cosmic energy. He has manifested the Universe by His own power. Every human being – man and woman is divine perfect and has divine strength, divine intellect and super consciousness.

One has inner infinite power. One has the soul, which is a fragment of God like electron and proton of atom. The soul is immortal. Body is mortal. One has to awaken the inner infinite divine power which is dormant, covered and influenced by illusion (Maya – the power of God to play with this Universe –creation). One can tune one's will with God's will. One can have self-realization. Enlightened persons have heard the voice of God. They have realized the will of God. Their realizations have been incorporated in scriptures. In some scriptures like the Gita, voice of God and talks of God to His disciple Arjuna were recorded.

Scriptures give insight into the will of God.

One can realize God's will without studying scriptures. There have been many such persons in India like Paramahansa Shri RamaKrishna, Saint Tulsidas, Meera Bai, Sri Chaitanya Mahaprabhu, Guru Nanak, Saint Kabir and so on.

Faith

(a) There is no standard of faith. Basic foundation is that faith must be ingrained with love. There must be a combination of faith and love. Scriptures have not prescribed any standard faith. It is laid down that faith must be steady, unshakable unwavering even when calamities seize one from all sides. He must have faith that God is His savior. God has His plan. In each suffering, God has His purpose. Love is infused with faith. In love, the believer does not want anything in return. He craves to live in the presence and consciousness of God. The believer remains absorbed in the thought of God. He believes that he is not the doer, God is the doer. In all his thoughts and actions he finds that God is there. He consecrates every thought and deed to God. He says "O My beloved God My life is Thine, My goal is thy love". He dedicates his life to the service of God. He attunes his will with God's will. There is no standard of faith in scriptures. It is all about relation with God. One can have relation of son / daughter-father, son / daughter-mother, husband-wife (like Meera Bai), servant – master, friend, teacher-disciple.

In Hindu mythology, a young boy named Prahalad was forced to sit on fire as he was calling the name of Lord Narayana (God Name). He was thrown from the peak of a hill. But, his faith remains unshaken. At all times he was saved from death by his God - Narayana.

(b) Paramhansa Sri Ramakrishna, teacher of Swami Vivekananda had not studied any scriptures of any religion. He had self-realised God of all religions. After realisation, he said that all religions through different paths and procedures lead to cosmic God, who is the God of all religions. All religions are the different rivers flowing from various places but merged with oceans.

(c) Hindu religion says "Have faith in yourself, in all and in God". Affirm that you are a perfect and infinite soul. Be not a slave of habit. Be one with universal unity despite diversity. Core of the lesson of scriptures is faith, love and service. Faith can move the highest mountain. It can stop the storm. Scriptures have laid various ways of faith. One can adopt to according to one's own nature. One can have inborn-faith. One can have self-realization from faith and love.

Purpose of Life

All men and women are divine and perfect. They have the souls embodied in mortal bodies. Soul is immortal. God is our father, mother and friend. Parents want their children to be good, free from enviousness and jealousy. They should live in peace and in harmony. They work hard without ulterior motive of selfishness. They love each other, their parents and God. They should be full of love. They should be sympathetic, compassionate, humble, egoless, empathetic, helping, serviceful and truthful. They must not engage in violence. Scriptures are the lighthouse. They dispel the ignorance. They ignite goodness. They extinguish the fire of evilness. They promote co-existence and co-operative spirit. All must work to the best of their ability without selfish motive for the welfare of humanity. Learn from Nature. All are in tune to serve the creation. Fruit laden branches of a tree bend down. It gives fruits even though people throw stones. So, a glorified rich person, a person of power should have humanity and be ready to serve people. Love God like a miser loving money. Love God like a lover loving his sweetheart. Love God like a drowning person loving restlessly crying for life. Cry for God's love tears flowing profusely in His love.

Self-realization or study of scriptures or message of teachers can create faith and love. Listen to your own feeble voice of conscience every moment. Unity in diversity is the law of God.

Ekoham Bahusyam – "I am One Let There be Many" - Casteism

Caste systems are different ranked, hereditary, endogamous occupational groups that constitute traditional societies in certain regions of the world.

Initially caste was determined by a person's occupation. Over a period of time this becomes more rigid and people started determining the caste based on heredity or by birth.

India's caste system however, is among the world's oldest forms of surviving social stratification. The system which divides Hindus into groups based on their 'Karma'(act) and 'Duty' which were related to Hindu religion.

Puraana

There are many theories like traditional, racial, political, occupational, evolutionary etc which try to explain the caste system in India.

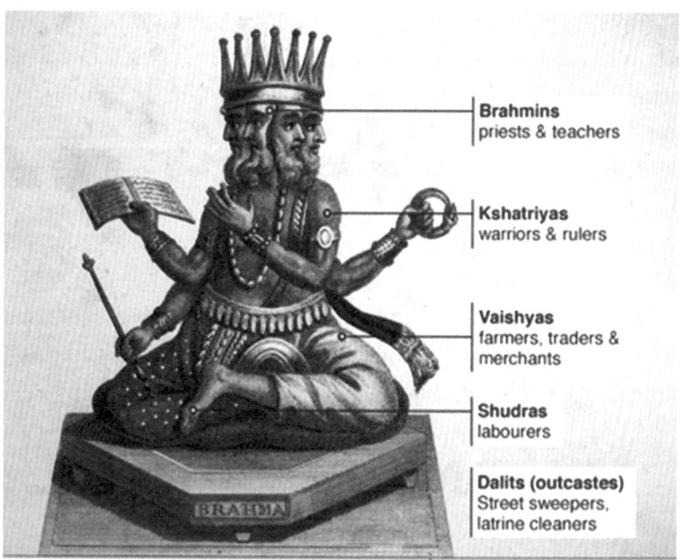

Brahma and the Origin of Caste

According to the traditional theory, Brahma, the creator of the universe had created the caste system based on classification of jobs. Different castes were born out of various body parts of Brahma. From his mouth came the Brahmins, from his hands the Kshatriya, from his stomach the Vaishyas and Sudras came from his feet. Puranas give some examples about the caste system. Caste system was not so rigid at that time. The life history of Devarshi Narada is a relevant example of that matter.

The Bhaghavat Purana describes the story of Narada. In the previous birth Narada was a Gandharva who had been cursed to be born in earth for singing glories to the demigods instead of the Supreme Lord. Puraana says that he was born as the son of maid-servant in his next birth. But originally his mother was not a maid-servant. She was the Queen of Kanyakubja, wife of King Drumila, named Kalavati. King Drumila along with his wife, performed penance on the banks of the river Ganges for an offspring. They met with a great sage named Kasyap. Kalavati pleased him by her worship and with his blessings she became pregnant. King Drumila decided to spend his life in the forest and later he gifted his wealth to the Brahmins and died in the forest. Kalavati returned to the village and lived as a slave in a Brahmin's house. In due course she gave birth to a child. On the birth of the child it rained heavily on the land and because of that the Brahmin master of Kalavati named the child Narada, meaning he who gives water. He turned out to be a great devotee of Lord Vishnu. Even though he was a Daasi-putra, Narada became a great sage and received blessings from the Lord Vishnu. He became well-known as a great devotee and messenger of Lord Vishnu.

अहं पुरातीतभवेऽभवं मुने दास्यास्तु कस्याश्चन वेदवादिनाम् ।
निरूपितो बालक एव योगिनां शुश्रुषणे प्रावृषि निर्विवक्षताम् ॥

aham puratitabhave&bhavam mune dasyastu kasyascana vedavadinam|
nirupito balaka eva yoginam susrushane pravrushi nirvivakshatam||

O Muni, in the last millennium I was born as the son of a certain maidservant engaged in the service of brahmanas who are following the principals of Vedanta. When they were living together during the four months of the rainy season, I was engaged in their personal service.

उच्छिष्टलेपननुमोदितो दविजैः सकृत्स्म भुञ्जे तदपस्तकिल्बिषः ।
एवं प्रवृत्तस्य विशुद्धचेतस-स्तद्धर्म एवात्मरुचिः प्रजायते ॥

ucchishtalepananumodito davijaih sakrutsma bhu~jje tadapastakilbishah|
evam pravruttasya visuddhacetasa-staddharma evatmaruchih prajayate ||

Once only, by their permission, I took their remnants of their food, and by so doing all my sins were at once eradicated. Thus being engaged, I became purified in heart, and at that time the very nature of the transcendentalist became attractive to me.

ज्ञानं गुहयतमं यत्त् साक्षात्भगवतोदितम् ।
अन्ववोचन् गमिष्यन्तः कृपया दीनवत्सलाः ॥

j~janam guhayatamam yattat sakshatbhagavatoditam |
anvavocan gamishyantah krupaya dinavatsalah ||

As they were leaving, those Bhakti-Vedantas, who are very kind to poor hearted souls, instructed in that most confidential subject which is instructed by the Personality of the Godhead Himself.

Vedic Period

The Varna system prevalent during the vedic period was mainly based on division of labour and occupation. Rig Vedic literature stresses very significantly the differences between the Arya and non-Aryans (Dasa), not only in their complexion but also in their speech, religious practices, and physical features. Vedas contain no word that can be considered a synonym for 'Caste'. The two words commonly considered to mean 'caste' are 'Jaati'

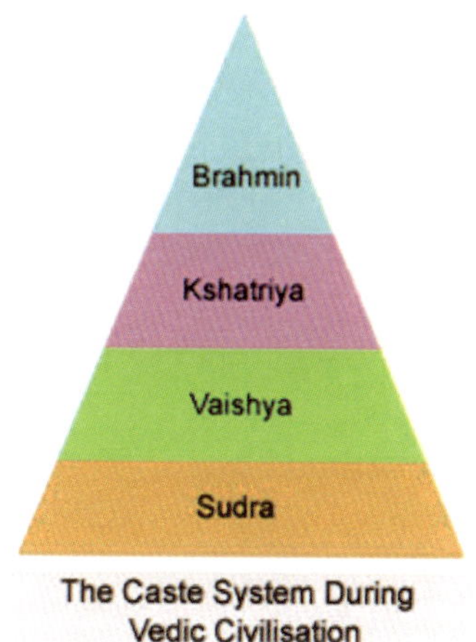

The Caste System During Vedic Civilisation

and 'Varna'. However the truth is that, all the three mean completely different things. Jaati means a classification based on source of origin. Nyaya Sutra states, "समानप्रसवात्मिकजाति:" or those having similar birth source from a 'Jaati'. An initial broad classification made by Rishis four fold: Udbhija (coming out of ground like plants), Andaja (coming out of eggs like birds and reptiles), Pindaja (mammals), and Ushmaja (reproducing due to temperature and ambient conditions like virus, bacteria etc). Similarly various animals like elephants, tigers, lions, rabbits from different 'Jaati'. In same manner, entire humanity forms one 'Jaati'. A particular Jaati will have similar physical characteristics, cannot change from one Jaati to another and cannot cross-breed. Thus Jaati is creation of Iswar or God.

"Varna" means one that is adopted by choice. Thus, while "Jaati" provided by God, "Varna" is our own choice. The actual word used for Brahmin, Kshatriya, Vaisya, Sudra is "Varna" and not "Jaati". Purusha Sukta is in 31st chapter of Yajurveda. It denotes the actual meaning of the traditional theory that different castes took birth from the various body parts of the creator Brahma. The mantras of Purusha Sukta's ask question and simalteniously gives the answer that, "Who is mouth? Who is hand? Who is thigh and who is leg?" The answer is - Mouth stands for Brahman, Hand stands for Kshatriya, Thigh for Vaisya and leg for Sudra. The mantra does not say that Brahmins "take birth" from mouth. It says Brahmin is mouth and it is same for Kshatriya, Vaisya and Sudra. So, Brahmin means intellectuality which come from brain, head or mouth that can think and speak. Kshatriya or defence personnel from the hands that protect. Vaisya or producers and businessmen from the thigh that support and nurture (thigh bone or Femur produces blood and is strongest bone). Sudra or labours force from the legs that lay the foundation and make the body run. In Vedic culture, everyone is considered to be born as Sudra. Then based on his or her education, one becomes a Brahmin, Kshatriya and Vaisya. This completion of education is considered to be a second birth or "Dwija" or twice-born which indicates the above three Varnas. In Vedas, Sudra means a hard-working person. For this reason Purusha Sukta calls them as foundation of entire human society. Slokas from Yajurveda related to caste system:

तं यज्ञं बर्हिषि प्रौक्षन् पुरुषं जातमग्रतः ।
तेन देवा अयजन्त साध्या ऋषयश्च ये ॥ 9 ॥

tam yaj~jam barhishi praukshan purusham jatamagratah|
tena deva ayajanta sadhya rushayasca ye||9||

They initiated into yajna the Purusha born in earliest time. SAdhyAs and Risis initiated him into various jobs.

यत्पुरुषं व्यदधुः कतिधा व्यकल्पयन् ।
मुखं किमस्यासीत् किं बाहु किमुरु पादा उच्येते ॥ 10 ॥

yatpurusham vyadadhuh katidha vyakalpayan|
mukham kimasyasit kim bahu kimuru pada ucyete||10||

When they initiated Purusha how many portions did they make? What was his mouth? What were his arms? What are the names of thighs and feet?

ब्राह्मणोऽस्य मुखमासीद्भाहू राजन्यः कृतः ।
ऊरू तदस्य यद्वैश्यः पद्भ्यां शूद्रो अजायत ॥ 11 ॥

brahmano&sya mukhamasidbhahu rajanyah krutah|
uru tadasya yadbhyaksham sudro ajayata||11||

The Purusha was Brahmana from his mouth, he was made Rajanya from his arms. From his thighs, he became the Vaisyas, from his feet he was produced as the Sudra.

चन्द्रमा मनसो जातश्चक्षोः सूर्यो अजायत ।
श्रोत्राद्वायुश्च प्राणश्च मुखादग्निरजायत ॥ 12 ॥

candrama manaso jatascakshoh suryo ajayata|
srotradvayusca pranasca mukhadagnirajayata||12||

He was born as the Moon from his mind, and sun from his eyes; as vAyu and prANa from his ear, and from his mouth as agni.

नाभ्या आसीदन्तरिक्षं शीर्ष्णो द्यौः समवर्तत ।
पद्भ्यां भूमिर्दिशः श्रोत्रात्तथा लोकां अकल्पयन ॥ 13 ॥

nabhya asidantariksha h sirshno dyauh samavarttata |
padbhyam bhumirdisah srotrattatha loka ra akalpayan ||13||

From his naval he was midspace; he was the sky from his head; Earth from his feet, and from his ear the Quarters. Thus they classified the body of purusha.

Many examples exist of change of Varnas in Vedic society.

(a) Aitareya Rishi was son of a daasa or criminal but became a Brahmin of higher order and wrote Aitareya Brahmana and Aitareya Upanishad. Aitareya Brahmana is considered critical to understand Rigveda.

(b) Ailush Rishi was a son of Daasi, researched on Rigveda and made several discoveries. He was also an Acharya.

(c) Satyakaam Jaabaal was the son of a prostitute but became a Brahmin.

(d) Prishadh was son of King Daksha but became a Sudra. Further he did tapasya to achieve salvation to after repenting. (Vishnu Purana-4.1.14)

(e) Nabhag, King of Nedishtha became Vaisya. His son Dhristi became Brahmin. Further his son became Kshatriya.

(f) Matanga was son of Chandaal became a Brahmin.

(g) Trishanku was a King became a Chandaal in his afterlife.

(h) Ravana was born from Pulastya Rishi but became a Rakshas.

Vedic society considers all humans to be one single Jaati or race, upholds the dignity of labour and provides equal opportunity for all humans to adopt the Varna of their own choice.

Upanishad

Casteism has also been discussed in Upanishad. Vajrasuchi Upanisad is a medieval ear Sanskrit text and a minor Upanishad of Hinduism. It is identified as a Vedanta text and attached with Saamaveda. This text discusses the four Varnas (caste system) – Brahamana, Kshatriya, Vaisya, Sudra, but this social division does not depend on Jiva (life, soul), Deha (body), Jati (birth), Jyana (knowledge), Karma (deeds), Dharmic (virtues or performer of rites).

The Jiva does not make anyone a Brahamana, because with rebirth the Jiva migrates from one body to another. But this Jiva remains the same individuality while the body changes.

Every human beings body is same. It is made up of the same five elements. Basically the colour complexion of a human body depends on the area they have lived. So Deha or body does not make anybody Brahmana.

Various sacred books tell that many great Rishis born in various casts and diverse origin, such as Vyasa from a fisherman's daughter, Kaushika from Kusa grass, Valmiki from an ant hill etc. Regarding their birth origins, they achieved greatness. So Jati or birth cannot determine one as a Brahmana.

Jnana or knowledge does not determine one as a Brahmana. People who belong to the other Varnas like Kshatriya, Vaisya, Sudra can also acquire knowledge through which they are able to establish themselves in the society. Rishi Viswamitra was Kshatriya. By the knowledge of scriptures and meditation, he had acted as Rishi Bola, Brahmin or Saint.

Karma or deeds do not make a Brahmana, because all living beings perform the same deeds, past and future embodiments are common and everyone is impelled by past.

Dharmic actions are not restricted to just the Brahmanas. They can be performed by all the Varnas. Anyone can perform religious rituals.

According to Vajrasuchi Upanishad, a Brahmana is the one who has realized his Atman (innermost self, soul). A Brahmana who knows that the Atman is truth, is knowledge, is bliss and is eternity and is free from every desires.

Chandogya Upanishad also said about the Caste system. Those who did good Karma (work), they will quickly attain some good birth like a birth of a Brahamana, Kshatriya, Vaisya etc. But those, whose conduct has been evil, will quickly attain an evil birth like a birth of a selfish and dirty person, or a dog or other which is very evil. So Chandogya Upanishad explained that every human being is taking birth on the basis of their work and the division of Varna depends on it.

Brihadaaranyaha Upanishad explained about Caste System. According to Puraana, various castes are born out from the different body parts of Brahma who is also the creator of this Universe. But Brihadaaranyaka Upanishad in its fourth chapter(Part-One) explains that, either through Vedic rites associated with meditation on a deity or through meditation alone anybody can attain the position of Prajaapati who had created this World and through His wondrous of Maayaa He created "male and female" without effecting his own individual existence. This text explains that Prajaapati or Brahma projected the Gods – the superhuman beings; Fire from His mouth, Indra, Varuna and the others God from His arms, the Vaayus, Rudras and others from His thighs and Pushan from His feet. After the different bodies were manifested Atman (Consciousness) entered into them all and worked in the body through the different organs. When the Atman is known all things are known. But if anyone ignores the Atman he will be caught in the eternal loop of Sansaara which is governed by the laws of Caste (Jaati). In the beginning all people belonged to the Brahmin caste. But society cannot flourish without a protector; so the military or Kshatriya caste was created. But there cannot be any social well-being without wealth; so the Vaisya caste was created. And since manual work is necessary to sustain the social structure, the Sudra caste came into being. In order to control the fierce nature of the military, Dharma or justice was promulgated. All being from the phenomenal universe – from the gods to the insects – must perform their respective duties to others for the happiness and welfare of all. So as per Brihadaaranyaka Upanishad the division of caste happened on the basis of responsibility and not by birth.

Satyakama Jabala

ChandogyaUpanisada said about SatyakamaJabala in chapter four. Satyakama was a little boy and his mother was Jabala. He desired to spend his life as a Brahmachari in a Tapovan. So he went to his mother and said about his wish that he wanted to get trained for the highest knowledge. He asked his mother about his ancestry. His mother was very happy to hear this. But she could not say the name of Satyakama's father, because she did not know who the father of Satyakama was. She told her son that she was very poor and she served many men in many countries as a slave girl. She had never been married. She said that she was Jabala and Satyakama was her son. If his Master asked him about his ancestry then he must said that he was the son of Jabala. He was SatyakamaJabala and it was his identification.

Many scholars refused to accept him as disciple. After that he reached at the Tapovan of Rishi Goutama. He was a great sage. Satyakama wanted to be his disciple. Rishi Goutama asked about his lineage. He told exactly what his mother said and identified himself as SatyakamaJabala. The sage was impressed with the honesty and purity of the little boy. He said that none other than a Brahmin could be so pure and honest. Rishi Goutam accepted Satyakama as his disciple affirming God abides in all. Despite unknown identity of

parenthoodSatyakama established himself as a great illuminate soul under a great master on the basis of truth and devotion.

Ramayana

First great Indian epic is Ramayana where Caste system explained through various incidents.

Casteism is not the message of Ramayana. Rather Ramayana condemns it, and it promotes harmony. One character of Ramayana is Shabari. The epic describes her as a true devotee, a saint, a yogi and who was given the greatest blessings by Sri Rama. Based on her faith and devotion she was waiting for Rama's arrival.

Lord Rama eating berry after tasted by Shabari as to sweetness

When Sri Rama entered in her ashrama she was bewildered. She wondered how to pay him obeisance. Sri Rama addressed her 'Bhamini' which means respected lady. Rama said that he considered relationship only on devotion. Rama had eaten Indian Berry after being tasted by Shabari, a low caste woman. A person may be of higher status in terms of caste, family, religion, wealth, knowledge, intelligence etc. but if he or she had no devotion to God, the person was just like clouds without water. The message is that God only recognises true devotion and not the caste, wealth, status etc. of a person.

Lord Rama's Feet Being Washed by the Kewat (Boatman) from Lower Caste

Another character Kewat, a boatman, belonged from low caste, Rama allowed him to touch his holly andkingly body by allowing him to wash his feet, is also depicted as a great devotee and servant. He was ready to sacrifice his life for his master Sri Rama. He was very wise with intuition and intellect who gave advice to the royal secretary and even to Sri Rama's brother Bharata, later on when Bharata had come in search of his brother Rama to take Him back to Ayodhya. He belonged from a lower caste still he was honoured by Sri Rama and his family. Sri Rama called Kewat his friend and brother like his other brothers. That examples show that Sri Rama, his family and the

Lord Rama taking Hanumana a living being - a subordinate in his loving arms

people of Ayodhya had respect and love the real devotees of Sri Rama irrespective of their caste and social background.

One of the main characters in Ramayana is Veer Hanumana who was the ultimate devotee of Ramachandra. He belonged from the ape dynasty though Rama respected and loved Him as His younger brothers Lakshmana andBharata. Lord Rama said to Hanumanji, "O Hanumana, you are twice as dearto me as Lakshmana and dear to me like Bharata."

Mahabharata

The great Indian epic Mahabharata told about Caste system. At that period the four Varnas clearly existed. But the main thing of Mahabharata is, it gives us both – the problem and the solution also. The caste system during this period was austere as per as liberal. Shantanu, the King of Hastinapur married a lady named Satyavati who was an adopted child of a fisherman chieftain, Dusharaj (also a ferryman) on the bank of river Yamuna. But originally she is the Princess of Chedi. She was the daughter of the Chedi King Vasu (also known as UpariCharaVasu), and a cursed Apsara (celestial nymph) who was turned into a fish named Adrika. But in society she was known as the daughter of a fisherman. Still she was married by the King of Hastinapur and became the Queen of Hastinapur. As a young woman, she met with a great sage namedParaasara before her marriage with Shantanu.Satyavati fathered a son name Vyasa out of wedlock.Vyasa was their spiritual son. Sage Paraasara made a spiritual ambience and the great sage Vyasa took birth. Despite belonging to upper caste sage Paraasara fathered a son with a fisherman's daughter who belonged to a lower caste. Vyasa the son of sage Paraasara and Satyavati was a great sage and also the writer of the great Indian Epic Mahabharata.

Satyavati then married Shantanu, the king of Hastinapura. Satyavati's father agreed to the marriage on condition that Satyavati's son would inherit the throne of Hastinapura. But King Shantanu disagreed with that. Because he already declared that his eldest son Devabrata (Bhisma) was the heir to the throne. Bhisma was

Lord Krishna eating skin of banana being given with love by a daasi (servicemaid)

the son of Shantanu and his first wife Ganga. After hearing this Devabrata took an oath that he never married and he never claimed for the throne. Then the marriage occurred and Satyavati gave birth to two sons of Shantanu – Chitrangada and Vichitravirjya. After Chitrangada's death his younger brother Vichitravirya was crowned king, while Bhisma ruled on behalf of him under Satyavati's command. Vichitravirya married the princesses of Kashi-Kosala: Ambika and Ambalika, who were won by Bhishma in a Swayamvara (marriage choice). The childless Vichitravirya met with an untimely death from tuberculosis. To continue the dynasty further Satyavati called her son Vyasa. Then Dhritarastra, Pandu and Vidura took birthspiritualy from Ambika, Ambalika and a maid of Ambika respectively. Vyasa wasthe father of a son who's mother was a "Daasi" and she was belong from a lower caste. The name of that son was Vidura. Dhitarastra and Pandu were his two elder brothers. After that he elected as the Prime Minister. The Prime Minister of the state Hastinapur was Vidura who was very intelligent and wise person identified as 'Daashiputra'.But he was designated as Prime Minister of the State. Vidura belonged to lower caste still Lord Krishna preferred to accept food from him and his wife Sulabha. Krishna had even eaten skin of banana as in deep love and devotion. Vidura's wife was throwing Lord Krishna Eating Skin of Banana Being Given with love by a Daasi (Servicemaid) pulp and offering skin to Krishna.

Some systems try to discriminate the people through their birth but this era did not support the caste system on the basis of birth but on the basis of occupation. Knowledge was very important at that time. Another very important character of Mahabharata is Karna who was originally known as Vasusena. He is one of the central characters in this epic. Karna was the adopted child of Adhiratha and Radha. Adhiratha was the charioteer of King Dritarastra of Hastinapur. They named him Vasusena. He also known as Radheya, son of Radha. But originally Karna was the son of Surya and Kunti, born to Kunti before her marriage with Pandu. For the sake of reputation of her being a vergin girl, Kunti had flo the child Karna in a river. The adopted Parents of Karna belonged to a lower caste. So socially he belonged to a lower caste. ButDuryodhana, the son of Dhritarastra,the Prince of Hastinapur considered him as one of his best friends and declared him the King of the state Anga. He was also known as "Angaraj". During the war of Kurukshetra,Karnacame to know the original story of his birth from his mother Kunti. Without knowing the actual identification of Karna, the Prince of Hastinapur, Duryadhana admitted him as his friend considering him to be only competent person to defeat Arjuna and gave him a social identity of a King, Kshastriya.Later Karna had known that he was the son of Kunti, a Kshatriya.

One of the most important events was the birth of Lord Krishna in a Kshatriya family but he represented YaduVansa which is socially known as a lower caste.In the Srimadbhagavat Gita, the sacred scripture of the Hindus we find that Lord Krishna in chapter 4 mentions about Castism. He says that he has created the four varnas namely Brahmin, Kshatriya, Vaisya and Sudra according to the work they performed in the society. However, he has given a message of respect each other. He has emphasized on the division on the basis of work and not on the basis of birth. In the Gita Lord Krishna says about caste system.

Srimadbhagavad Gita

चातुर्वर्ण्यं मया सृष्टं गुणकर्मविभागशः ।
तस्य कर्तारम् अपि मां विद्धय अकर्तारम अव्ययम् ।।

chātur-varṇyaṁ mayā sṛiṣhṭaṁ guṇa-karma-vibhāgaśhaḥ
tasya kartāram api māṁ viddhyakartāram avyayam

"I have created this fourfold order (4 Varnas/ Castes namely – Brahmins, Kshatriyas, Vaisyas and Shudras) according to the work of engagements and work being done.

ब्राह्मणक्षत्रियविशां शूद्राणां च परंतप ।
कर्माणि प्रविभक्तानि स्वभावप्रभवैर् गुणैः ।। 41 ।।

brāhmaṇa-kṣhatriya-viśhāṁ śhūdrāṇāṁ cha parantapa
karmāṇi pravibhaktāni svabhāva-prabhavair guṇaiḥ

"O Arjuna, the activiries of the Brahmanas, Kshatriyas, Vaisyas and Sudras are clearly divided according to the qualities born of their own nature.

शमो दमस् तपः शौचं क्षान्तिर् आर्जवम् एव च ।
ज्ञानं विज्ञानम् आस्तिक्यं ब्रह्मकर्म स्वभावजम् ।।

śhamo damas tapaḥ śhaucham kṣhāntir ārjavam eva cha
jñānaṁ vijñānam āstikyaṁ brahma-karma svabhāva-jam

"The actions of a Brahmin arising from his own nature are serenity, self-control, austerity, purity, tolerance, honesty, knowledge of the Vedas, wisdom and firm faith."

शौर्यं तेजो धृतिर् दाक्ष्यं युद्धे चाप्य् अपलायनम् ।
दानम् ईश्वरभावश्च क्षात्रं कर्म स्वभावजम् ।।43।।

śhauryaṁ tejo dhṛitir dākṣhyaṁ yuddhe chāpy apalāyanam
dānam īśhvara-bhāvaśh cha kṣhātraṁ karma svabhāva-jam

"The actions of a Kshatriya born of his own nature are heroism, exuberance, determination, resourcefulness, no trace of cowardice in battle, generosity and leadership."

कृषिगौरक्ष्यवाणिज्यं वैश्यकर्म स्वभावजम् ।
परिचर्यात्मकं कर्म शूद्रस्यापि स्वभावजम् ।।

kṛiṣhi-gau-rakṣhya-vāṇijyaṁ vaiśhya-karma svabhāva-jam
paricharyātmakaṁ karma śhūdrasyāpi svabhāva-jam

"The actions of a Vaisya born of his own nature are agriculture, cow protection and trade; also the actions of a Sudra born of his own nature consists of service to Brahamanas, Kshatriyas and Vaisyas."

But Lord Krishna's commandment is ignored while Bharatwasi worship Him till today. Unfortunately today in our society the caste division is not based on quality or action of work, rather it is based on birth or heredity.

With the passage of time, the caste system which was not prevalent has now accelerated. A certain class of people with vested interests merge the system of Casteism with Hinduism.

Manusmriti

Caste system has also been defined by Maharshi Manu in his book titled "Manusmriti". Here Manu founded Caste System. Manu asserts that Brahmin can become Sudra and Sudra can become Brahmin. Similarly, Kshatriyas and Vaisyas can also change their Varnas. Manusmriti acknowledges and justifies the Caste System as the basis of order and regularity of society for the purpose of jobs, engagements, programme.

Maurya Dynasty

In the later period of India, basically in the period of Maurya Dynasty, minister and the political adviser of the great King Chandragupta Maurya, Kautilya described Caste system in his book Arthasashtra. Through his perspective Caste happened on the basis of birth. There are four Varnas in the society and an individual's placement in the varna system defined their education, social and economic status and also their choice of work. King Chandragupta Maurya was not Kshatriya. Kautilya, the Brahmin made him a King.

Goutam Buddha

Goutam Buddha also said about Caste System. Buddha makes no compromise with conventional and orthodox views of fixed social hierarchies. Not only does he open the door of enlightenment to all, regardless of call or creed, but he also emphasizes the inherent equality of all, considering caste prejudice to be one obstacle of the path of enlightenment. All people, irrespective of caste, stands as equals before the moral law. Reward or punishment meted out in accordance with positive or negative karma, not according to caste. People are born in heaven or hell as per their karmic balance. Everyone is capable of moral and spiritual development and everyone can develop within himself loving thoughts towards all beings free from hatred and ill-will. There is only one criterion for a person's true status, and that is the criterion of moral and spiritual progress. Such progress is open to all equally, and thus there can be no reality of classifications of worth created by human beings. A person is always

capable of transformation. Since there is no valid ground for caste distinction, Buddhism rejects these obsolete and anachronistic customs without reservation, imparting teachings that preach the unity and equality of all people.

Adi Shankarachariya

AdiSankarachariya was one of a great Indian philosopher and theologian of 8th century B.C. consolidated the doctrine of Advaita

Vedanta. He also established the main current of thoughts on Hinduism and as well as on the Caste System. AdiSankarachariya never supported caste system, by birth or by profession. There was a story behind his thought on caste system. Once while in Kashi, Adi Shankarachariya and his disciples were going to the temple after taking a bath in the Ganga, there was a person coming in opposite direction. He belonged to a caste of cemetery dwellers, which was considered as lowest among the caste hierarchy. He was a chandala. The disciples of Shankarachariya ask the man to move aside as he was unclean. To which the man responds, 'Should I move my body which is composed of the five element as yours or the soul which ever pure?' listening to this, AdiShankara fell at the man's feet and even proclaimed that man was his Guru. In his book "Nirvana Sataka" AdiSankarachariya says that, 'he isnot his religion or his lineage, he is

eternal joy, he is Shiva'. This is the beauty of Advaita Philosophy, according to which everything is just one in different manifestation.

Mahaprabhu Shri Chaitanya Dev

Lord Mahaprabhu Shri Chaitanya appeared in the late fifteenth century, 1486. He took birth at Bengal when the Pathana Muslims ruled over the India. ShriChaitanya started "Sankirtan" at Navadwip city. At that time Chand Kazi was the magistrate of the city. Chand Kazi was against "Harinaam Sankirtan". The people, who sang "Sankirtan", were tortured by Chad Kazi. And he also tried to convert Hindu into Muslim. After hearing that Mahaprabhu Shri Chaitanya became very angry. It was an unbearable sin and Shri Chaitanya Dev decided not to forgive him. He arranged a great "Hari Naam Sankirtan" which was the first public performance of Sankirtan. It was a big carnival. The carnival reached in front of the house of Chand Kazi after walking around the entire city. Chand kazi was frightened to hear the sound of the "Sankirtan". Chaitanya Dev sent some respectable members to bring Chand before Him. Chand Kazi realized his sin and he surrendered himself in front of Lord Chaitanya. After that Chand became one of His great devotees. It is the Bhakti Movement of Lord Mahaprabhu Shri Chaitanya. He involved all the people of His community, even who also belonged from different lower castes and different religions, in His "Naam Sankirtan". He removed all the barriers between the higher caste and lower caste and the religion. In that way Mahaprabhu Shri Chaitanya established the purity of the society and spread it all over the world. Chaitanya and Nityananda scattered the name of Hari to everyone, including the pariah (a social group of southern India who are not accepted by a society), and embraced them all. The superiority or inferiority of a man does not depend on his caste or his position in society. It depends upon his character and purity.

British Rule in India

When the British Raj began to take power in India in 1757, they exploited the caste system as a means of social control. During the 1930s and 40s, the British Government made laws to protect the untouchables and low-caste people. Within Indian society in the 19th and early 20th there was a move towards the abolition of untouchability.

After Independence India become a democratic, socialist and

secular country. According to this policy there is a separation between religion and state. Practicing untouchability or discriminating a person based on his caste is legally forbidden. Along with this law the government allows positive discrimination of the depressed classes of India. But with all this positive discrimination policy, most of the communities who were low in the caste hierarchy remain low in the social order even today. There also exist upper caste and lower caste and communities who were high in the social hierarchy remain even today high in the social hierarchy.

Sri Ramakrishna

Social reform happened at that time. Some social reformers tried to remove various social problems created by caste system in Indian society. In Sri Ramakrishna's language, the caste system can be removed by one means only, and that is the love of God. Lovers of God do not belong to any caste. The mind, body and soul of a man become purified through divinelove.

Swami Vivekananda

Swami Vivekananda, the main disciple of Sri Ramakrishna was one of the social reformers told about Caste system. He opined that Caste is a social system and not religious one. The caste system is opposed to the religion of the Vedanta which teaches that all are manifestation of

All Human Being Are Manifestation of God

God all are His children. All are perfect and divine. Oh God! Thou infinite reflection is in all living beings.

Caste is a social custom, and all the great preachers of India have tried to break it down. Swamiji, in his days of pilgrimage, smoked Hookah from an old man who was from the lower caste. He was a scavenger. Swamiji was able to realise his inner vision of Universal oneness. Supreme Lord abides in all. From Buddhism downwards, every sect has preached against caste system which has evolved. Caste is simply the outgrowth of the political institutions of India and narrow minded, selfish, greedy people; it is a hereditary trade guild. There is neither existence nor non-existence, all is Atman or Souls. Shake off all ideas of relativity; shake off all superstitions. Everybody is pure and divine by their very nature. In Vedas, Darshanas, Puranas

Swami Vivekananda is Smoking from The Hookah of an Untouchable

or Tantras it is never said that the soul has any gender, creed or caste. In one word Swamiji told that Caste is a social custom.

Overall View About Caste System

In the Vedic period there was no discrimination between the four varnas as we see today. Especially the Sudras participated in all religious rituals during Vedic period which become progressively restricted in the later times. In the medieval period, the three key domains dominated were meals, marriage and right to conducting religious worship. Marriage outside caste was forbidden strictly due to which sometimes many people married within their own jati (caste). Anyone can take food from a Brahmin hand, but a Brahmin become sinful if he or she accepts food from lower caste. In terms of worship, only the priestly class-Brahmins were allowed to conduct religious services. Kshatrias and Vaisyas were allowed to offer worship inside temples but Sudras were prohibited to access temple. They can worship Lord Vishnu or any deity of Hindu Sanatan Dharma. But the Hindu villagers tried to keep their identity through caste system. In British era, British exploited caste system as a tool to maintaining their rule over India. British made Brahmins their ally by restoring some of their privileges revoked by the Muslim rulers. During the 1930s and 40s when the antibritish activities were high, the British Government made laws to save the untouchables and similar low caste people by grouping them under the special category called "Scheduled castes" to create a division among the people. Their principle was divide and rule.

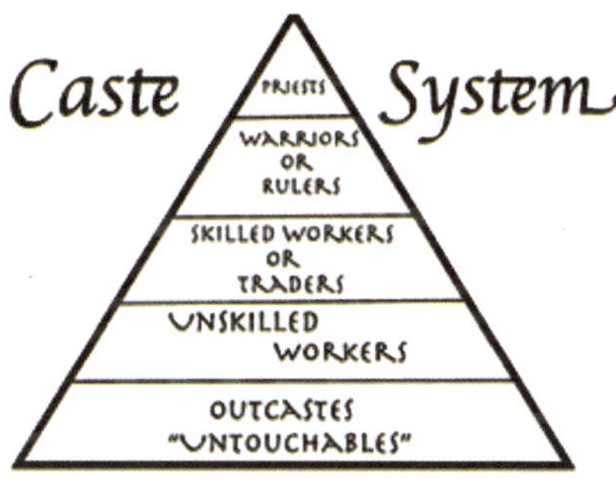

Conclusion

न जात्याब्राह्मणश्चात्रक्षत्रियो वैश्यवच ।
न शूद्रो नच वै म्लेच्छो भेदिता गुण कर्मभः ।। (शुक्रनीतिसार 1/37)

अर्थः मनुष्य जन्म से ब्राह्मण, क्षत्रिय, वैश्य, शूद्र अथवा म्लेच्छ नही होता, इन सबके भेद का कारण गुण-कर्म है।

In this world, no one is a Brahmin (Brahma), Kshatriya (a warrior caste), Vaishya (caste doing trading/business) and Shudra (low caste) by birth but on the basis of quality (Guna) and deeds and actions (Karma).

योधीतविद्यः सकलः च सर्वेषां गुरुर्भवेत् ।
नचजात्याऽनधीतोयोगुरुर्भवति ।। (शुक्रनीतिसार 4/3/21)

अर्थः जो कला सहित विद्या को जानता है वही सबका गुरु होने योग्य होता है। जो पढ़ा गुणा नहीं है वह जाति विशेष में जन्म लेने से गुरु होने का अधिकारी नहीं है।

A person who has profound knowledge about every perspective should be considered as a Guru or teacher. A person, who belongs to a community or race where the light of education hasn't reached yet, cannot establish himself as a Guru.

Bharat's saints like Surdas, Saint Kabir, Saint Tukaram, Saint Thiruvalluvar and Saint Ramdas, Saint Ravi Das came from the humblest sections of society and they are revered to this day by all irrespective of caste.

Lord Krishna said in Bhagavad Gita in the battlefield on the division of society based on the skill, jobs, occupation for relatively greater stability, service, efficiency and dignity to the individuals. It was also to transgress hereditary skill acquired in the family. It is for economic and social system. There was no untouchability.

God has manifested human being in His own image. God is the force within all. God is alone. He manifested in many :

।। एकोहम वहुस्याम ।।

"ekohaṃ bahusyām"

In the great religious epic "The Ramayana", saint Tulsidasa wrote, "Siya Ram Mai sab jag jani": The whole world is full of Lord Rama-Sita –incarnation of God and Goddess.

Lord Krishna said' "I am seated in the hearts if all beings."

|| सर्वभूतहर्तिरता: ||

|| सर्वस्यचाहंहृदसिन्नविष्टो ||

"sarvabhUtahiterataaH ||

sarvasyacaahaMhRudisanniviShTo" ||

Lord Krishna also said,

|| मयातत्मदिंसर्वव्यंगद्वयक्तमूर्तनि ||

|| मत्स्थान सिर्वभूतानिचाहंतेष्ववस्थति ||

mayātatamidaṁsarvaṁjagadavyaktamūrtinā |

matsthānisarvabhūtāninachāhaṁteṣhvavasthitaḥ ||

Means, The entire Universe has been manifested from My form. All beings are dependent upon Me but I am not dependent on them.

All being are children of God. Discrimination on the basis of birth is in fact disrespect to the children of God. Sanatana Dharma – Hinduism believe in Pantheism that God is in everything.

Discrimination on the basis of caste has been outlawed in India, it still exists in the community today.

Liberation in thought is very important. No one is untouchable. All are children of God – All are perfect, divine having immortal soul embodied in the mortal body.

Dr. H. P. Kanoria

Swami Vivekananda

Swami Vivekananda was a great spiritual and socio-economic reformer with this unique equation in mind that has infused spirituality into humanity, patriotism, socio-economic reformation and women empowerment.

Application of his philosophy is very essential to present conflicting spiritual and socio-economic conditions of the world.

His patriotic fervour fused into his burning spirituality. "Service to Mass" is "Service to God." A few lines of his poem "The Living God" are quoted as under:

"He who is in you and outside you
He who works through all hands,
Who walks on all feet,
Whose body are all ye,
Him worship, and break all idols!
Ye fails ! Who neglect the living God
And His inspired reflection with which the world is full."

Love is religion. Love is God. India will be raised with the power of spirit. He inspired Rockefeller to use his wealth for serving mankind.

Parents

Love parents as you love God. Mothers' love has no boundary. Mother is your first guru. Never hurt parents, specially mother.

Pure Foods

Food contains all the energies that go to make up the forces of our body and mind. There are certain kind of foods that produce a certain change in the body and mind. The misery we suffer is occasionally by the food we take. After a heavy and indigestible meal, it is very hard to control the mind. After drinking a large quantity of wine / alcoholic beverages, a person is unable to control the mind.

Meat should be avoided. It is not pure. One gets pleasure for a moment and another creature, who is also a manifestation of God, has to give up its life. It would be rather better if every man who eats meat, kills the animal himself but instead of doing so, society gets a class of persons to do that business and then people hate such class of persons. In England, no butcher can serve on the jury, the idea being that he is cruel in nature.

Individuality / Youth

As a Nation we have lost individuality. Every youth must develop his personality with characteristics of individuality. A youth has his role on the stage of the world. He must play his role efficiently and to the best perfection. So the youth must be self motivated to do hard work, have integrity, discipline, faith and love for all and the Supreme Lord.

"Work, work the idea, the plan, my boys, my brave, noble, good souls – to the wheel, to the wheel put your shoulders! Stop not to look back for name or fame or any such nonsense. Throw self overboard and work".

My child, what I want is muscles of iron and nerves of steel, inside which dwells a mind of the same material as that of which the thunderbolt is made. Strength, manhood, Kshatra Virya plus Brahma Teja. Never sacrifice your own faith.

Be courageous and fearless. Face the brutes. "Face the Maya". Face the Death. Cowards can never be victorious. Have faith in yourself. You are the children of God. You are the sharer of immortal bliss. Be a lion and not a sheep.

"My sons, all of you be man. This is what I want. If you are even a little successful, I shall feel my life has been meaningful."

Nation

"My India, Arise! Where is your vital force? In your immortal soul? Throw away weakness, superstition and rise to hail a new India."

India preached the spiritual oneness to the whole universe. India lives in its villages. The national sin is the neglect of the masses. We have forgotten the doctrine of Vedanta, the doctrine of Universal equality. Women have been neglected. Look at our girls becoming mothers in their teens. We are horrible sinners. Look at female foeticide.

Manu said that "The Gods are pleased where women are held in esteem." We worship "Shakti", but we neglect women. All the wealth of the world cannot help one little Indian village, if the people are not taught to help themselves, work hard, have faith in themselves, cultivate obedience have unity, have discipline, have conviction of power of goodness, absence of jealousy and suspicion, education, moral, technical, intellectual ability. Help each other. Do not be narrow minded and narrow hearted.

India will be raised not with the power of flesh but with the power of spirit. India is a sleeping dragon. When it will awake, move and rise, no power on earth can stop its glory. Lord is with his / her righteous children.

Women

There is no chance for the welfare of the world unless the condition of women is improved. It is not possible for a bird to fly on one wing. India of the Vedas time entertained a great respect for women amounting to worship. The conditions of women in Mughal ruled and British ruled India were deplorable.

Swami Vivekananda is the first monk to uphold and do work for the freedom and equality of women and realising her importance for the functioning of home and society. He visioned that Indian women would be a combination of the western spirit of Independence, freedom and dynamism with Indian values of austerity, purity and chastity. His English disciple Bhagini Nivedita played a major role in promoting the rights of women in rural India. He said that women have as much ability, rather more than men.

The rise of outstanding women administrators, statesmen, scientists, writers and spiritual teachers is gradually proving the truth of these prophetic words of Swami Vivekananda. Women all over the world are coming forward with a combination of the mother's heart and hero's will. There should not be tortures / abuses and violence against women.

They should not remain as an object of sex and commerce.

Caste

Swami Vivekananda said that in religion there is no caste. Caste implies a social institution. Do not blame Hinduism or Vedanta. Vedanta philosophy is of universal equality. But, curse power and money mongers.

In Gita, Lord Krishna had given a vivid description – Brahmans who are knowledgeable, wise, rich in study of scriptures, followers of righteousness; Kshatriyas – fighters, defenders, administrators, protectors of society and nation; Vaishyas – businessman, traders, industrialists; Sudras – for service. Society's classification was based on the jobs being done by each individual. There was no lower caste or upper caste. After returning to India, Swami Vivekananda said to an English friend, "India I loved before I came away. Now the very dust of India has become holy to me, the very air is now to me is holy, it is now the holy land, the place of pilgrimage, the Tirtha."

Swami Vivekananda : "I believe in God, and I believe in man. I believe in helping the miserable. I believe in going even to hell to save others" "I may have to be born again because I have fallen in love with man".

I do not believe in a God or religion which cannot wipe the widow's tears or bring a piece of bread to the orphan's mouth" "We want truth to come to us. Love will make every word talk like thunderbolt".

The truth of all religions

Hinduism

Hinduism is Sanatana Dharma. It means eternal law.

Philosophy of Dharma is – Righteousness, Love, Service, Austerity, Simplicity and Faith in the Divine Lord.

Artha (money) is the means of living. It is not the aim. Dharma precedes Artha. To earn money in righteous way without hurting others, without cheating others, without grabbing others' means of livelihood and possession. Kama denotes love and lust. Love for all and is righteous ways of love, satisfies natural instinct of Kama (lust) for ongoing creation. Lust is to be limited. Indulgence is bad. To be lion, it is to be limited. So, Righteousness (dharma) precedes artha (money) and kama (lust & love).

Moksha means liberation. Human body is manifestation of infinite parambrahma. In duality, as human being, we enjoy Brahma (Supreme Lord) like one enjoys sugar. In non-duality a person is merged with the Lord. Liberation means to realise this ultimate truth and merge in the Lord while following the path of Dharma, Love and Service.

Scriptures of Hinduism are based on Sruti (revealed) and Smriti (remembered). Main scriptures are four Vedas, Upanishads, Puranas, Mahabharata, Ramayana, The Bhagwat Gita a treatise from the Mahabharata spoken by Lord Krishna to Arjuna is the essence of the teaching of the Vedas, finally Hinduism. Hinduism believes in "creation, sustenance and destruction of world by Divine Lord". Reincarnation based on Karma Yoga, Rajas Yoga, Bhakti Yoga and Gyan Yoga is the teaching of Lord Krishna.

The syllable Om represents Parambrahma. Om is the divine sound at the time of creation of the world when the world was void. Scriptures give insight and philosophical teaching to the living world and how to realise the ultimate truth and reality with all happiness in austerity and simplicity.

Max Muller and Josh Woodroffe translated Vedas & Upanishads in English for the knowledge of the world. Enlightended teachers like Sri Tulsidas, Sant Kabir, Sri Sri Aurobindo, Paramhansa Ramkrishna, Paramhansa Sri Yoginandji, Swami Vivekanandji, Swami Rama have been awakening the true meaning of existence and love, the magnetic force balance the cosmic creation. Epic Ramayana sways the common masses, influences their devotion to God and establishes the righteous living and destruction of person/ persons who follow the path of unrighteousness.

Hindu believes that there is a spirit – Him the sword cannot pierce – him the fire cannot burn – him the water cannot melt – him the air cannot dry. Human should be eternal and immortal, perfect and infinite and death means only a change of centre from one body to another.

Vedic sage proclaimed "Hear you children of immortal bliss, come out of darkness, delusion, and know him. You are not sinner. Like all rivers flowing to sea, all various paths of religion lead to one cosmic / divine power / God. It is oneness. It is universal oneness.

Jainism

Lord Mahavir was the 24th Tirthankara or Prophet of the Jain religion. His preaching is Ahimsa (Non-Violence), Anekanta (Non-Absolutism) and Aparigraha (Non- Possession).

Liberated souls are the supreme in this world.

"Do not injure any and do good to all that you can. Man has to bear his sorrow all alone. Attachment and aversion are the root causes of karma and karma originates from delusion". Dharma is essence. The ten virtues are forgiveness, right faith, right knowledge, right conduct, giving protection to living creatures, supreme forgiveness, humility, straightforwardness, truthfulness, purity, self restraint, austerity, renunciation, detachment, continence. "The soul verily is Brahman. Fight with your own self. One who conquers one's self by one's own self alone experiences supreme bliss"

"Conquer anger by forgiveness, pride by humility, deceit by

straightforwardness and greed by contentment." "Mediate on one's soul after controlling one's diet, posture, sleep and gaining knowledge wholesome and healthy food, in lesser quantity."

"Be free from fear and let others be free from fear." There should be no colour, no taste, no smell, no touch, no gender. The pure soul is free from the activities of mind, body and speech. It is full of infinite knowledge and perception, firmly established in the self.

Mahavir said that possession of an object itself is not possessiveness; the attachment to an object is possessiveness.

A monk in search of the supreme path of liberation resembles a lion (in fearlessness) an elephant (in dignity) a bull (in strength) a deer (in uprightness) a beast (in freedom from attachment) the wind (in being companion-less), the sun (in brilliance), an ocean (in serenity) the mountain (in firmness), the moon (in coolness) a diamond (in luster) the earth (in patience) a serpent (in being homeless) and the sky (independent, limitless, vast, humanity is the foundation of the Jain faith.

Thus, Jainism prescribes a path of non-violence for all forms of living being in the world. Self effort is essential for progress of soul on spiritual ladder to divine consciousness. One has to conquer own inner enemies. Every living soul is potentially divine. The universe and dharma are eternal, without beginning or end. The universe undergoes process of cyclical change. Soul incarnates in various life forms during its journey over time.

Jains do not believe in an omnipotent supreme being the creator. They believe in an eternal universe governed by natural laws. Compassion for all life both human and non-human is care to Jainism. Lord Mahavir was the last Tirthankara, preceded by 23 others to attend enlightenment. Jain rituals have been influenced by Hindu Philisophy. Hindu Holy books contain beautiful narration about Lord Rishabdev (first Tirthankar).

Lately there are sects in Jainism – Digambars and Svetambars. "Svetambars believe that women may attain liberation while digambaras do not believe in it. Holiest symbol is swastika. Other is Dharma-Chakra and Sidha-Chakra. Jain monks do research an obtain higher – education. "Do not injure any, do good to all that you can."

King Nami, believer of Jainism said, “Fight with yourself! Why fight with external forces? He who conquers himself through himself will obtain happiness.” He who is desirous of pleasures will not get them and will come to a bad end at last.

Christianity

The Christian faith is essentially faith in Jesus as the Christ; the son of God, the saviour. It is centered on the life and teachings of Jesus as presented in the New Testament. Resurrection of Jesus after three days of his death is the most important event. According to the gospels of Mathew and Luke, Jesus was conceived by the Holy Spirit and born from the Virgin Marry.

Trinity is an essential doctrine of Christianity – “Father, son and the holy spirit”. God is believed to be infinite. Trinity is also being defined as one God in three persons. Bible is the holy book. It is in two parts (The Old Testament & the New Testament). Christians assemble for communal worship on Sunday, the day of resurrection. The Cross is one of the most widely recognised symbols in the world.

Golden Rule

Do not do to others what ye do not wish done to yourself; and wish for others too. • Thou shalt love God above all things, and thy neighbour as thyself. • Blessed are the pure in heart, for thy shall be filled. • Blessed are they which do have hunger and thirst for righteousness, for thy shall be filled. • Do not fear them who kill the body; fear him who is able to destroy soul. • Judge not, that you be not judged. • Seek first the kingdom of God and His righteous-ness and all these things will be added to you. • Be not be afraid, only believe. • Oh father forgive them for they know not what they do. • Be you therefore perfect, even as your father heaven is perfect. • The light of the body is the eye; if therefore your eye be controlled, thy whole body shall be full of light. • Nature provides equity in life sustaining water, air, natural products balancing the entire earth. • Listen to own feeble voice of conscience every now and then.

Buddhism

Buddhism had its origin in the teachings of Gautama Buddha of the 5th century before Christianity became the world religion. Buddha saw truth by intuition and realisation. He was born in a royal family. Being moved by seeing an old man, a diseased person, a dead body and a sannyasin, he was moved and plunged into deep thought. After 6 years of renouncing everything, desired enlightenment dawned upon him. He preached full forty five years. He is not only the light of Asia but "the light of the world". Swami Vivekananda said, "He was the ideal karmayogi acting without motive, he was the greatest man ever born beyond compare."

Five Precepts : One has to abstain from killing, stealing, adultery, lying and liquor.

Eight Fold Path : Right understanding, thought, speech, action, livelihood, effort, mindfulness and concentration.

Buddha looks equally with a kind heart to all the living beings.

The Tathagata has found the middle path. To satisfy the necessities of life is not evil. To keep the body in good health is a duty for otherwise we shall not be able to trim the lamp to wisdom, and keep our mind strong and clear.

Judaism

Judaism is the 'religion, philosophy, and way of life' of the Jewish people. Originating in the Hebrew Bible (also known as the Tanakh), Judaism is considered by Jews to be the expression of the covenantal relationship which God developed with the Children of Israel.

Judaism is a monotheistic faith as it believes in only one God. Often this God is beyond our ability to comprehend, but God is nevertheless present in our everyday lives. Some connect with God through prayer, others see the divine in the majesty of the natural world, others may not think about God on a daily basis. Humankind in Judaism is the divine image of God. For this reason every person is equally important and has an infinite potential to do good in the world. People have the free will to make choices in their lives and each of us is responsible for the consequences of those choices. Judaism believes that Jews are uniquely connected and all Jews are part of a global Jewish community.

The Torah is Judaism's most important text which contains stories and commandments that teach about life and death. It contains the 10 Commandments as well as the 613 commandments (mitzvot). The Ten Commandments that all Jews consider to be the most important are:

- I am the Lord your God
- You shall not recognise the gods of others in My presence
- You shall not take the Name of the Lord your God in vain
- Remember the day of shabbat to keep it holy
- Honour your father and your mother
- You shall not murder
- You shall not commit adultery
- You shall not steal
- Do not give false testimony against your neighbour
- You shall not covet your fellow's possessions

Sikhism

Sikhism is founded on the teachings of Guru Nanak Dev and ten successive Sikh gurus in the 15th century Punjab. The word Sikh comes from the Sanskrit word 'sishya' meaning disciple and 'siksha' meaning instruction.

Sikhism has faith in "Waheguru" using the sacred symbol of "Ikonkar", the universal God. Holy scriptures are the Guru Granth Sahib (Adigranth) and Dasam Granth.

Sikhism believes in equality of all humans. God is one, but He has innumerable forms. God is love. God is unity. The same God resides in the temple, in the mosque and outside as well.

Spiritual union with God is the ultimate aim of life. They believe in an endless cycle of birth i.e reincarnation.

Sikhism accepted some of the basic doctrines of Hinduism. God is Absolute, All pervading, and external. He is the creator, the cause of causes. Life is not sinful in its origin. God himself takes human form. To make His will your own will is the means to achieve Him. Give up to His supreme will. He cannot be comprehended by reason, one can never have contentment even with the riches of the world. All things are manifestation of His will. Discover untold spiritual riches within yourself. God is the only doer. Remember Him day and night. So pure is God's name. Whoever obeys God, knows the pleasure of it, it has own heart. God's name is the ocean of peace.

Guru is God like in power as creator, protector and destroyer. In Hinduism "Guru Brahman Guru Bishnu Guru Shiva Guru's God (Govinda both are standing, whom should I salute first).

Three essentials for spiritual realisation of soul to God - Satguru, Satsang at holy assembly & prayers and Satnaam – chanting name of God. Like other religions Sikhism says, "Conquer your mind for victory over self ; victory over self is the victory over the world."

Third Guru Amar Das's son in law Ram Das founded the city of Amritsar, the Harmindar Sahib, the holiest city of Sikh. The 6th guru Har Govindji created "Akal Takht (the throne of timeless one) serving as the supreme decision making centre of Sikhdom. Guru Tegh Bahadur was executed by Aurangzeb for helping to protect Hindus. Govind Singh ended the line of human gurus and now the guru granth sahib serves as the eternal guru, with its interpretation vested with the community.

Nanak taught that ritual, religious ceremonies or idol worship is of little use and Sikhs are discouraged from fasting or going on pilgrimages. Gurudwaras are open to all, regardless of religion, background, caste or race. Guru Nanak's japji is a prayer. Jap meaning recitation of the divine name to combine all negative thoughts out of the mind. Sikh's religion does not permit divorce. Khalsa (meaning pure) is the name given by Govind Singh to all Sikhs who have been baptized or irritated by taking a ammrit in a ceremony called ammrit sancar. Guru Nanak said, "As fragrance abides in the flower, as the reflection is within the mirror so does the lord abide within you. Why search for him without?"

The ray has merged in the sun, The wave in the sea The light has merged in the light And man is fulfilled.

That which you practise day and night has been written on your forehead. How clear is the path of one who believes! He lives with honour, with honour he leaves walks straight on the highway, nor wanders in the byways. And is to Dharma, the duty bound when hands feet and body are soiled water washes them pure.

When the mind is polluted by sin and shame it is cleaned by love of your name for him you cannot hide your shame. When He the saver sees all within. If compassion be your mosque faith your prayer mat.

Islam

Arabia about the time of Muhammad's birth in Mecca in AD 570 was in a state of religious unrest. There was urgent need of moral reform. At the age of forty, Muhammad received his first "divine revelation" in the solitude of the mountains near Mecca. Onward he felt he had a mission in life to life to the people from moral degradation. He proclaimed himself as the messenger of God to mankind. Swami Vivekananda said, Christianity is increasing due to service and Islam is multiplying by sword. He suffered every kind of indignity when he began to denounce the worship of idols and observance of superstitious practices. He migrated to Madina. He sent missionaries to all parts of Arabia and even to neigh-bouring countries including Egypt and Persia.

Prophet Muhammad's lessons

• Have faith in God • Abandoning that which God disapproves • Purity and hospitality • Free from malice towards anyone • To love him who loves God • To hate him who hates God • To do unto all men and women as you would wish them to have done unto you • Speak the truth • Perform what you promise • Be chaste • Serve humanity – feed the hungry, serve sick • Resign to the will of God • Acquire riches in lawful manner • Love neighbour • Hold the oppressor from oppression • Whoever does good to you, return the same to him

• Whoever does good to you, return the same to him • Giving alms, out of the little one owns • God is merciful. He is gracious. He is pure. He loves the pure • Adore God. He sees you • God is humble. Be humble • God is unity. He likes unity • One will enter heaven, if one has faith in heart equal to a single grain of mustard seed • Faith is a restraint against all violence • He who knows his own self, knows God • With knowledge man rises to the heights of goodness and to a noble position.

Sufism

Sufism is defined by its adherents as esoteric, inner, mystical branch of Islam. Another name for a Sufi is dervish. Sufi means purity, truth and wisdom. Sufis trace their origin to an inner circle of disciples of the Prophet Muhammad, to whom he taught secret and hidden truths, not revealed to all. Living with total dedication and devotion to God, they realise God within their hearts, experiencing mystic visions and unity with the divine by the means of love and devotion towards the truth. This is called the 'Tarigat' – the spiritual path or way towards God. Through continuous meditation and contemplation one attains intuitive insights. One reaches the height of ecstasy through devotional music. Live in poverty to avoid material desires. And following path of truth, meditation, contemplation, living in austerity, singing songs of love in bliss ecstasy have the Union with divine. Muslims believe that they will become close to god in paradise after death and the final judgement. Sufis believe that one can become close to God and experience him while one is alive. The Sufi surrounds to God in love over and over.

The essential messages are remembrance of God - let go the consciousness of other things and forget all except god, until one can exclaim - 'All that I have read and know I have forgotten, only awareness of the friend now remains constant'. Sufi loves all beings as manifestation of god and serves them service to others means service to God. Sufi prays - "Thy light is in all forms. Thy love in all beings / In a loving mother, in a kind father, in an innocent child, in a helpful friend, in an aspiring teacher / Allow us to recognise that in all Thy

Holy names and forms as Rama, as Krishna, as Siva as Buddha / Let us know Thee as Abraham, as Solomon, as Zarathushtra, as Moses, as Mohammad and in many other names and forms known and unknown to the world." May the messages of God reach far and wide illuminating the whole humanity as one single brotherhood as Lalan Fakir, the famous Sufi Fakir sang-

The man who holds his beloved in his mind', Can do without the rosary. He enjoys solitude or

I am the end of all knowledge
I may not be I
If you know the real I
You will also know the unknown
And I merges with I

Taoism (Daoism)

It is the main stream of traditional religion in China. The word Tao (or Dao) translates as the 'path or way' of life In Chinese religion and philosophy, Tao emphasises three jewels—'compassion, moderation, humility.' Taoist thought generally focuses on nature, the relationship between humanity and the cosmos, health and longevity and wuwei (action through inaction) which is considered to produce harmony with the Universe.

Robinet asserts that Taoism is better understood as a way of life than a religion. "Man is a macrocosm for the Universe. The body ties directly into the Chinese five elements". The five organs correlate with the five elements, five directions and the seasons. Man may gain knowledge of the Universe by understanding himself. Various rituals, exercises and substances are said to positively attract one's physical and mental health. They are also intended to align one spiritually with cosmic forces or enable ecstatic spiritual journeys.

Some of the essence of Taoism and Hinduism appears to be the same. Lord Krishna told Arjuna, 'Action is inaction and inaction is action.' One of the means to be near Divinity: 'Five elements and five organs are to be regulated.'

Zoroastrian

Thee only do I know to be Supreme. All other I dismiss from this my mind. He who is known as Ahura Mazata with duteous deeds we worship Him alone we know thee as supreme above all lives. O pilgrims for the shrine! Where go come back! Come back! Ye, where? The beloved is here! His presence in all your neighbourhood both bless. Why will ye wander in the wilderness!

Confucianism

In reality, it is not a religion. Confucius was a philosopher, moralist, statesman, educationist and above all a saint but not a religionist. China has not suffered the calamity of a religious war. The Chinese have welcomed every visiting religion from outside and assimilated it by a gradual process of humanisation. Confucius said that with heaven and earth, there is no past nor present and no beginning nor end. The best way for human life is to follow nature and to be harmonised with it. Know to serve living beings, then think of serving God. All beings are just like the flowing water, changing and changing without a moment's cessation. A virtuous man has three awes: first awe for heaven's decree: then; second awe for a great man, third awe for the saint's words. His teachings urge one to be loyal and filial, faithful and moral, to know propriety and righteousness, to value shame and purity and to practise all ways of self-culture. The wise and the able should be chosen to rule: faithfulness and peacefulness cultivated by and maintained among all. Man must not only love his own parents and his own children, but also endeavour to give the aged rest and comfort, make the grown ups work and serve and help the young grow in body and mind. How to realise Perfect Beauty and Perfect Good is based upon the cultivation of individual personality.

China's ruling Communist Party embraces Confucianism for use in shaping what it likes to call a 'harmonious society', but it has also stoked the nationalist sentiments that sparked objections to the church in Qufu.

Bahai Religion

The Bahai Faith is a, founded by Bahaullah in nineteenth-century, emphasising the spiritual unity of all humankind. In the Bahai faith, religious history is seen to have unfolded through a series of divine messengers. The followers of Bahai religion believes -

• All humanity is one family • Women and men are equal • All prejudice - racial, religious, national, or economic - is destructive and must be overcome • We must investigate truth for ourselves, without preconceptions • Science and religion are in harmony • Our economic problems are linked to spiritual problems • The family and its unity are very important • There is one God • All major religions come from God • World peace is the crying need of our time

All religions

Essence of all religions is humanity which revolves around righteousness, action, creation, sustenance, happiness and ultimate self realisation to who am I and who is He. Human is called social animal. But it forget the same by overcoming greed and so on. Animals are better grateful. All you know the story of "Alexendra, the slave and lion". On being treated of his wound, lion though hungry for days did not eat Alexendara.

Hinduism is ageless, sanatana - a religion of wisdom, love and hope for all. It does not divide, but unites, does not injure but heals, does not kill but saves. If you attain to God and his kingdom of righteousness, all other things shall be added unto you.

One God and Father of all, who is above all and through all and in you all.

Ye who are seeking God! You are He! Ye need not search! He is ye very much! Why will ye seek for what was never lost? There is naught – else than ye! Be not in doubt. "The wise see in their heart the face of God. And not in images of stone seven clay, who in themselves, alas I can see him not. They see to find him in some outer spot".

To conclude

Religion everywhere served the purpose of supporting the moral & social principles which have made men civilised. To all religions. My salutation again and again or my salutation to the truth of all religions.

O Woman

O Wedded Woman! Unite and become the guiding light of this new family. Endowed with Dharma (righteousness), intelligence, understanding and love.

Care and respect for all the members of the family.

Share their joys and sorrows.

Attend to the well being of all.

Bring happiness and prosperity to this house.

Be free from greed, selfishness, ego, possessiveness, me and mine.

Speak and behave with harmony and sweetness.

Be all unanimous and of one accord.

Be not separated from one another; talk to each one sweet words with love.

Serve and hold in high esteem parents and elders.

Serve, share and love youngers with intelligence and understanding.

With love share food and other things and treat all children equally with your children.

Be honest and loyal to the husband and family.

Have positive thoughts and vibrations.

Never pay heed to negative opinions against in-laws.

Perform household duties while progressing in career.

Be courageous, generous and benevolent.

Achieve Bliss and Admiration.

The Supreme Lord by His mystical powers blesses both with sublime love, prosperity, health, happiness and humble fame.

Dr. H. P. Kanoria

- Based on the Holy Vedas

Why depressed? Why weep?
Why be an addict?

Talk to God

Dr. H.P. Kanoria

We are the children of God. We are the sharers of immortal bliss. We are holy, perfect and divine beings on Earth. God is our father, mother, brother and honest friend.

Why do we not talk to God? When we are depressed or meet failures, become a victim of wrong habit and evil friends? Do not weep or cry. Seek His light. You have a motivating force inside you. Do not doubt yourself. Read scriptures of all religions. You will find saints and prophets-many had talked, have been talking and shall remain talking with God. They have become Sun and Moon to give light to human beings.

Whenever you are in trouble, pray - "Lord, you are within me and all around me. I am in the castle of Thy presence.

Thou art my father. Thou art my light."

Talking with God is a definite fact. In the Bible, it is said that Lord appeared to Solomon in a dream by night. God said, "Ask what I shall give thee". Solomon said, "Give thy servant an understanding heart." And God said unto him, "Because thou hast not asked for long life, nor hast asked riches for thyself, nor hast asked the life of thine enemies, but hast asked for thyself understanding to discern judgement: Behold I have done according to thy words.

So I have given thee a wise and an understanding heart. And I have also given thee that which thou hast not asked, both riches and honour."

David, too, held many conversations with the Lord. He asked God, "Shall I go up against the Philistines and will Thou deliver them into mine hand?" God said unto him, "Go up for I will deliver them into thy hand."

All scriptures tell us that God will communicate with us (Jeremiah 29:130). "Ye shall seek me and find me when ye shall search for me with all your heart. The Lord is with you while ye be with Him and if ye see Him, He will be found by you; but if ye forsake Him, He will forsake you." (Chronicles 15:2)

Jesus Christ said, "I and my father are one!" Swami Shankara said, "I am Spirit and thou art that." God through His cosmic consciousness is aware of Himself in every atom creation.

Jesus said, "If thine eye be single, thy whole body shall be full of light." When you concentrate at the point between the eyebrows, the current in the two eyes reflects as one light and you behold the spiritual eye. "Behold, I stand at the door and knock; if any man hears my voice and opens the door, I will come into him and will sup with him and he with me." (Revelation 3:20)

Lord spoke to Moses. He gave him the 'Ten Commandments'. Lord talked to Prophet Mohammad on the hills of Medina. Allah directed him to save human beings who were then seized with a series of evils and vices. On being queried by Narendra Dutta (later Swami Vivekananda), Prof. Hasty of Scottish Church College had said, "Go to Dakshineswar. Sri Ramakrishna talks to mother Kali. He feeds Mother Kali. He relates to disciples about what Mother Kali tells Him."

After his father's demise, Vivekananda was in great financial difficulties even to meet simple domestic needs. Sri Ramakrishna asked him to go and ask Mother Kali. He simply asked for wisdom and service to humanity. Ramakrishna said to him that as he was told by Mother Kali, he would not have difficulty in getting simple food and basic necessities of life.

In Hindu scriptures, we find that Lord Krishna had talked to Arjuna, Lord Vishnu talked and blessed Prahlad and Dhruba. There are numerous instances. Sri Ramakrishna used to say that you should have faith and love in God and God will come, talk and help you. He said that a boy named Gopal was afraid of joining school as he had to pass through a dense forest. He was afraid of giants residing there. His mother told him not to fear, but invoke 'Madhusudan' (Lord Krishna). He would help you cross the forest. Having faith in his mother's words, he called 'Madhusudan' with longing, love and faith. Madhusudan came and helped him in all the ways.

God does appear to us in person. He is as real and actual as we are. The Lord is talking to us through vibrations. Luther Burbank talked to the flowers. God is calling us and speaking to us, but we do not hear Him. Though God hears all our prayers, he does not always respond. Our situation is like that of a child who calls for his mother, but the mother does not think it necessary to come.

St. Francis said, "Heaven is within us." When he was young, he heard God's voice, "Where are you running Francis? You cannot escape. I turned, but saw no one. I began to run again. I heard the voice again saying Francis, is this why you were born? To sing, make merry and entice the girls?" Francis continued to listen to the voice of God inside him. He then became the great Saint and the son of God.

God talks to everybody – the good and the bad and not only to saintly persons or boys or girls. God has come to you in many ways in life. But, one does not listen. God continues his efforts for years and years. Neale Donald Walsch in his three volume book "Conversations with God" has written how God communicates with all of us.

Love God in silence. God does not possess our love, he craves for our love. Swami Tulsidas said in Ramcharit Manas, "Love him as a miser loves money, as a drowning person loves breath."

When you yearn for God with intensity, He will come to you. Sri Sri Paramhansa Yogananda said, "You are His child. Do not pity yourself. You are loved. You must see His love for it encompasses eternal freedom, endless joy and immortality."

Swami Vivekananda said:

Thy Love I fear
Thy knowledge, man! I value not.
It is Thy love that shakes my throne.
Brings God to human tear
For love, behold the Lord of all
The formless, ever free.
Is made to take the human form
To play and play with thee
What learning, they of Vrinda's groves
The herdsman, ever got?
What science, girls that milked the kine?
They loved and me they bought.

Let us be righteous, courageous and love Him and His creatures. God alone knows His mysterious divine play. We are part of that play. Let us drink the wine of love of God instead of alcohol and drugs as God dwells in everyone to test the Truth of it. Each one has to eat and drink for oneself; much more think for oneself, so one has to think, feel and enjoy the bliss of God.

"Our duty is to encourage everyone in his struggle to live up to his own highest ideal, and strive at the same time to make the ideal as near as possible to the truth"

–Swami Vivekananda

Spirituality for Success

Dr. H. P. Kanoria

Spirituality encompasses humanity. It is internal law of creation. It is inherent nature. Every human being is infinite, perfect and divine. Soul is immortal. Creation is His manifestation. God was alone. He said "एकोहं बहुस्याम", I am one, let me become many.

I am one-alone, from this one, let there be many – this is the teaching of the Upanishads. Every human being is in His image endowed with love, virtues, ocean of strength, infinite knowledge and Infinite Power. He is our Father, Mother and Friend. Inner power needs to be awakened and ignited. One has to listen to own feeble voice of subconscious. The goal of life is to manifest divinity that we are bestowed with.

Spirituality is the essence of life. It awakens the inner power. It develops body, mind and soul. It ignites the spirit with strength and joy.

It infuses the eternal law of hard work with joy without the expectation of fruits. It gives insight, perception and intuition in complexity of life in the context of the material world.

Spiritual thoughts give strength to stand with poise and renewed strength during the storms of failures and depression. It strengthens one to overcome failures and to climb the ladder of success. Life becomes joyful and free from stress. In Spirituality, life is enlightened. Failures become stepping stones. It sharpens the memory. It gives new vitality. It imbibes faith in self and in all. It disciplines and balances the life. If you break the word Spirituality it is 'Spirit' and 'uality' that is Spirit is your quality. It is to recognise that you in Spirit and I in Spirit are the one same reality.

Swami Vivekananda said: "Manifest spirituality within you. Mark, if you give up spirituality the result will be that in three generations you will be extinct".

In the battlefield, Lord Krishna told Arjuna, who was in

depression due to the emotional grief of killing of relatives, elders and others for the kingdom that you have the right to perform your respective duties honestly, but do not try to control the results. Results of work should not be the motive. So, failures or success is not in one's control. Every human being has to work hard with rapt concentration in a righteous way.

Success is not only achievement in the material world. There has to be inner happiness, peace and stream of service and love. Failure and success are a part of the journey of life. Former President Dr. Prof. Abdul Kalam in his book, "The journey of my Life" wrote, "I firmly believe that unless one has tasted the bitter pill of failure, one cannot aspire enough for success. I have seen both sides of the coin and have learnt life's toughest lessons when I have been in the pit of despair that failure brought with it". Spirituality can guide us through the process of developing consciousness. Spiritual development within the mind, body and soul can help us sweep off failures and dive into the ocean of success. Dr. Kalam had inspiration from an acclaimed Enlightened Guru when he was in depression on not being selected for a job. One will have to learn the culture to bear failure and success. Success is not simple. Hard work with concentration is required. Holistic success gives joy which is universal. Control life. Make it simple. Moral integrity is essential. Focus your mind and feel the power of God within you. Success is assumed. Watch your time. Do not waste time. Mind must remain undefeated with source of fresh power from God. Analyze your failure and its causes and benefits from experience.

KonosukeMatsushita's spiritual philosophy in management in his book, "Not for Bread Alone" is the reason of its great success. Steve Job, a college dropout was working in Apple. He was dismissed by a new and very educated CEO who considered Steve as uneducated. Steve had bad times. He used to have his food at Iskcon every week. His intuition and insight was awakened through spirituality in India. He was reappointed with due respect. He then developed Apple. He made Apple a 600 billion company. Mark Zuckerberg, co-founder of Facebook said that he had spiritual awakening in India. Therein he had intuition.

To conclude, let us have tremendous faith in ourselves. In you is infinite power, unbounded wisdom and indomitable energy. Rouse power in yourself by positive thought and positive prayers. You will have success after success. Have the bow of determination.

According to the New Testament, "Whatever things you desire when you pray sincerely, believe that you have received them and you will have them". Let us affirm that I have divine power, I have infinite knowledge, I am success, I am success.

May God bless us and give courage and endurance.

Jai Bharat! Jai Vishwa! Success to all! Happiness to all!

Mother Earth

Truth, Eternal Order, that is great and stern.
Consecration, Austerity, Prayer and Devotion.
Uphold the Earth.
The Earth has many heights, slopes and unconfined plains.
In the Earth lies the sea, the rivers and other waters.
In her food and cornfields have come to be.
The Earth bears plants of various healing powers.
May she provide vast space for us.
May she confer on us the finest of her harvest.
May she give us cattle and crops.
May she give us magnificence and lustre.
The Earth bears all sustaining, treasure-beraing places.
The Earth bears the sacred Universal fire.
May the Supreme Lord and talented sages give us spiritual wealth and wealth.
Never sleeping cosmic powers protect Mother Earth without erring.
May Mother Earth pour on us riches in many turns and endow us with lustre.

Dr. H. P. Kanoria

- Based on the Holy Vedas

Rishi Sri Aurobindo

Dr. H. P. Kanoria

Rishi Aurobindo Ghosh was born on August 15, 1872 in a Kayastha family in the city of Calcutta in Bengal. His father Dr. Krishna Dhan Ghosh was a surgeon and his mother Swarnalata Devi was the daughter of Brahmo religious reformer Rajnarayana Basu. The meaning of Aurobindo (Sanskrit) is lotus. He took his education in England along with his brothers. His father studied medicine at King's College. All his three sons studied in an English school and then in London. Dr. Ghosh aspired that all his sons would pass the prestigious Indian Civil Service. Only Aurobindo passed the scholarship examination of King's College of Cambridge Universityh and stood first. In ICS examination, his rank was 11 out of 250 competitors. He spent two years in King's College but he did not want to serve the British. So he did not appear at the horse riding examination. Rather he joined the Maharaja of Baroda - Sayaji Rao Gaekwad III. He transferred to Baroda College as a teacher of French and later he was promoted to the post of Vice Principal. He published the first of his collection of poetry 'The Rishi from Baroda'. He started taking interest in the policies of India's freedom struggle against the British Rule.

God's call: Aurobindo said, "In Jail I waited day and night for the voice of God within me to know what He had to say to me, to learn what I had to do. Later a call had come to me from God to put aside all activity to go to seclusion and to look into myself so that I can enter into closer communication with Him."

"When I was in my pride of my heart as to suffering of my work in my absence, it seemed to me that He said to me again and said, 'The bonds have no strength to break, I have broken for you, I have another thing to do for you, I have brought you here to train you for my work. Then he placed the Gita in my hands. His strength entered into me and I was able to do the Sadhna of Gita.' I realised that what Lord Krishna demanded of Arjuna and He demanded of those who aspire to do His work to be free from repulsion and desire to do work for Him without the demand for fruit, to renounce self will and became a passive and faithful instrument in His hands to have an equal heart for high and low, friend and enemy, success and failure yet not to do His work negatively."

"Indian has always existed for humanity and not for herself and it is for humanity and not for herself that she must be great. India shall not fear. This trail is not against you and you shall not fear. The case itself is not only a means of for my work and nothing more. Sri Chittaranjan Das, who abandoned all his practice came to defend me. He sat up half the night and day for months and broke his health to save me." Aurobindo wrote, "I heard the voice of my Krishna telling me that I had brought Mr. Das to save you." I listened to His voice within me again and again. "I am guiding therefore fear not. Turn to your own work for which I brought you to jail and when you come out, remember never to fear, never to hesitate. Remember that it is I who is doing, neither you nor any other. Therefore, whatever clouds may come, whatever dangers and sufferings whatever difficulties, whatever impossibilities, there is nothing impossible, nothing difficult. I am in the nation and its uprising and I am Vasudeva, I am Narayana and what I will, shall be not what others will. What I choose to bring about, no human power can stay."

Health: Sri Aurobindo said that the body cures itself. He even said that doctors create disease and then cure it. The doctor is able to cure the patient more by the patient's faith in him than by his treatment. The body needs medicine for its cure because over the ages the body has become used to taking medicine and has come to believe in the medicine.

Education: Sri Aurobindo felt that if one learns one subject with certain thoroughness, his education will be complete and he has the essential equipment to acquire any other subject by himself. He felt that history and biographies are great educators. The school they founded in the Ashram for the children of the devotees teaches English and French and awards no degree so that she does not rise as other countries do, for self or when she is strong to trample on the weak. She is rising to shed the eternal light entrusted to her over the world. Nationalism is not a creed or religion. When Sanatana Dharma declines, nation declines." In the words of Aurobindo, "Krishna made me realise the central truth of the Hindu religion. He turned the hearts of jailers who allowed me at least to walk outside the cell for half an hour in the morning and in the evening saving me from the suffering in confinement. It was Vasudeva Krishna who surrounded me. I walked under the branches of the tree in front of my cell, but it was not tree, I knew it was Basudeva, it was Krishna whom I saw standing there and holding over me His shade. I lay on the coarse and felt arms of Krishna around me the arms of my friend and lover I looked around the thieves, the murderers, the swindlers in jail. But, I found Narayana in those darkened souls and misused bodies. Krishna spoke to me, "Behold my friend, my lover smiling the people among whom I have sent you to do a little of my work. During prosecution, I saw Vasudeva in magistrate and counsel for prosecution. My lover Krishna asked me, "Now do you fear?" He said, "I am in all men and I overrule their actions and their words. My protection is with you and you completion of the higher level.

Truth: Truth is self-existent. The truth of supermind can penetrate ignorance and reach its basis of truth (nothing on earth can exist without a seed of Truth) and unite all such truths and build upon them. The body and its inconscient base would not yield to the overmental force, but could not resist the onslaught of the supramental truth. Sri Aurobindo also showed her that Krishnavatar already came from overmind.

Rabindranath Tagore met Sri Aurobindo during his 24 years of silence and pronounced, "The world is with you." He saw Aurobindo resplendent with the supermental energy. He wanted that the world know Aurobindo's Yoga and his work. Sri Aurobindo's close spiritual collaborator Mirra Richard came to be known as 'The Mother' simply because Sri Aurobindo started to call her by this name. Aurobindo attained Samadhi on December 5, 1950. The golden light slowly entered his body and stayed there for three full days and then gradually withdrew into peace and silence that are said to be the body of the transcendent Divine.

Famous Quotes

- I have three madness – love for God, love for Mother and love for Nation. My blessing to humanity for playing the respective roles on the stage of the world as destined by God.

- He is in me, round me, facing everywhere self-walked in ego to exclude His right. He has become my substance and my breath. He is my anguish and my ecstasy. In my heart's chamber lives the unworshipped God.

God calls O Children!

God calls O Children!
Become instruments of my will.
Be firmly established in the world.
Earn honestly by honest hard work and share generously.
Be on the path of own inner wisdom and law.
Never gamble, never be addict, never be selfish.
Never waste, never be proud of wealth.
Be wise in using wealth.
Goddess of Wealth, Mother Lakshmi does not stay in home of such person.
Know that the wheels of the wealth-chariot are ever rolling.
Riches come today to one, tomorrow to another.
O Children! Have the habit of working hard honestly with vigour and vitality.
The law of Providence is such that the wealth earned through evil means is scattered away.
The wealth earned through pious means flourishes.

Dr. H. P. Kanoria

- Based on the Holy Vedas

Vishwakabi Rabindranath Tagore

Dr. H. P. Kanoria

Swami Vivekananda said that God does not punish. He does not take revenge. Our misfortunes are the result of our own action to humanity and nature. During his stay in San Francisco in late 1916, Tagore escaped a ghastly assassination attempt by Indian expatriates after failure of an argument. Yet Tagore wrote songs lionising the Indian independence movement, namely 'Where the mind is without fear' (Chitto Jetha Voi Shunna) and 'If they answer not to the call walk alone' (Jadi tor dak shune keu na ase tabe ekla cholo re). He campaigned successfully to open Guruvayoor Temple to Dalits. Civilisation must be judged and prized by how much it has evolved and given expression to it by its laws and institutions, the love of humanity.

A few lines of his devotional songs are –

"This is my prayer to the Lord, Strike, strike, at the root of penury in my heart Give me the strength lightly, to bear my joys and sorrows,

Give me strength to make thy love fruitful in service Give me the strength never to disdown the poor or Bend knees before insolent might.

Give me the strength to raise my mind high abovedaily trifles.

Give me strength to surrender my strength to thy will with love."

Spirituality for Rabindranath Tagore isthe dynamic principle that touches every aspect of life and is the guiding principle that 'leads human existence from partiality to fullness.' Life is a journey, for Tagore, achieves its fulfillment through the creative interaction of an artist or a poet, and not through renunciation of the world. Tagore stresses the need to respond to the call from within,from "the man of the heart." It is this inner intimacythat also enables one to experience unity with the external world.

God can be found through personal discovery and human service. He called for a new world order based on transnational values and ideas.

The Universe

The Outer Space illuminated with suns and galaxies proclaims His cosmic existence.

With the strength of His Divine fervor the universe is created.

The most powerful object in creation is the Sun.

The most radiant possession of the Universe is the Earth.

Spiritual and material splendors symbolize the two principal attributes of the Supreme Being.

Realizing His power we pray.

O Supreme Being, inspire us and guide us to attain Sublime Bliss.

Bless us to progress in every respect in this Universe.

Bless us with everlasting peace and happiness in every way.

Bless us to be on path of thy righteousness and devotion.

Bless us with the nectar of thy love forever.

Dr. H. P. Kanoria

- Based on the Holy Vedas

Maha Yogiraj
Sri Shyamacharan Lahiri
Mahasaya - a yogi with family

Dr. H. P. Kanoria

Sri Lahiri Mahasaya was incarnated on 30th September, 1828 (some disagreements as to date), in an orthodox Bengali brahmin family in Ghurnigram village near the town of Krishnanagar, in the Nadia district of West Bengal.

Lahiri Mahasay called his Guru "Babaji," who was "a fully realised, immortal being who had lived in a human body for almost 600 years. He is alive even today." He would proudly speak of the glorious yogic abilities of his Guru. In order to dispel the doubts of unbelievers, when he called his guru Mahamoni Babaji Maharaj, Babaji appeared in his subtle body and his asana. On one occasion Lahiri Maharaj along with his disciple Swami Yukteswarji came to know from Babaji that his age was over 500 years. Babaji told them that it is possible by the power of yoga sadhana to maintain the body in that way, even though there may be some changes every 100 years.

The essence of Maha Yogiraj's teachings:

- Kriya is truth and the rest is false. Kriya practice opens the eye of wisdom.
- When the tongue is raised, the senses are subdued.
- Om is radiant light. When this light is spread throughout the body, all is seen; then there is no desire to speak or to look.
- Air (Breath) is the Lord.

- When the breath is tranquil day and night, then Om realises the real state of Ram Mantra.
- Dualism is the root of all suffering.
- You yourself do not know what will render you good.
- Whatever one thinks at the time of death, accordingly one becomes that; likewise if you become Satchitananda (blissful) at the time of leaving the body, then you become yourself, the ultimate self.
- If one meditates always on the Lord, all his other worries are taken care of by the Lord himself.
- Looking at the middle of the forehead, which is above the nose and the eyebrows, is a bit difficult; if one stabilises on this he attains the state of Samadhi.
- Always remember that you belong to no one, and no one belongs to you. Reflect that some day you will suddenly have to leave everything in this world, so make the acquaintanceship of God now.
- Attune yourself to the active inner guidance; the Divine voice has the answer to every dilemma of life. Though man's ingenuity for getting himself into trouble appears to be endless, the infinite success is no less resourceful. Om!

Guru Govind Singh

Dr. H. P. Kanoria

Guru Gobind Singh was born on on Poh 7, 1723 sk/22 December 1666 at Patna, in Bihar, to the Ninth Sikh Guru Tegh Bahadur and his wife Mata Gujri.

When he was at the age of five year he was escorted to Anandpur (then known as Chakk Nanaki) on the foothills of the Sivaliks where Gobind Rai started studying Punjabi under Sahib Chand. Persian under Qazi Pir Mohammad, Braj, Hindi and Sanskrit. An expert warrior was employed to train him military skill, horse riding. In early 1675 when he was nine, a group of Kashmiri Brahmins driven to desperation by the religious fanaticism of the Mughal General Iftikar Khan visted Guru Tegh Bahadur for his assistance against persecution from Islamic Mughal ruler emperor Aurangzeb. Tegh Bahadur sat in reflection on what to do. The young Gobind in the company of his friends said in an innocent manner "Grave are the burdens the earth bears. She will be redeemed only if a truly worthy person comes forward to lay down his head. Distress will then be expunged and happiness ushered in. None could be worthier than you to make such a sacrifice" In Delhi, Emperor Aurangzeb asked Guru Tegh Bahadur to convert to Islam.

When he refused, he was beheaded on 11th Nov 1675 at Chandni Chowk in Delhi. Bhai Jaita narrated the incident to his followers that guru had sacrificed his life to protect the freedom of worship of the Hindu. Teg Bahadur dedicated his life not his faith. History tells us how India was ruled by invaders. It was selfishness, jealousy, envy and disunity of rulers and people. Trusted relatives, friends, assistants betrayed their brave men of justice and strength. Guru Gobind Singh fought many battles with Rajput.

On Guru's repeated calls Daya Ram, a Sobti Khatri of Lahore, arose and humbly walked behind the Guru to a tent near by. The Guru returned with his sword dripping blood, and asked for another head. At this Dharam Das, a Jat from Hastinapur, came forward and was taken inside the enclosure.

Guru Gobind Singh made three more calls. Muhkam Chand, a washerman from Dvarka, Himmat, a water-carrier from Jagannath Puri, and Sahib Chand, a barber from Bidar (Karnataka) responded one after another and advanced to offer their heads. All five were led back from the tent dressed alike in saffron-coloured raiment topped over with neatly tied turbans similarly dyed, with swords dangling by their sides. Guru Gobind Singh then introduced khande da pahul, i.e. initiation by sweetened water churned with a double-edged broad sword (khanda). Those five Sikhs were the first to be initiated. Guru Gobind Singh called them Panj Piare, the five devoted spirits beloved of the Guru. These five, three of them from the so-called low-castes, a Ksatriya and a Jatt, formed the nucleus of the self-abnegating, martial and casteless fellowship of the Khalsa. All of them surnamed Singh, meaning lion, were required to wear in future the five symbols of the Khalsa, all beginning with the letter K.

On invitation of Aurangzeb Guru proceeded to meet him. On the way, Guru got the news of the Emperor's death. Later in 1707, he went to meet Bahadur Shah, Aurangzeb's successor and was received with honour. Emperor called him "You shall be called Hind ka Pir" At Nanded (South) Guru was stabbed twice by men of Nawab Wazir Khan of Sirhind. Though the Guru was mortally wounded, he killed Jamshed Khan with his sword. Guru called upon his followers "My end is near,Please bring Holy Granth Sahib the scared book of the Sikhs. He declared that the holy book Granth Sahib shall be the Guru of Sikhs. He passed away on 7th October, 1708 at the age of 42 years.Since then Holy Guru Granth Sahib is the Guru of Sikhs and not any person. The Word as contained in the Guru Granth Sahib was henceforth, and for all time to come to be the Guru for the Sikhs.

Kabir: His life was His message

Dr. H.P. Kanoria

Kabir (1440-1518) was a great saint and mystic poet of India. Kabir was born to a Brahmin widow at Lahartara near Kashi (Varanasi) in 1440. The widow abandoned the child at Lahartara Talab (pond) to escape dishonour associated with births outside marriage. He was saved and brought up by a family of poor Muslim weavers Niru and Nima.

Philosophies

Kabir's message appealed to the poor and oppressed. David Lorenzen describes the primary purpose of this legend as a "protest against social discrimination and economic exploitation". He had universal view of spiri-tuality. Vehemently opposed dogmas both in Hinduism and in Islam. He advocated the simple natural way to oneness in God.

He spurned the Hindu societal caste system and idol worship. He opposed many customs of Islam.

Poem

Kabir was a social critic and Bhakta. He had tried to open the eyes and hearts of Hindu & Muslims to the true meaning and realisation of Ram/Allah/God.

"Tell me, O Pandit, what place is pure-where I can sit and eat my meal?

Kabir says only they are pure

Who have completely cleansed their thinking".

***

Adi Granth

"O Mullah, Make your mind your Mecca

Your body, the Ka'aba

Your self interest, is the Supreme Master

In the name of Allah, sacrifice your anger, error, impurity.

Chew up your senses, become a patient man

The Lord of the Hindus and Turks is one and the same.

***

Allah-Rama

Kabir did not honour the world's conventions, such as caste, the four stages of life, the six philosophical systems- He showed that yoga, ritual sacrifice, fasting and charity were trival and base without the practice of devotional worship. Swami Vivekananda and Ramprasad, the great spiritualist, were also advocating "Love, Love, Love Hari/Allah/Godno need of other practices. Their songs are full of this messages.

***

Kabir on Mother & Son

Hari, you are the mother, and I'm your son.

Why do not you forgive me my faults?

Whenever a son commits a wrong,

His mother doesn't take it to heart.

If the child is in pain, the mother is in pain.

***

Kabir's saying

"The man with a truthful heart is best. There's no happiness without the truth". Judge your actions with your own mind. Make only honest transactions. Falsehood is harmful at the very source. So, acquire the diamond of truth.

Kabir says "God is with you. Why look for Him elsewhere? He is in our possession. He is not in temple, not in mosques, not in the Ka'aba, not on Kailash, not in rites, not in rituals, not in yoga or renunciation. It takes a moment's search to find him. He is the very breath of our breaths. The man of knowledge understands the creator is different from a form or without a form. The creator's love remains invisible. The man who comprehends both love and renunciation, only looking into His heart - His very heart, where Karim and Rama reside and only he can realise God. Musk lies in the musk deer's own nave. But it roams in the forest to seek it. Alike, God pervades heart to heart. But man of world do not conceive. He searches here and there. Kabir says "He found Ram pervade in his heart. He exists profuse in each place. Kabir says that the ways of his creation are something else. It changes a pauper into a king, it turns an emperor into a beggar. Rama is the King. Whatever He does is beautiful.

Kabir-couplets

The company of the righteous, other sorrows doth mitigate

While company of the unrighteous, is grief for all the trivial hours eight

Bad Company

Kabir tells that one should always have good company, not have bad company for a moment.

Do not befriend one who is a fool

A righteous man condemns wholesale

A liquor filled pot made of gold

Man eats the fruit of whatever kind of company he doth keep.

***

Do not trust a man who speaks very sweet as he may not be a righteous man. A righteous person does not cause grief and pain to others.

Kabir says

"Speech is priceless, if you speak with knowledge

Weigh it in the scales of the heart

Before it comes from the mouth"

"Use the strength of your own arm

Stop putting hope in others

When the river flows through your own yard

How can you die of thirst"

Kabir was against slaughtering of animals particularly the cow, which he denounced. To Kabir, it is the same God; earnestly sought after in all religions. It differs in the way they call upon him. God is one. Man can have a relationship of love and affection and even a Union with Him. Turn to God and surrender to Him. Kabir says "I have purchased Him with my soul (Heart). And now that I recognize him as mine own. I have met God who dwelleth in the Heart; my mind shall now no more wander. I have drunk the brimful cup of love. My soul is being dyed with God's life. Kabir had some first experience of God like those of Moses in biblical story and Prophet Muhammad in Quran. Kabir was the pioneer of Hindu Muslim Unity, Social Reformer and true lover of God. Follow messages of Kabir. Be happy. Let all be happy.

Hinduism – The Eternal, Universal Tolerance, Acceptance and Righteousness

Dr. H.P. Kanoria

Swami Vivekananda, a true Sannyasi (monk), a great reformer, a preaching nationalist, an illuminated soul, lived a reformist active life of nine and half years. He expanded the Hinduism amidst thunder applauded by four thousand people assembled in World Parliament of Religions on Monday, September 11, 1893 at Art Institute in Chicago, US. Addressing 'Sisters and Brothers of America' and thanking all the organisers in the name of the mother of all religions

and millions of Hindu people irrespective of classes and sects, **Swami Vivekananda** said with the voice of lion, "**I am proud to belong to a religion – Hinduism, which has taught the world both universal tolerance and acceptance. We accept all religions as true. My nation had sheltered the persecuted and the refugees of all religions like Zoroastrians and all nations of the earth.**"

The Hindu religion, the oldest surviving religion without beginning and end is perpetual and eternal (sanatana). It is based on divine revelation and realisation. It was the communication with cosmic entity (God) by the several enlightened rishis, saints, sages and seers who were on their journey of enlightenment through service to merger with divinity, being one with God.

In the Persian language, people who were living near the river bank of Indus were 'Sindhu' or later 'Hindus.' All revelations and the Four Vedas were recorded in 'Sruti' or 'Smriti.' There were other major scriptures – the Ramayana, the Mahabharata, Vedanta, Puranas, Upanishadas and the Bhagawad Gita.

For years, the spiritual treasury and the spiritual laws were discovered by the enlightened souls just as the law of gravitation existed before its discovery and would exist even if all humanity forgot it. So it is with the laws that govern the spiritual universe. The moral, ethical and spiritual connection between two souls and the relation between the individual spirit and the father of all the spirits were there and would remain forever.

The Vedas teach us that creation is without beginning or end. Science has proved that the sum total of cosmic energy is always the same. So it can be concluded that there has been creation at all times. The Veda declared, 'I am a spirit living in a body, I am not the body. The body will die but I shall not die. I shall go on living. I had also a past. The soul was not created, for creation means a certain future dissolution.' If then the souls were created, they must die. Why? If they are all created, why does a just and merciful god create one happy and another unhappy? There must have been causes then before his birth, to make a man miserable or happy and those were his past actions. A soul with a certain tendency by laws of affinity would take birth in a body which is the fittest instrument for the display of the tendency. This is in accord with science that explains everything by habit. Habit is formed through repetition. So, Hindus believe that they are the spirits. Lord Krishna in Gita said, "Him the sword cannot pierce, him the fire cannot burn, him the water cannot melt, him the air cannot dry."

नैनं चिन्दन्ति शस्त्राणि नैनं दहति पावकः ।

न चैनं क्लेदयन्त्यापो न शोषयति मारुतः ।।2-23।।

nainam cindanti sastrani nainam dahati pavakah |
na cainam kledayantyapo na soshayati marutah ||2-23||

Weapons cannot cut it nor can fire burn it;
water cannot wet it nor can wind dry it.

देहिनोऽस्मिन्यथा देहे कौमारं योवनं जरा ।

तथा देहान्तरप्तिर्धीरस्तव न मुह्यति ।।2-13।।

dehino&sminyatha dehe kaumaram youvanam jara |
tatha dehantaraptirdhirastatra na muhayati ||2-13||

Just as boyhood, youth and old age are attributed to the soul through this body, even so it attains another body. The wise man does not get deluded about this.

A Hindu believes that every soul is a circle whose circumference is nowhere, but the centre is located in the body. On death, the centre changes to another body. The soul is not bound by the conditions of matter. It is free, unbounded, holy, pure, perfect, immortal and infinite. The present is determined by past actions and the future by the present.

Swami Vivekananda said in his address, "Hear, ye children of immortal bliss! Even ye reside in higher spheres! I have found the ancient one who is beyond all darkness, all delusion. Knowing Him alone you shall be saved from death over again. Allow me to call you, brethren by that sweet name – heirs of immortal bliss – yea Hindu refuses to call you sinners. It is sin to call a man sinner; it is a standing libel on human nature. Come up, O Lions - shake off the delusion that you are sheep; you are soul, immortal, spirit free, blest and eternal. Ye are not matter, ye are not bodies. Matter is your servant, not you the servant of matter."

The Veda declares that there is one by whose command the wind blows, the fire burns, the cloud rains and death stalks upon the earth. He is everywhere - the pure and formless one, the Almighty and the all merciful. Thou art our father, thou art our Mother, thou art our beloved friend, thou art the source of all strength, give us strength. He is worshipped through Love, love for his love's sake. Live in this world like a lotus leaf. Soul is divine. When fruits ripen, they fall down. Likewise, when the soul becomes perfect and enlightened, it frees from the bondage of body matter. Bondage can fall off through the mercy of God. Mercy comes on the pure. God reveals Himself to the pure heart. The Hindu sage says, "I have the soul; I have seen god, I have talked to God." Paramhansa Ramakrishna had talked to Mother Kali. A Hindu believes in realising, not in believing, but in being and becoming one with Him. On attaining perfection, one likes a life of bliss infinite. He then lives with God, the soul becomes perfect and absolute. It becomes one with Brahman – "The existence of absolute knowledge and bliss absolute." The ultimate of happiness being reached when it would become a universal consciousness.

Science has proved that physical individuality is a delusion : really, my body is one little continuously changing one in an unbroken ocean of matter. Unity (Advaita) is the necessary conclusion of the other counterpart, the soul. Science is in finding unity. Its goal is to reach perfect unity. Chemistry's goal is to discover one element out of which all others could be made. Physics discovers one energy of which all others are but manifestations. Science of Religion becomes perfect when it would discover Him, who is one life in a universe of death, Him who is the constant basis of an ever-changing world. One who is the only soul of which all souls are but delusive manifestations. Through multiplicity and duality, the ultimate unity is reached. Religion can go no further. This is the God of all sciences.

मया ततमिदं सर्वं जगदव्यक्तमूर्तिना ।
मत्स्थानि सर्वभूतानि न चाहं तेष्ववस्थितः ।।9-4।।

maya tatamidam sarvam jagadavyaktamurtina |
matsthani sarvabhutani na caham teshavasthitah ||9-4||
The whole of this universe is permeated by Me as unmanifest Divinity, and all beings dwell on the idea within Me. But really speaking, I am not present in them.

The entire universe has been manifested from my form. All beings are dependent upon me but I am not dependent upon them.

अथवा बहुनैतेन किं ज्ञातेन तवार्जुन ।
विष्टभ्याहमिदं कृत्स्नमेकांशेन स्थितो जगत् ।।10-42।।

athava bahunaitena kim j~jatena tavarjuna |
vishtabhyahamidam krutsnamekamsena sthito jagat ||10-42||
Or, what will you gain by knowing all this in detail, Arjuna? Suffice it to say that I hold this entire universe by a fraction of My Yogic Power.

I retain this world by a single fragment of myself.

Manifestation and not creation is the word of science today. The Hindu is glad but what he has been cherishing in his bosom for ages is going to be taught in forcible language with further light from the latest conclusions of science.

Hindu uses an external symbol when he worshipped. It helps him to keep his mind fixed on the Being to whom he prays. He applies all attributes of God to the images. It is not polytheism. He finds attributes of One to manifestations of many. He associates the ideas of holiness, purity, truth, virtues, omnipresence and such ideas with different images. Hindu's religion is centred in realisation. Man is to become divine realising the divine. Idols are only the support.

Scriptures say, "External worship, material worship is the lowest stage, struggling to rise high, mental prayer is the next stage and highest is the realisation of the Lord. Hindu travels from lower to higher truth and from truth to truth." Sri Krishna, an incarnation of the Lord said, "I am in every religion as the thread through a string of pearls. Wherever thou seest extraordinary holiness and extraordinary power raising and purifying humanity, know there that I am there". Every religion is evolving a god out of material man. It is the same light coming through glasses of different colour. Paramhansa Sri Ramakrishna said, "I am Krishna, I am Ram", when he was asked who you are. Paramahansa Yogananda talking to disciples at SRF Hermitage, Encinites, California said, "Everything is God. This very room and the Universe are floating like a motion picture on the screen of my consciousness. I see nothing but pure spirit, pure light and pure joy. The picture of my body and your bodies and all things in this world are only rays of light streaming out of that one sacred light. As I see that light I behold nothing anywhere but pure spirit."

यावानर्थ उदपाने सर्वतः सम्प्लुतोदके ।
तावान्सर्वेषु वेदेषु ब्राह्मणस्य विजानतः ।।2-46।।

javanartha udapane sarvatah samplutodake |
tavansarveshu vedeshu brahmanasya vijanatah ||2-46||

A Brahmana, who has obtained enlightenment, has as much use for all the Vedas as one who stands at the brink of a sheet of water over flowing on all sides has for a small reservoir of water.

"After obtaining a large reservoir of water, there is no use of a small reservoir of water. Likewise, all the purposes and contents of Vedas are of no use for One who has obtained enlightenment."

Swamiji said, "At present the word Hindu means anything bad, never mind, by an action let us be ready to show that this is the highest word that any language can have. Hindus stand for everything that is glorious, that is spiritual. Children of ancient Aryans, have the same pride through the grace of the Lord. You may have the same pride, may that faith in your ancestors come into your blood, may it become part and parcel of your lives, may it work towards the salvation of the world. All the fortunes and miseries of the world will pass over without hurting us, and we shall come out of the flames like Prahlad; so long as we hold on the grandest of inheritances and spirituality. We are the children of Almighty, we are sparks of the infinite divine force. Losing faith in one's self means losing faith in God."

Spirituality in India is Upalabdhi - realisation. God has been seen by ancients as well as moderns. The words of love alone will come out of that heart, which has realised the truth and realised the blissfulness. Lord Krishna talked to Arjuna, his beloved disciple. He told him about Yoga "Union". It is union between a man and the whole humanity and union between himself, God and love. He said that there are four types of Yoga – Karma Yoga, Jnana Yoga, Raja Yoga and Bhakti Yoga. Karma Yoga is the attainment of God through selfless action/actions without attachment and expectation of fruits. King Janaka attained realisation. So you should make on the path of progeny, perform selfless action just for the sake of people.

कर्मणैव हि संसिद्धिमास्थिता जनकादयः ।
लोकसंग्रहमेवापि सम्पश्यन्कर्तुमर्हसि ।।3-20।।

karmanaiva hi samsiddhimasthita janakadayah |
lokasamgrahamevapi sampasyankartumarhasi ||3-20||

It is through action without attachment alone that Janaka and other wise men reached perfection. Having in view the maintenance of the world order too, you should take to action.

Jnana Yoga (Yoga of knowledge) : To the Yogi of knowledge, God is the life of his life, the soul of his soul. God is own self, nothing else remains which is other than soul.

Lord Krishna told Arjuna, "Free from attachment, fear and anger, fully absorbed in me, being purified by knowledge and mediation may help to attain union with my being."

योगी युञ्जीत सततमात्मानं रहसि स्थितः ।
एकाकी यतचित्तात्मा निराशीरपरिग्रहः ।।6-10।।

yogi yuj~jita satatamatmanam rahasi sthitah |
ekaki yatavittatma nirasiraparigrahah ||6-10||

Living in seclusion all by himself, the Yogi who has controlled his mind and body, and is free from desires and void of possessions, should constantly engage his mind in meditation.

Rajayoga (Yoga of Concentration): It is controlling of the mind. He deals with concentration. Lord Krishna said, "A Yogi who wants to concentrate on God should restrain his mind, live alone in a private and quiet place, should be free from the bondage of desires and feeling of possessions and should constantly meditate on God."

आत्मौपम्येन सर्वत्र समं पश्यति योऽर्जुन ।
सुखं वा यदि वा दुःखं स योगी परमो मतः ।।6-32।।

atmaupamyena sarvatra samam pasyati yo&rjuna |
sukham va yadi va duhkham sa yogi paramo matah ||6-32||

Arjuna, he, who looks on all as one, on the analogy of his own self, and looks upon the joy and sorrow of all equally-such a Yogi is deemed to be the highest of all.

Bhakti Yoga (Yoga of devotion): This is Yoga of love-love-love alone. A man in love uses all sorts of rituals, flowers, incense and so on. Paramahansa Ramakrishna used to feed Mother Kali, talked to Her in love - ecstasy. Emotional natures do not care for abstract definitions of the Truth. His love is childlike for mother. His love is selfless, no expectation, no attachment to world except God. Wherever the heart expands, He is there manifested. Mahaprabhu Chaitanya, Saint

Bamakhapa, Swami Trailanga, Mirabai all were great lovers too. Kabiguru Rabindranath Tagore in one of his songs writes, "I will call you Maa, Maa like a little child in emotional pleasure of his being able to speak. I will cite God's name with tears, and smile but not in any expectation." Lord Krishna said, "One who by fixing him on me, steadfast in me, always worships and has supreme faith in me, is extremely merged in me. I consider then to be most devoted to me."

मय्यावेश्य मनो ये मां नित्ययुक्ता उपासते ।
श्रद्धया परयोपेता: ते मे युक्ततमा मता: ।।12-2।।

mayyavesya mano ye mam nityayukta upasate |
sraddhaya parayopetah te me yuktatama matah ||12-2||

Sri Bhagavan said : I consider them to be the best Yogis, who endowed with supreme faith, and ever united through meditation with Me, worship Me with their mind centred on Me.

Lord Krishna said, "Concentrate your mind on me, my devotee and offer your homage on to me. This way you will attain me. I promise this as you are very dear to me. God appears in this world in His original true form by His Divine Potency.

Lord Krishna says, "Whenever there is a degradation of religion and righteousness and surge in irreligion and unrighteousness, at that time I move myself. For the protection of the pious and to annihilate the wrongdoers, as well as to re-establish religion and righteousness, I manifest myself, era after era." In Bhagawad Gita, Lord Krishna said a realised person works for the welfare of all beings : Those holy men whose sins have been least, who are working for the welfare of other beings, those who are self restrained and have cleared all these doubts and dualities attains the eternal happiness or God. Hindu believes in welfare of all. He works for the welfare of all. Swami Vivekananda said, "The Hindu's Universal Religion, it so happens, will have no location in place or time. It will be infinite like God. The sun of Universal Religion will shine on all followers of all preachers and religions. It will have no place for persecution or intolerance in its polity.

It will recognise divinity in every man and woman. Its whole force will be central making humanity realise its own true, divine nature."

Love your religion, be humble and respectful to other religions. You are infinite. The body is manifestation of spirit which is youthful.

Have faith in yourself and God. Affirm you are not a sinner. You are a perfect and infinite soul. Come out of the bondage of habit. Be not the slave of habit, but be master of body matter – habit. March on the path of perfec-tion, realisation and unity with the ultimate cosmic infinity – God. Be one with the universal unity. Unity in variety is the plan of nature. Love, but face brutes. Be not fanatic, but face fanatics. Love your religion, but respect other religions. If you are a Christian, be Christian, if you are a Hindu, be a Hindu. Keep harmony and peace.

Motherland

Let us work with devotion for the glory of the Motherland.

Let us work hard for our countrymen speaking different dialects.

Let us give due respect to the faith and aspirations of the people.

Countless are the resources of Mother Earth.

From Motherland flow the rivers of wealth in hundreds of srteams.

Motherland gives bounty of food, herbs, plants and space.

From time eternal, Motherland is giving life to Her children.

We owe debts to Her.

Let us sacrifice our lives for the protection of Motherland.

Let us have loyalty to Motherland irrespective of religions.

Let us worship Motherland as we worship God.

Let us work hard with devotion and righteousness.

Let us create and generate wealth for prosperity and happiness of all.

Let us protect Motherland from enemies and global warming.

Let us worship Motherland as we Worship God.

Dr. H. P. Kanoria

- Based on the Holy Vedas

Meditation

Dr. H.P. Kanoria

Hinduism as Sanatana Dharma is without beginning or end and the Vedas remain the source of Sanatana Dharma. The scriptures say, Lord Vishnu–was alone. He said, एकोहम बहुस्याम – ekoham bahusyam. "I am one, let there be many." Thus started the multiplicity on this globe.

The entire teachings of the Vedas can be summed up in one grand sentence: तत् त्वम् असिः अहं ब्रह्मास्मि "tat tvaM asi: ahaM brahmAsmi— "Thou Art That"—I am Brahman" meaning, "I am the Spirit living in a body, I am not the body. The body will perish but the Spirit remains eternal." The body is composed of the five elements: space, air, fire, water and earth. Lord Krishna in the Bhagvad Gita (chapter II/23) says , "Weapons cleave it not, nor does the fire burn; waters drench it not, nor does the wind dry." The soul is always divine, pure, perfect, immoral and infinite.

Om is the most powerful ultimate knowledge of Brahman (God). Before the existence of the Universe, there was the sound Om — Aksharabrahman. Om stands for the pure consciousness. The mission of men is to discover the Supreme "self". The Spirit is all pervading. It alone exists as that which enlivens actions and perceptions, emotions and thoughts.

Meditation is focusing on the thought of the Supreme and in identifying with Him. To realize the Self within is to attain enlightenment and immortality. In the Bhagvad Gita, Lord Krishna says (Chapter X/20)

अहमात्मा गुडाकेश सर्वभूताशयस्थितः ।
अहमादिश्च मध्यं च भूतानामन्त एव च ।।10/20।।

ahamatma gudhakesa sarvabhutasayasthitah
ahamadisca madhyam ca bhutanamanta eva ca.

O Gudakesa (Arjuna) I am the Self, who abides within all things seated in the hearts of all creatures. I am the beginning and middle and also the end of all beings. The regular practice of meditation leads to the conquest of the mind and to attach it constantly with God. As one can see the reflection of the man in water when it is still, one can only realize the self when the mind becomes tranquil. Meditation is the Science of realizing God. The best way to meditate is as below:

1. Sit in solitude with a mind of a Yogi and control your senses and free yourself from desires and attachments, try constantly to contemplate on the Supreme Being, as light in the center of two eyebrows.

2. Sit in a comfortable position. Inhale and exhale. Chant Om. Deep short meditation is better. Concentrate the mind on a single object controlling the thoughts and activities of the senses.

3. Hold the waist, spine, neck and head erect, motionless and steady; fix the eyes and the mind steadily on the tip of the nose.

4. Be serene and fearless, with a firm vow of celibacy. Fix the goal to reach the Supreme God, i.e. to realize God. Concentrate on the glory of the Lord. Shut your eyes to worldly affairs.

5. Constantly direct your thoughts on the Divine. With the mind thus subdued, one attains everlasting peace and supreme bliss.

6. Be moderate in eating, recreation, working, sleeping, walking and every aspect of life. Meditation destroys all sorrows, thus disciplining the mind. One becomes content in Parabrahman (God), with a purified intellect. Thus, one frees oneself from the feeling of "I and My". We see that the same Atman is present in all beings. Grace from above is essential to make this meditation effort a success.

7. God's grace is unlimited. He showers His grace on His devotee both in favorable and unfavorable circumstances.

8. All actions, spiritual and worldly, are to be carried out with absolute devotion to God. With this, all malice is removed. Behold the Lord everywhere and for everyone. Patanjali Yoga describes the methods of meditation is details.

The ultimate aim of meditation is to invoke the energy centres of the body. There are seven chakras (energy centers) in our body. These are: Mooladhar (the root of the spine), Svadhishthana (the scared prostatic), Manipura (the solar plexus — navel), Anahata (the heart), Viscidia (the throat), Ajna (the third eye), and Sahastra Padma (the crown). With mediation they are activated and balanced.

The benefits of meditation are manifold. It frees the soul from the bondage of worldly affairs, helps to heal all ills, removes misconceptions, achieves success, develops positive thinking, reduces stress, develop the faculty of intuition, eliminates addiction, if any, develops humility, promotes better control of emotions and physical well-being to allow the being in perpetual bliss— Ananda.

Realisation

Find the eternal object of quest within soul. Not to search in ignorance and groping in helplessness. Turn gaze inward, realise the bright light of faith.

The lasting truth is shining around.

With rapturous joy, find the soul of Universe, the eternal object of quest.

Find the object of search within own heart.

Inner vision is illuminated by this new realisation.

Resolve with courage to crush the deceitful.

Overcome violent urges with firmness as those are enemies.

Through rigorous discipline and strict austerity.

Burn the passionate desires.

Always have noble thoughts in mind, never express bitter words.

Get rid of jealousy from heart and eschew violence.

Rise above material desires.

To the divine path of spiritual experience.

And behold the light divine, guiding towards eternal joy.

O God! Help us to be ever on the divine path with faith and love in Thee.

Dr. H. P. Kanoria

- Based on the Holy Vedas

Address of Dr. H.P. Kanoria at the 9th World Confluence of Humanity, Power and Spirituality on 16th December, 2016

Hon'ble President of India, Revered Religious Leaders, Honourable Global Leaders, Dignitaries, Brothers & Sisters. Dear Youth, Jai Hind Jai Vishwa.

Happy Day, Happy Ensuing Christmas and New Year.

We are privileged and honoured to have admist us, the Hon'ble President of India of our beloved country; I express my gratitude to him. I had the privilege of knowing Sir since decades. I can emphatically say that he is truly a spiritual enlightened soul, who has embraced all religions with equality & humanity.

I feel extremely blessed by the Sri Sri Paramahansa Ramakrishna, Maa Sharada, Swami Vivekananda for enabling Srei Foundation to organize the world confluence of humanity, power and spirituality from almost a decade to foster humanity through service and spirituality, harnessing the oceanic potential of human beings, with faith in self, in all and God.

The World Confluence of Humanity, Power and Spirituality along with ASSOCHAM and Times Foundation have been organizing this World's Noble Confluence with global mission and vision of Sach Bharat and Spirituality at work since last year. The confluence has been applauded globally for being graced by political and religious leaders and other eminent personalities from all walks of life.

Spirituality infuses humanity and the spirit to do hard work with the best of ability selflessly without any motive. It develops our intuition to holistic reality which is not driven by material senses and emotions. Service to humanity becomes ideal of life. Swami Vivekananda was denied Nirvikalpa Samaadhi – union bliss with God by his preceptor Paramahansa Sri Ramakrishna, He was told that service to humanity is worship to God. Jesus Christ said, "Only right in the world is to give, to serve. Be content to serve on. Serve the world". The world stands in obeisance objects. Material beings will be at your beck and call. Have a sense of gratitude. Spirituality makes one humble. Fruit laden branches bend. A great man lives in humanity and in service.

It gives strength to remain self-poised, self-pleased despite surmounting criticism. He performs his duties without fear and favour. God conspires to help such righteous person. Spiritual manifestation will always glorify whatever one does. Swami Vivekananda said, "Spirit manifest divinity within you. It is the vision of one's own self in all beings". It ignites the spirit to honour woman as soul of both is immortal, embodied in a different form of body. Humanity is the essence of all religious Service to God's creation and to live in harmony, peace, love, co-operative spirit with interfaith is the essence of eternal law. Unity in diversity is the manifestation of the creator. All rivers flowing from several countries merge with oceans and the oceans return water in the form of rain to nurture God's creation. Spirituality is essential at workplace. It fosters collective efforts with cooperative spirit.

The collective action does miracle. It brings the vibration of joy and the spirit of righteousness at work. It gives insight and intuition to deal with complex problems and to be innovative. It gives strength to stand with poise during the storm of depression and recession. One does not miss the worldly pleasure and enjoys the abundance of divine bliss also.

Our Hon'ble Prime Minister Shri Narendra Modi ji has given the call for Swacch Bharat, Digital India, Swasth Bharat and glorious Bharat. The Nation is committed to achieve these.

The world is facing serious problems of poverty, dissatisfaction to globalization, rising nationalism to protect one's own people, global warming, hunger, violation of human rights, terrorism and interfaith fight. Spirituality has to be infused with materialism for the welfare of humanity and the universe. SAVE MOTHER EARTH, HELP NOT FIGHT, ASSIMILATE, NOT DESTROY. Bring harmony and peace not dissension. Neglect not the loving God – the Man and Woman who are the infinite reflection of God. Love, serve and work with devotion while living on path of righteousness. Let us Awake, Arise and Work hard for inclusive and sustainable growth to provide basic needs of the increasing and growing population at a pace higher than that of current economic growth. Let the world have the cosmic cooperative spirit. Youth have to be ignited with spiritual manifestation and do not be only self-materialistic and egoistic. Unity is divinity is the core of Universe. We have to learn from the nature.

Let us march ahead imbibing spirituality to serve humanity and to be humane.

We express our gratitude to the Hon'ble President of India. My heartiest thanks to all for their gracious presence.

Peace, Peace, Peace.

Jai Hind, Jai Vishwa.

Family Life

God calls, O Children!

Adapt Dharma (Righteousness), Artha (Wealth), Kama (Family) and Moksha (Liberation).

O man and women when married as husband and wife.

Look at each other with love and affection.

Live together happily without malice with one spirit.

Be considerate and affectionate towards each other.

Live joyously in home with children, grand children and great grand children.

Follow the path of duty, justice, love and spirituality.

Beget noble and brave children.

Both be wise, benevolent and live to inspire all with blissful life.

Never go against inner voice of soul.

Develop intellect by devotion and prayers.

Be respectful to elders and loveable to youngers.

Have magnanimous hearts.

March ahead and progress with common aim and goal.

Dr. H. P. Kanoria

- Based on the Holy Vedas

Address of Dr. H.P. Kanoria at the 6th World Confluence of Humanity, Power and Spirituality on 27th December, 2014

Revered religious leaders, Hon'ble Political leaders, eminent personalities on Dias and in audience, Brothers & Sisters, Dear Youth.

Wish you all a very happy and prosperous Holy Christmas and ensuing New Year.

I welcome all to the 6th World Confluence of Humanity, Power and Spirituality.

I am grateful to all for gracing the Confluence.

I convey my delighted thanks to the many students of schools and colleges of World who have participated in essay writing on (a) Spirituality for Success & Happiness (b) Spirituality – a panacea for happiness & Value.

We are the children of God; we all are equal in his eyes. We are the infinite, perfect, immortal children. We have oceanic power and wisdom. The infinite library of the Universe is our own mind. I am a spirit living in a body. Spirituality balances the trinity of power, money and authority.

Spirituality awakens the inner power. It connects God in our heart and mind. Spirituality serves the purpose of supporting the moral and social principles which have made men civilized. It strengthens you for adventures of life. It gives strength to be on the journey of life with joy and giving joy to others.

Your spiritual manifestation will always glorify whatever you do.

A spirituality grown up person does not miss the worldly pleasures. He has abundance of Divine bliss too.

Swami Vivekananda, "Spirituality manifest divinity within you. It is the vision of one's own self in all beings.

Mark, "If you give up spirituality the result will be that in three generations, you will be extinct."

The river of material joy dries up quickly, if there is no perennial source of spiritual water. When divinity draws the weakness vanish of their own accord as the petals drop off when the flower develops into fruit.

Change yourself. World will change. You are the cause of everything that happens to you. We are the product of our own thoughts and desires. We are our own architect.

Women and men are both children of God. All possess the immortal soul and are the sharer of immortal bliss. Soul does not have a gender. Women are reflections of the divine love. Swami Vivekananda said that if you do not respect woman, who are the living embodiments of divine mother, do not think that you have other ways to rise. It's the mother who is the first Guru of the child. God rejoices where woman are respected. Many enlightened souls like Saint Tulsidas were inspired by women (Tulsidas by his wife Ratna). Women have the capability to acquire the spirit of heroism. In the present day it is necessary for them to learn self-defence and learn heroism.

We all possess within us the seed of spiritual fruition. We must nurture and foster it. Let noble thoughts come to us from everywhere.

Hindu believes in "Vasudeva Kutumvakam", world is one family.

ॐ सर्वे भवन्तु सुखिनः
सर्वे सन्तु निरामयाः ।
सर्वे भद्राणि पश्यन्तु
मां कश्चिद् दुःख भाग्भवेत् ।
ॐ शान्तिः शान्तिः शान्तिः ॥

oum sarve bhavantu sukhinah
sarve santu niramayah|
sarve bhadrani pasyantu
mam kascid duhkha bhagbhavet|
oum santih santih santih ||

May all be happy (sukhinah);
May all be healthy (niraamayaa)!

May all look (pasyatu) to the good of others;
May none suffer from sorrow (dukkha).
Om Peace, Peace, Peace.

World Peace! Nation Peace! Family Peace.

We can call the creator by different names. Vibration, feeling inside us is of love, empathy, sympathy, harmony, peace, Creator is watching us. God is the only soul of which all souls are but delusive manifestations. The entire Universe has been manifested from Him (God). All beings are dependent upon Him.

Every religion is evolving a God out of a material man. All different types of worships and prayers reach one and the same Lord as waters of all rivers reach the same ocean.

Spirituality creates the international bondage and one family, one world.

Let us march ahead with the flag of humanity and unity through spirituality to serve the purpose of creator. World must have whole education imbibed with spirituality and secularism.

Let us arise, awake and work hard till death to serve the Humanity.

Om! Amen, Amin, Ek Omkar, Ahura Mazda.

World Confluence of Humanity, Power and Spirituality

The World Confluence of Humanity, Power and Spirituality is being held every year with great success since 2010. So far 10 confluences were held, 6th-10th January, 2010; 2nd-4th January, 2011; 2nd-4th January, 2012; 22nd-23rd December, 2012; 28th-29th December, 2013; 27th-28th December, 2014 in Kolkata; 22nd-23rd December, 2015 in New Delhi; 7th May, 2016 in Mumbai; 16th-17th December, 2016 in New Delhi; 22nd-23rd December, 2017 in Kolkata. This programme is the first of its kind in the world with a conglomeration of important issues on humanity, power (inner & outer) and spirituality. Several distinguished luminaries whose hearts echo with humanity from different communities and religions across the world, shared their views that every religion propagates service to humanity, and that moral and social principles have its own paths leading to one cosmic reality. Various religions are like flowers of different colors to be tied with a cord of love into a beautiful bouquet to be offered at the altar of truth. Diversity with unity is inherent in nature.

This is a spectacular confluence where all streams of thought converge irrespective of religious persuasion, inclusive of all disciplines whether belonging to science or humanities, sacred or secular, social or cultural, political or economic, where distinguished luminaries share their thoughts and life's experiences, highlighting unity in diversity and diversity in unity. It remains the task of this conference to bring home the values of enlightenment in practice as life's journey within one's own self, and through love and service to the society at large.

Swami Vivekananda observed that **the world needs spirituality to establish fearlessness** in the new generation, self-discipline, hard work and selfless service to the nation. He asserted, "Manifest divinity within you", and added, "Mark, if you give up spirituality, the result will be that in three generations you will be extinct."

The former President of India, late Dr. A.P.J. Abdul Kalam, who inaugurated the 4th World Confluence of Humanity, Power and Spirituality rightly quoted at the confluence, "Spirituality can eradicate corruption not legislation."

The World Confluence accords a special place to women who are a source of inspiration, love and selfless services. He said that women have great abilities and a great role to play in the world's advancement, which also finds voice in the UN Millennium Goals to which we are committed. They are the architects of the future generation. The world will be happy if they are happy.

Children and youth are the future of the country and their consciousness has to be transformed through spiritual alchemy to gain inner power so as to cope with life's challenges with faith in self and the creator, and to serve humanity. Positive energy has to be aroused to maintain life's balance by having faith in self, creator and service. To inspire the youth, the confluence program included on the margin interschool debate, sit-and-draw and essay writing competitions related to service to humanity amongst different age groups followed by prize distribution. On Swami Vivekananda's 150th Birth Anniversary the confluence started.

Conferring the Swami Vivekananda Srei Samman Awards for Outstanding Service in the field of:

(i) Education

(ii) Work for the Deprived and the Disadvantaged

(iii) Contribution for Health

(iv) Development and Research
(v) Literary Excellence
(vi) Crusader for Humanity
(vii) Crusader for Women

To recognize the best practice and to motivate organizations we have also given the "Sach Bharat Samman" to three organizations. These were selected through a panel of eminent jury members. Ernst & Young was the process partner for this Award.

The topics of our previous confluences are as follows:-

1. Humanity, Power & Spirituality
2. Service to Humanity
3. Service to Humanity and Nature
4. Essentialism of Spirituality to Blossom Life and the Nation
5. Reflection of Your Inner Self through Spirituality, Humanity and Power
6. Essentialism of Spirituality for Humanity
7. Spirituality fosters Humanity
8. Spirituality - A Panacea for Happiness & Values
9. Spirituality - A Panacea for the Growth of the Nation
10. Spirituality in Business & Nation's Governance
11. Spirituality @ Work
12. Spirituality unfolds Humanity
13. Spirituality and Nature- Climate Change
14. Spirituality in an Exponential World
15. India's Strength is its Spirituality
16. Spirituality - A Panacea for Governance and for the Growth of the World

The Confluence is not religion oriented. Emphatically it is for humanity, peace, harmony and happiness. It is to ignite our consciousness, sub consciousness, and super consciousness to the divinity within us. "Jeev Seva is Shiva Seva" (Service to humanity is service to the Lord) Paramhansa Ramakrishna said to Swami Vivekananda, "Narendra, serve humanity with faith in the creator."

Mission

- To live and let live in peace, harmony, love - following the path of righteousness protecting Mother Earth.
- Having faith in own religion while respecting other religions.
- Awakening the inner power & ignite human power.

Vision

- A world with happiness, peace, harmony, austerity, simplicity, prosperity & good health for all.
- Trinity of Power (money, authority, muscles) to be imbibed with Humanity & Spirituality.
- Economic growth in synchronization with human facet.
- Awakening woman power - reflecting God's love.

Love, Peace, Unity, Humanism

Dr. Hari Prasad Kanoria

May God of all the religions bless the nation and the world with peace, harmony, love, unity, righteousness, food, austerity, and simplicity. May Mother Earth, and the socio-economic growth provide the minimum necessities for a living.

Every human being is infinite, perfect and divine. God has created us in his own image with his virtues and love. He is the universal Father. He has also created illusions of greed, lust, jealousy, anger and so on. He has given free will to remain virtuous. Evil has overtaken humanity and it is drifting away from virtues. Humanity is seized with poverty, terrorism, destruction, tortures, wars, power struggles, food crisis, global warming, religious fanaticism, global financial crisis, etc. (Excessive consumerism by a section of the population, amassing wealth, and natural resources by some providing others to live and grow). Weakness is exploited. Fear is dominating, curbing the potentiality of human beings. Nature is excessively exploited leading to class imbalance. Majority have been suffering with stress, anxiety, depression and others submerged in bad habits, such as, excessive food intakes, lust, greed, alcoholism, smoking and so on. This is leading to an unequal distribution of wealth and power, resulting in the division of the society between the haves and the have-nots. Thus, when man acquires the trinity of power, that is, wealth power, muscle power, and the power of authority; he gets imbalanced. Nature brings equality in life by sustaining water, air and natural products, thereby balancing the entire Earth.

Human power has two aspects; inner power and outer power. Inner power is infinite but since it is dormant, it needs to be awakened and harnessed. In today's society, one has to listen to one's own feeble voice of conscience and remind oneself of the words from the Vedas that declare, "I am a spirit living in a body. I am not the body. The body will die, but I shall not die."

Guru Nanak once said, "Friend! Bear no hate to anyone. One God dwells in every heart." St. Paul once also said, "Overcome evil with good." Whereas, Mohammad had said, "Recompense evil ,conquer it with good." Hinduism states that with kindness we can conquer rage, with goodness, we can conquer malice, with generosity we can defeat all meanness, and with truth we can defeat lies and deceit. All religions have been serving the purpose of commanding moral and social principles.

Both women and men are children of God. The Soul does not have any gender. Both are the infinite soul embodied in peace and love. Women are the reflection of God's love. In love, they surrender to men. They have been subjects of humiliation, suffering, physical abuses and mental tortures. Women have to awaken themselves. They need not be dependent. They have strength mightier than that of men. History confirms their courage and strength with examples of Laxmi Bai of Jhansi, Rani Padmabati of Rajasthan and so many. In the past also women were full of wisdom. Margaret Thatcher, Kiran Shaw, Lata Mangeshkar, Kalpana Chawla, Prativa Patil, P.T. Usha and many have shown their strength, wisdom, entrepreneurial skill, leadership and what not. Swami Vivekananda said, "Educate women and let them manage themselves".

Women are the source of inspiration, aspiration, love and selfless service. All of us need to awaken women power within us, i.e. tolerance, restraint and love.

Children are ignited by spirituality and inspired to be alchemists to have virtues as given by God.

Spirituality inspires and aspires. Spirituality serves the purpose of supporting the moral and social principles which have made men civilized. Spiritual bliss is also the vehicle that allows us to gather the extraordinary scientific truth, logic and intuitive power. Let us then march at the vanguard of civilization with the flag of harmony, and vow to live and let live; be happy and let others be happy; to have bread and let others have bread; give dignity to women. All these are reflection of Gods' love.

Fear him who is able to destroy the 'soul'. All religions have been serving the purpose of commanding moral and social principles.

THE LIVING GOD

Swami Vivekananda

He who is in you and outside you,
Who works through all hands,
Who walks on all feet,
Whose body are all ye,
Him worship, and break all other idols!

He who is at once the high and low,
The sinner and the saint,
Both God and worm,
Him worship—visible, knowable, real, omnipresent,
Break all other idols!
In whom is neither past life
Nor future birth nor death,

In whom we always have been
And always shall be one,
Him worship. Break all other idols!

Ye fools! who neglect the living God,
And His infinite reflections with which the world is full.

While ye run after imaginary shadows,
That lead alone to fights and quarrels,
Him worship, the only visible!
Break all other idols!

Ethics Springs from Divinity

Dr. H.P. Kanoria

We are divine and perfect. Values and ethics spring from divinity. Divinity and spirituality imbibe the values, ethics, fearlessness, courage, selflessness, spirit of cooperation, spirit of helping, self-control, nonviolence, truthfulness, egoless, humbleness, perseverance, endurance, integrity, calmness, patient hearing, modesty, free of greed, hard work, austerity, contentment, simplicity, enthusiasm, loving, empathy, sympathy, forgiveness, enterprising, courteous , caring and team work. All these factors need to be integrated with the leaders, management, team and all the personnel, stakeholders and customers.

Spirituality is the essence of life. It awakens the inner power. It develops body, mind and soul. It ignites the spirit with strength and joy. It infuses the eternal law of hard work without expectation of fruits. It gives insight, perception and intuition in complexity of life in context with the material world.

Business and enterprise has to face storms and at times tsunamis which are the internal and external factors which create conflict. It is important how to come out successfully from the conflicts and tsunamis of enterprise, national and global competition. Values and ethics give strength to face the same with firmness and humbleness. Failures become the stepping stones to success.

Former President Late Dr. Professor A.P.J Abdul Kalam said, "I firmly believe that unless one has tasted the bitter pill of failure, one cannot aspire enough for success. He said that I have seen both sides of the coin. I have learnt life's toughest lesson when I have been in the pit of despair that failure brought to me".

To the men of ethics and values, the soul helps to dive into the ocean of success. Hard work with concentration is required to control life, make it simple and modern. Integrity is essential. Focus the mind and feel the power of God within you.

Analyseyour failure, its causes and benefit from the experience.

In the words of Mr. Winston Churchill, "Never, never, never give up. It is essential to have faith in self, in all and in God."

Swami Vivekananda quotes, "Everyhuman being has infinite power. Manifest spirituality within you".

Steve Jobs (developer of Apple), Mark Zuckerberg (co-founder of Facebook) had spiritual awakening in India. They developed the intuition and were successful.

Enthusiasm is the mother of effort. Without it nothing great was ever achieved. Risk taking after full analysis is essential for the growth of an enterprise. Self-control is the foundation of all virtues. One needs to conquer oneself, instead of others.

Enviousness and jealousy are like acid that burns you from inside. Tolerance and forgiveness is essential to win the confidence of all.

God conspires with those who work for the welfare of all, creating and generating wealth for the welfare of creation. Lord Krishna had conspired with Arjuna breaking His own promises.

Swami Vivekananda said, Love reflects love. Life is a joyous journey. Love and service is all that matters to worship Him.

I quote from the Universal Prayer written by me, "Life is a joyous journey, Love and service that matter, all worship to Thee. What we sow, we must reap, no one but us to blame".

Fearless we are marching ahead to make Bharat World. We surrender our will at the altar of thy will. Work, work for the Nation and the world.

Based on the Holy Vedas – Walk the divine path for greater wisdom and divine glory. God escorts. He is a constant companion to those who are inspired to work hard. On them does he constantly shower the joy of His blessings.Engage in noble and beneficial work.

Let us work with devotion for the glory of the Motherland. Let us work hard for our countrymen speaking different dialects. Let us give due respect to the faith and aspirations of the people. Let us sacrifice our lives for the protection of Motherland. Let us work hard with devotion and righteousness. Let us create and generate wealth for prosperity and happiness of all.

Lord Krishna advised His disciple Arjuna to work hard with devotion for the welfare of creation. Do not look for the fruits of action. Be free from the bondage of duality. Even during activity in the material world, all action must be done in service of humanity. Engage in activities in His consciousness than to be a Sanyasi. With control of mind and senses, work with devotion in consciousness of soul and Krishna.

Realise that you are not doing anything at all. You are being an instrument of God. Perform duties without attachment and expectation of fruits while surrendering to God.

Awake and arise O Divine people! The Lord defends only those who work hard righteously and those work for the benevolent cause Become brave and strong. God helps them to conquer their adversaries.

Be self-sufficient, O Man!

Be not slave to any outside help.

Listen to such words that enable to conquer inner foes.

Be so illustrious that all approach you for guidance.

Be self sufficient to architect own destiny.

Realise the virtues of self-reliance and self-sacrifice.

Be inspired by the wisdom of seers which are true and effective.

Follow their instructions with full faith.

Along with leaders of Nation resolve to keep a strict vigil over the

safety of our motherland.

Acquire happiness through the joy of worship - devotion.

And the cultivation of virtuous qualities.

A true devotee is always soft in speech.

And considerate towards others.

Keep away from the evils of violent anger at all stages of life.

O God! Bless us with divine fragrance.

And purify our speech.

Bless us to speak sweetly.

So, a broad understanding, a broad outlook toward life, a sense of belongingness with all the people in the world, caring and commitment, alone can bring integrity in social and private life.

To conclude, let us have tremendous faith in ourselves. We have infinite power, unbounded wisdom and indomitable energy. We have to rouse power in ourselves by positive thought and positive prayers. We will have success after success. Let us have the bow of determination.

May God bless us and give courage and endurance.

HOLY VEDAS

Be ever happy. Cheer up. Soul is the reflection of ever joyous spirit. Soul is the essence of happiness itself. Happiness depends mainly upon mental conditions. Change thoughts, circumstances will change. Own nature creates thoughts. Change that nature which creates unhappiness. Start thinking only of those thoughts which will bring health and happiness. - Sri SriParamahansaYogananda 'Where there is light.'

The Vedic verses enable one to enjoy the glory of God in this creation. Enjoy the full charm of dawn a little before sunrise, rising sun, thrilling evening, the calmness of night, cool and refreshing, beauty of starts set like pearls and diamonds on a blue background - sky. A constant struggle between our divine tendencies and our devilish ones. The incessant conflict between Truth and Non-Truth, between Good and Evil or Enlightenment and Nescience, Knowledge and Ignorance. In the verses, we invoke the Supreme Reality, the Sole master of creation and the living beings. The Supreme Divine is an architect producer of everything within a human being. He (God) is within all. Yajurveda, 'It moves, it moves not, it is far and it is near. It is within all this and it is outside all this". - Upanishads

Song/Prayer -

O Blissful Mother!

Thou art the source of all happiness.

Remembering and chanting thy mystic sweet name Ma Kali, Ma Kali.

My mind, heart and soul in fill with joy and bliss.

My body thrills.

I dance and dance lifting both hands.

Chanting Ma Kali, Ma Kali, Ma Tara making the universe resound thy sweet name.

Mother, thou art far and thou art near.

When I look at Thee with love and tears in eyes, thou art near me.

Thou art within, outside, front, back, left and right.

I move as thou move me.

Mother be ever with me thy little child.

ॐॐॐॐॐ

Man's own intelligence controls the atoms of his body. Don't live in the closed chamber of mental narrowness. Breathe in the fresh air of vital thoughts and views of spiritually progressive minds. Expel poisonous thoughts of discouragement, discontentment and hopelessness. Feast unstintingly on the creative thinking within and others who are good. Take long mental walks on the path of self-confidence. Exercise with the instruments of judgement, introspection and initiative. - Sri SriParamahansaYogananda 'Where there is light.'

A Vedic verse about creation - unmanifest to manifest - "The golden embryo existed prior to all. It was source of everything that was born. It was the sole lord of existence. It maintains or upholds everything that exists between earth and heaven only to that Lord and none else, shall we offer our affection and homage". We have to invoke and evoke for our personal fulfilment of our life. The Supreme Reality is our concern every moment. We might ignore Him, and so we usually do, but He does not neglect us. - *The Holy Vedas*

Song/Prayer-

O Loving Mother!

How thine illusion dare to invade thy child, me.

Tell thine illusion not to disrupt my love for Thee.

The five elements are constantly disrupting with six passions and ten organs of perception and action.

The hungry play of energy earth, air, fire, water, space.

Mother! Mother! Mother! How I can bear this mundane existence.

I hold thy abiding presence, at the centre of awareness.

Bless me Mother, Bless me Mother to amuse with Mother every moment.

Mother! Flee all intruders with thy ferocious glance.

ॐॐॐॐॐ

The mind is the King. Like nutritive food, give nutritive thoughts to the mind. Deny your mind thought of sorrow. Man had divine nature. Assert divine heroic self. Do not blame God. Freedom is yours. Use will power to be happy and remain happy. Make effort to change. Persevere to conquer all difficulties. Do not blame others for troubles. Arouse the sleeping hero in yourself. Improve yourself. The self-improving man is the increasingly happy man. People around will be happier. - Sri SriParamahansaYogananda 'Where there is light.'

God Himself is unmanifest, but He is manifested behind His Divine Art. The effulgence behind His creation is His effulgence. The mighty force behind nature's force is His force. He is the light behind light. He is the Supreme Activity behind all activities. We admire His forces. We proceed to the unmanifest Reality, the Supreme Source of Enlightenment and Bliss. We invoke our Lord in terms of attributes and function. We try to establish personal relationship with Him. The tiny soul and Supreme Lord-Self are both mutual friends and companions.

- *The Holy Vedas*

Song/Prayer -

O Blissful Mother!
Awaken my heroic power to tame my mind.
O my mind sing Om Ma Kali, Om Ma Kali, Om Ma Kali,
Experience sheer delight at feet of Ma Kali,
Whole Body and universe resound with Her name.
Taste everywhere the sweetness of own pure essence.
And attain liberation now.
O my mind! Do not fly here and there like a strange winging creature.
Listen to my command and heartfelt plea.
Seek from own true divine nature,
The four traits of highest aspirations, righteousness, power, delight and illumination.

ॐॐॐॐॐ

Do not have negative approach to life. Avoid it. Enjoy loveliness all around us. Enjoy the beauty of nature. Enjoy their charm and glory. Remember three little monkey-figures that depict the maxim, 'See no evil, hear no evil, speak no evil.' Have the positive approach. Good and evil, the positive and the negative both exist in the world. Keep the conscious positive. Fear not negative - use discrimination to analyze wrong thoughts and then dump them. - Sri Sri Paramahansa Yogananda 'Where there is light.'

Om (A-U-M) the all comprehensive syllable - potential creativity, sustenance and dissolution. Man, his entire body complex is a huge sovereignty by itself with the soul as Supreme ruler and the sense organs as his subordinates. Yajna is not fire-ritual. It refers to man's dynamic activity to explore and utilize Nature's resources for our common good. A concerted, coordinated and well planned effort for human good is yjana. This is sacred act and hence is technically known as sacrifice, a selfless act. - *The Holy Vedas*

Song/Prayer -

With the innate cry Om Kali, Om Kali, Om Kali.

Tears of love flowing abundantly.

Mother rises through kundali to the crown of my head.

My Soul's light to rise.

The gateway to total illumination.

The whole body is so sweetly reeling.

With Mother's own drunken love.

Body, mind and soul dance and submerged in Mother's love.

Love Bliss is all round.

ॐॐॐॐॐ

Life has a bright and a dark side, for the whole world of relativity is composed of light and shadows. Look only for the good in everything. Thinking, reading and repeating statements of truth will help to establish a positive attitude. Repeat prayers and concentration with concentration. This will help to think in right way. The ever new joy of God inherent in the soul is indestructible. - Sri Sri Paramahansa Yogananda 'Where there is light.'

We are born on Mother Earth. Mother set us secure and happy. The Mother, Goddess has stored treasure of gold, gems etc. in many places. She has given us riches and opulence. She grants great passions to us bestowing them with love and favour. She is the wife of Lord Vishnu. Rightly I am the son of Earth. Earth is my Mother (Atharveda 12.12) - Vedic verses refer to the glory of God in is His creation to establish a personal link with Him in the innermost core of heart where one can feel His throb, Hear His voice and see His enlightenment. Man's natural religion is eternally with Him. - *The Holy Vedas*

Song/Prayer -

O Mother Kali! By thy grace, my mind has plunged in thy love ecstasy.

I imbibe the nectar of timeless awareness.

My whole body is so sweetly reeling with Mother's own drunken love.

Now, I abide day and night beneath the red soled feet of my Mother Kali.

Delight is absolute reality.

Delight of non-duality. Delight of oneness.

Oh! It is delight of Mother's wonderful intimacy.

Child and Mother! Mother and child.

ॐॐॐॐॐ

You are in image of God. We should behave like God. Have the evenness of mind. Be absolutely calm and free from all anger. Let nothing take away peace. Resurrect from the littleness of life, the little things that disturb. Remove moods from mental mirror. Do not make yourself miserable. Keep mind beautiful and fragrant with divine thoughts. Think and treat mind as a garden. Cultivate the heavenly scented blooms of peace and love. God comes only when life is sweet with thoughts of service and love. - Sri Sri Paramahansa Yogananda 'Where there is light.'

The Vedic verses uphold high moral values of life. God is truth personified, purity personified, love personified and bliss personified. We crave to imbibe within us a bit of His qualities. The Vedic Dharma (religion) is thus morality based Dharma based on truth and its acceptance for life i.e path (Shraddha) austerity (Tapas) piety (Daya) and selfless service and dedication (Yajana), generosity (Dana), Peace

(Shanti), Friendship (Mitrata), Fearlessness (Abhaya) and mutual understanding (Saumanasam).These are the essential qualities of complete reliance on God. O the lone alambana or skambha, the pillar of strength. - *The Holy Vedas*

Song/Prayer

O Blissful Mother Kali!

This cosmos floats on the elixir of ecstasy of thy love.

That flows from the sound of thy name Ma Kali, Ma Kali, Ma Kali.

Mother thou lift hearts from the common birth of selfishness.

To the noble rank of selfless lovers.

O loving Mother! Graciously bless me never abandon the life of dedication to thee, My Mother.

ॐॐॐॐॐ

Introspect each day. Make conscious effort to create some positive interest. Beware of indifference which ossified progress in life by paralyzing will power. Have right thinking. Lead to a healthy, active and moral life. Pray for greater faith in the healing power of God. Analyse the problem of failure. Think of success. Resolve to conquer mood. Analyse the cause. Do something constructive about it. Creative thinking is the best antidote moods. Be not in a negative or passive state of mind. Be active physically or engage in creative thinking. Remain busy. Human intelligence is mad in the image of God's creative intelligence through which all things are possible. - Sri Sri Paramahansa Yogananda 'Where there is light.'

Man is not an individual. He is a social organism. God loves those who serve other beings – men, women, cattle and other creatures. His glory lies in being a member of a big family. Man is also bound by blood kinship – his parents, his wife, his sons, daughter and grandchildren. Human being has to be dynamic. He is expected to lead society from poverty to prosperity with a happy today and happier tomorrow. There is a purposeful benevolent bondage. Through the series of bondage man is expected to attain his fullness – his liberation or emancipation. Be free from shackles of body and sense organs. We shall revert to our self-effulgent form and enjoy divine bliss one becomes amrita or immortal. - *The Holy Vedas*

Song/Prayer

O gracious Mother!

By thy grace I will never allow the world's opinion.

To dim the delight of non-duality.

Nor draw away even subtly.

From Mother's wonderful intimacy, Mother's oneness,

My mother holds me for ever.

My soul remains in tune with my Mother.

ॐॐॐॐॐ

Visualise great things strongly which you want to accomplish. Employ steadfastly enough will power, creative ability and patience until dreams are materialised. Keep busy doing constructive things for own self-improvement and benefit for others. To enter God's kingdoms try also to do good for others every day. Feel the mood dispelling joy. Advance mentally, physically and spiritually. Happiness lies in making others happy forsaking self-interest. Own cup of happiness will be full in giving spiritual, mental and material service to others. - Sri Sri Paramahansa Yogananda 'Where there is light.'

The four Vedas contain the divine, infallible knowledge revealed to enlightened primal men by the grace of God to impart to humanity the words of Almighty God. The purpose of revelation was to enlighten and spread Godly knowledge to human being so that he may live a happy life in this world. Be aware of his innate divinity and try to realise eternal bliss. The Vedas are sacred heritage for all mankind, not only of India. Draw inspiration and guidance from Vedas to achieve harmony with the Creator. - *The Holy Vedas*

Song/Prayer

Divine authority of my Mother of Universe is absolute.

My blissful Mother is the supreme warrior of wisdom.

I bear the self-directing arrow of Her name Ma Kali, Ma Kali in the quiver of my heart.

I keep it keen by constant chanting Her name Ma Kali Ma Kali.

This mystic arrow of Her name Ma Kali remain victorious over the notions of me and mine.

Common intruders who steal away with the treasures of selfless devotion.

ॐॐॐॐॐ

On birth one cry, while everyone else smiles. Live a life that when leaves (departs from this world), everyone will cry, but one will smile. Attune consciousness to the ever existing, ever conscious, ever new joy which is God. Do not allow outside environment to touch inner peace. Abide in true state of the self, the soul's bliss, wisdom, love and peace. Do every task. Enjoy all good things with the joy of God filled with His intoxicating Bliss. Perform all action joyfully. - Sri Sri Paramahansa Yogananda 'Where there is light.'

The manifested Devahs as Agani, Indra, Varuna, Soma, Rudraetc are various powers and attributes of only one Supreme reality-Supreme Lord. See the divinity behind the splendor of all manifestation of Nature, the creator behind the creation.

Hymns on Creation – In the beginning was Hiranyagarbha (Golden Womb).

The seed of elemental existence.

Atharva 4.2.7

The only Lord of all that was born

He upheld the heaven and earth together

To what God other than Him, could we dedicate our life?

- *The Holy Vedas*

Song/Prayer

O Mother Blissful! I

I offer thee seven subtle centre of the pristine spiritual body.

O loving Mother blossom all the centres by thy love.

Let all subtle centres radiate with thy love.

The blooming drum of realization announces the Mother reality.

In My Mother's ocean of love I swim with Bliss.

Crying Jai Ma Kali, Jai Ma Tara, Jai Ma Kali.

My Bhole Baba Shiv, Ma Kali dance along with me.

All bliss love. Motherly sweet love. Sweet love.

ॐॐॐॐॐ

Be like a little child without resentment, without attachment, full of life and joy. Real happiness can stand the challenge of all outer experience. Bear the fructification of other wrongs and still return love and forgiveness while keeping the divine inner peace intact despite all painful thrusts of outer circumstances. Then, know the real happiness. Meditate every night and morning. Be silent and calm. With happiness within fulfill the demands of daily needs. - Sri Sri Paramahansa Yogananda 'Where there is light.'

The whole Universe existed in a state of paramanu (Atoms) invisible, subtle and un-manifested. The various elements were first evolved out of the homogeneous atoms of ether. In the beginning there was Hiranyagarbha – the light. The atoms of ether came closer together and united in the different proportion and formed molecules. This union necessarily implies the contraction of the primeval mass. Chemical union and contraction gave rise to a great deal of heat. Because of high temperature, the atoms had been broken down into nuclei and electrons; even earlier nuclei of the atoms had been reduced to their elements, the protons and neutrons. - *The Holy Vedas*

Song/Prayer

O my loving mind, consecrate your being to pure love.

Turn every thought to Maa Tara.

My Blissful Tara Ma bear me tenderly across the raging sea of separation and individuality.

Utterly dedicated to Mother's reality.

I cry aloud Ma Kali, Ma Kali, Ma Kali.

My Mother will clarify the inconceivable maze of relativity.

Neither wealth nor relatives, no religious rites can give me assistance and guidance.

Only Mother Tara provides profound solution.
So, I cry aloud in ecstasy Ma Tara, Ma Tara, Ma Tara.

ॐॐॐॐॐ

The sun of happiness burns within bosom. Open the window of calmness and find a sudden burst of the bright sun of joy within the very self. All knowledge depends upon the calmness of the mind. Interiorize attention. Train the mind to enjoy the beautiful scenery of thoughts in the invisible, intangible kingdom within. Don't search for happiness only in beautiful clothes and other luxuries. These will imprison happiness behind the bars of externality of outwards.- Sri Sri Paramahansa Yogananda 'Where there is light.'

In the beginning, there was neither sought nor aught.
Then there was neither sky nor atmosphere above.
When then enshrouded all this universe?
In the receptacle of what was it contained?
Then was there neither death nor immortality?
Then was neither day nor night nor light nor darkness.
Only the existence one breathed calmly self-contained
- *The Holy Vedas*

The whole of His universe is stationed in the Omnipresent and the Omnipotent God. We see Him in various forms. He brings light in all these worlds.

Him they call the Kala, Infinite, Pervading the Infinite space - Atharva Veda

Song/Prayer

This cosmos is the strange theatre where souls act.
Wearing various costumes and disguises.
This intricate play of transparent energy is initiated, sustained and dissolved by Ma Kali.
My Mother is the dream power of absolute reality.
I am resting on the vast lap of Mother's cosmic dream.
Abandoning obsession with self and hollow passion.
I sing the song of love of Ma Tara.

Meditating on Ma Tara's lotus feet, I see Her transparent intimacy.
Drunken in nectar of love, I dance crying Ma Tara, Ma Tara.
Tasting the unique sweetness of self-luminous awareness.

ॐॐॐॐॐ

Express gratitude to God for whatever is given. Do not feel bad when it is gone. Do not let feelings rule. Be not fussy about clothes or other possessions. Dress neatly in clean clothes. On receipt of some expensive gift or clothes, be not attached, be not uncomfortable of soiling, tearing or loss. Depend on God for happiness. External conditions cannot give happiness. Do not forget God. Remember Him at all times. Human being is made in God's image. Derive lasting happiness from God. - Sri Sri Paramahansa Yogananda 'Where there is light.'

Creation poses a great mystery. Vedanta teaches that beautifully in the verses in Rig Veda. There was neither existent nor non-existent. There was neither earth nor firmament. When there was nothing what could cover what and where and whose care did waters and bottomless deep then exist? There was neither death nor immortality then; there was no sign of night, nor of day. That one breathed without extraneous breath with His own nature. Other than Him there was nothing beyond. Only the Supreme person was there when there was non-existent and existent - *The Holy Vedas*

Song – Prayer

O my intimate friend Mind, Be not careless, remember ceaselessly.
Ma Tara, who delight absolute reality.
Do not fill with egocentric desires to waste the life.
Whether beaten by worldliness, negative thoughts and actions
Cross the ocean of delusion by crying Om Ma Tara, Om Ma Tara, Om Ma Tara,Om Ma Tara.
By calling Mother's name Ma Tara, all the senses will become paralyzed.
Immerse in the ocean of love of Mother Tara.

Divinity and Humanity will shine infused with Mother's love.

ॐॐॐॐॐ

God is joy itself. Be happy to find Him. Have greater attainment with Him. Perform the funeral rites for all sorrows. Be happy to know Him. Affirm - "Beginning with the early dawn, I will radiate my cheers to everyone, I meet today. I will be mental sunshine for all who cross my path." I see the good everywhere. I behold all things as the perfect idea of God's manifestation. I have made my mind to be happy within myself right now, where I am today. - Sri Sri Paramahansa Yogananda 'Where there is light.'

In the beginning there was darkness.

Intensified darkness, indistinguishable darkness.

- Holy Vedas

All this visible world was reduced to its primordial nature.

This primordial world which was enveloped by the All-Pervading Power of One.

Before whom the world of matter is trifle become One that is, came into existence.

Through the force of His intense activity and spiritual fervour.

- Rig Veda

Song/Prayer-

O Blissful Mother!

No longer I will be fooled by the alluring fruits of selfish motivation.

Knowing them to lack true sweetness.

Such false delicacies are filled with subtle poison that devastates consciousness.

Partaking them we lose spiritual sensitivity.

Most tender Mother Tara, I do not want to forget Thee.

Even for a single heartbeat.

Thou art my beloved mother, my matrix, my bliss.

Mother bless me not to consume negativity.

Loving Mother of unitive wisdom destroy all negativity and egocentric separation.

ॐॐॐॐॐ

Be at peace with immediate relations living everyday to have greatest joy-happiness after Divine Happiness. Handle the extremely complicated machinery of human feelings. Our happiness lies in the art of understanding the law of human behavior. Be not in hot water with friends and constant war with best beloved ones at home. Do Self-Reform. Self-Reform is the basic law of Human behavior. Lay the blame on ourselves. Get out of it fast and graciously. Do not increase the trouble by loudly, unkindly, discourtesy blaming others, even though they are to blame and at fault. Better set good example. Have self-righteous words. Do Self- Righteous works. - Sri Sri Paramahansa Yogananda 'Where there is light.'

In the beginning the Divine will arise, This was the first seed of the mind of the Creator. Those who can see beyond by putting their mind and heart together. Found the binding link of the existent in the non-existent. The non-existent existing in the existent. - *The Holy Vedas*

Song/Prayer -

O Mother! The fruits of mundane existence drive me insane.

Causing me to claim this universe as mine alone.

My loved ones, my sense organs, mine, all mine!

But where is the possessive ego to be found?

During deep meditation, I no longer encounter I.

Blissful Mother, please lead all humanity.

On the mystic way, unveiling thy identity.

Mother! Thou art alone real, Do not keep thy lovers wandering in the illusion of division and limitation.

ॐॐॐॐॐ

There will be no fight, if you refuse to participate. If someone speaks in hurtful language, "Say sorry, if I have done something to offend you". Be silent conquer wrath by coldness. Stop quarrels by keeping silence.

Dispel in harmony by being sweet of speech, shame discourtesy by being thoughtful of others. Give people kindness in return of unkindness. Never be mean. Have resentment towards none. Be friend to all. Christ was crucified. He prayed "Father, forgive them, for they know not what they do". - Sri Sri Paramahansa Yogananda 'Where there is light.'

The rays of the Divine will spread across the whole world.

They spread below and above

And the result was that small and big organisms bearing seeds were born.

As the existence of the Earth was dependent on the Divine will of the creator

The position of matter was lower than the spirit Which acted with Divine will

- The Holy Vedas Rig Vedas

Song/Prayer

O Blissful Mother! O Mother of infinity, what gift can I offer thee.

I perceive all lives and worlds are thine alone.

Why thy lovers present thee so many gifts?

Mother! Thou thyself are the mountain of inexhaustible abundance.

Yet thy husband Lord Shiva appears move as a beggar.

Contemplating my elusive Mother I am overwhelmed with ecstasy.

I cry My Mother My Mother, Mother of Universe, and Blissful Mother.

Thou art the Creator and preserver of the Universe.

Thou art the mystery.

Thy play is mystic, but showering love.

I plunge in thy love, never to come out of thy love.

Mother be gracious to keep me drown in the ocean of thy love.

I now, offer thee my love as gift not matter of thy Universe that belong to thee.

Thou want also my love as mine gift, nothing else.

ॐॐॐॐॐ

Inward civility, inner heartfelt courtesy and goodwill are the proper panaceas for all bad behavior. Do not talk of own viewpoint. Listen to other viewpoints and understand them. Do not enter into argument. Fools argue, wise men discuss. Control feeling, but follow the truth. Share the truth. In zeal to follow truth do not annoy others. Be silent if one is not receptive. Never compromise own ideals and inner peace. Be a force for doing great good in this world. - Sri Sri Paramahansa Yogananda 'Where there is light.'

Who truly knows and who can declare whence it cometh.
And whether it vanished?
- *The Holy Vedas*
The Divine people who know were born.
Much after creation into being.
Who knows whence it has come about.
When this creation has come.
Who holds or does not hold.
He who is its surveyor in the highest heaven.
He alone knoweth, yet doth He know?
Divine people had come much late after creation.
None knows when the creation cometh and vanisheth?

When this creation has come, who holds, who does not hold, one one knows who is unknown. - *Rig Veda*

Song/Prayer -

Mother of Universe!
Thou art unspeakable and unthinkable.
No one can comprehend thine countless revelations.
Thou art seated beside Shiva in quiet harmony.
Peacefully doing all household works even grinding leaves for Lord Shiva, thy Lord.
Sometimes thou dance with warrior's ecstasy on the vast breast of Absolute Reality, thy Lord, thy husband Shiva.
Sometimes thou manifest in the radiant cosmos.
In love rapture, I fall at thy lotus feet Mother.

I offer my whole being as gift.

Fulfill thy will through this body, mind and soul.

Take me back home holding me smiling both.

While I am crying Mother, Mother, Mother.

ॐॐॐॐॐ

Be courteous to immediate relatives. Real family happiness has its foundation on the altar of understanding and kind words. Not necessary to agree on everything to show kindness. Calm silence, sincerity and courteous words whether agreeing or disagreeing mark the person who knows how to behave. Start loving others to be loved - start respecting others to be respected. Sympathize with others to have sympathy from others. Be respectful to everyone. Behave as you want others to behave. - Sri Sri Paramahansa Yogananda 'Where there is light.'

The Supreme being is thousand headed, thousand eyed, thousand footed. He pervades the universe and all sides and extends beyond the ten directions. He indeed is all this, what has been and what will be. He is the Lord of immortality, transcending through material existence. Such is the magnificence, but the Supreme being greater than this. All beings are quarter of Him. Three quarters make up immortality in the Supreme Region. - *The Holy Vedas*

Song/Prayer -

Mother of Universe! Thou art remover of thy veil of enlightened sages.

They know and see the Mother of Universe in form and formless.

Thou were present in the form and formless with Ramakrishna.

Thine transparent presence dwells within every atom, every perception.

Mother Blissful, I don't want to know any theology, any philosophy.

I can only weep Ma! Ma! Ma!

Mother! Ma is the sweetest name, transcending all descriptions.

Mother! Bless me to call Thee Ma, Ma, Ma every moment and ever.

Mother! Bless me to lay forever atthy dark blue loving wisdom feet.

Mother! Hold me, thy child forever.

I will be lost without thine holding.

Just be smiling, congenial and kind. Do not wear a long face. Sincerity is the soul quality that God has given to us, but not all express it. Above all, be humble. Do not overwhelm others with strong nature. Be kind and considerate. Do not adopt artificial mannerisms. Be loving. Be helpful. Saturate with divine communion with divinity get along with everyone in all circumstances. - Sri Sri Paramahansa Yogananda 'Where there is light.'

Three quarters of the Supreme Being remain abstract.

One quarter part manifest again and gain.

And diversified in form, it moves.

To the animate and the inanimate world.

Through the Divine energy of the Supreme being.

This Dynamic Universe (Virat) come into existence.

In the course of the evolution of the universe,

The earth and other habitable planets came into being.

And souls manifested themselves in the form of living beings and thus life came into existence. - *The Holy Vedas*

Song/Prayer -

O mind, my ancient friend, this projected universe is only the faint reflection of reality.

By attempting to grasp reflected images.

We cheat ourselves of true experience.

Turn instead to the original

Discover the limitless treasure of delight.

Realise mother's love, mother's love is infinite.

Rapture in mother's love cry cry Ma MaMa.

Mother is the savior, Mother is the Reality.

Study people with open mind to understand them and get along with them. Recognise and appreciate their characteristics. Find out one's interest. Talk with him about that subject of his interest and not the subject of your interest. Do not talk too much about yourself. Try to speak on a subject that interests the other person and listen. This is the way to attract people. - Sri Sri Paramahansa Yogananda 'Where there is light.'

With the coming into being of the dynamic Universe.

The adaption of the primordial matter was made in the primeval activities.

Thus began the changes in the atomic composition of matter.

In the colossal cosmic sacrifice, substances to sustain life were produced.

As well as vegetation, grains, fruits, flowers and therapeutic substances that increase both energy and the life span.

This made it possible for animal life to thrive.

In the course of creation of the Universe.

The Rig Veda, The Sama Veda, The Yajur Veda and The Atharva Veda were revealed.

- *The Holy Vedas*

Song/Prayer -

Contemplate, Why we consume earth instead of nectar.
Convention instead of rapture.
Time instead of timeless.
Cut immediately and easily this illusion of bondage to the world.
The passionate words of a selfish lover,
At first tastes sweeter than honey.
But, they contain the poison of delusion.
Drain the cup of selfish love.
Taste only Mother authentic love; weep with spiritual tears.
Ma Kali! Ma Kali! Ma Kali!
Mother! Thou art union of relative and absolute.
Laughing daughter of the eternal snow mountain.

Do what thou will with me, thy child.

ॐॐॐॐॐ

Develop self-confidence. Find real self. Soul can never be inferior in any way. Do not have imagined weakness. Overcome weakness by efforts. Do not have either inferiority complex or superiority complex. Superiority complex arises from false pride or ego. Improve. Do not talk too much. Do not put your finger into everyone else's pie. - Sri Sri Paramahansa Yogananda 'Where there is light.'

Three kinds of animals came into being in the creation of universe. Four types of domestic animals. Human being have superior intellect. They are advanced of all living being. Some have Divine qualities, which were well versed in the knowledge of Vedas. They contemplated intensely on how to integrate and organise society. Highly intellectual Brahmans were recognized as the mouth. Kshatriyas, who were administrators and warriors, represented the arms. The Vaishyas who were artisans, traders and agriculturists corresponded to the abdominal region and the thighs, the Shudras were associated with the feet to serve. - *The Holy Vedas*

Song/Prayer -

O Blissful Mother! Transform my mind.

With the delicate light of the hearts' sincerity.

With this pure mind and heart, I meditate on thy lotus feet.

With thy grace I will attain final success in spiritual life.

The enlightenment of the whole -being including all its passionate intensity.

And attain bliss of thy love.

Rapture in Bliss of love I dance and cry Ma, Ma, Ma.

ॐॐॐॐॐ

Be considerate to others. Considerate means intuitive awareness of others needs. Practice consideration and goodness. Be like a beautiful flower that everyone loves to see. Be of pure mind. All and God love such man-woman. What you give, that comes to you. Hate, you will receive hate in return. Negative and inharmonious thoughts and emotions destroy one. Why hate or be angry with anyone. Love your enemies. - Sri Sri Paramahansa Yogananda 'Where there is light.'

The moon denotes the mind of the Supreme Being; the sun His eyes. The wind and breath issue from His ears; fire is produced from His mouth; human mind is similarly associated with moon; the sun symbolizes His eyes; the universe is conceived in the form of the intangible Supreme being. The central region identical with abdominal region corresponds to the middle space Anatariksha - the sky; the uppermost region the luminous outer space synonymous with the head, the lowest region correlating with the feet is identified as the earth (Bhumi). The entire planetary system of the Universe gradually evolved according to this scheme of Supreme Being. - *The Holy Veda*

Song/Prayer -

Mother of Universe, what else thou will display to me during this lifetime?

My soul journey across the planetary plane.

Bears no sweet spiritual fruit.

Even though I am the child of Thee, my universal Mother.

Utterly disillusioned by the world of convention.

I pray to Thee, my Mother Tara, bring my soul to the truth.

Mother pour awareness to me, thy child.

Not knowing what I do, I hold thy lotus feet with fervour of love.

ॐॐॐॐॐ

Command "Go away the voice of jealousy, fear or anger". These are not your voice. These are in collision with the cosmic delusion of Satan. Do not have negative feeling. Eradicate jealousy, fear and anger from within. Listen to the strangers voice within which tells to love and to forgive. Listen to voice within. Jealousy comes from an inferiority complex. Improve yourself. Develop yourself. Do not have feeling of inferiority complex. Constantly improve yourself. Instead of you seeking others, others will seek you. - Sri Sri Paramahansa Yogananda 'Where there is light.'

The Supreme Being proceeds ahead with yajna (task) of the creation of the universe. Solid substances displaying natural specific properties were offered as oblation (Ahuti). In this cosmic yajna, clarified butter or ghee symbolized spring, wood chips summer and corn autumn. Innumerable species/animal life came into existence of which human race is most advanced. Among mankind there were also seers, sages, hermits, ascetics, intellectuals and scholars. They set about the task of organizing society by disciplining man, the animal. Seven enclosures or disciplines or twenty sticks, samidha were utilized. - *The Holy Veda*

Song/Prayer -

O my mind! Be not in depression, I am not a motherless child.
I have a Mother who is the queen of the universe.
As a beloved child of the Mother of Universe, be utterly fearless.
My Mother is Supreme Sovereign.
There is no one and nothing I can fear.
For nothing and no one exists apart from Her; My Mother.
Do not indulge any longer in any thing - in worldly affairs.
Ceaselessly sing Jai Ma Kali, Jai Ma Tara, Jai Ma Kali.
My Mother will awaken me to non-duality.
In love Bliss, my Mother shall merge me with Her.

ॐॐॐॐॐ

Strive to improve. Learn to stand alone. Be secured in own virtues and self-worth. Words have an effect but not enough. It is what we are and what we feel within, what is in soul. These qualities have lasting effect. Always strive to be angel within. No matter how much others behave. Be sincere, kind, loving and understanding. - Sri Sri Paramahansa Yogananda 'Where there is light.'

The scholars and sages undertook function of organizing society. Significance and priority was given to the formulation of fundamental laws and behaviour that promoted social stability and cohesiveness. The creator is perfect. He possesses perfect power. He created perfect nature. The perfect universe derives life from the perfect Creator. Let us comprehend this perfect power. That bestows life on all beings.

- *The Holy Vedas*

Song/Prayer -

O Death! Know that I am not motherless child.

Know that my mother Kali is the queen of universe.

When you will come, my Mother Tara will be at the side of me.

I will not care about your torture, I will cry and laugh in my Mother's love Bliss.

My Mother will hold me, take me thy child with Her.

When time comes for me to return home, my mother will come.

Holding my hand, Mother will take me to Her home.

ॐॐॐॐॐ

If someone comes in anger, remain in charge of yourself. "I will not lose my temper. I will keep on expressing calmness until his feeling changes". When a loved one tries our patience beyond endurance, we should retire to a quiet place, lock the door and practice some physical exercise, then quiet ourselves and sit in a straight chair with spine erect, slowly inhale and exhale twelve times. Then deeply affirm mentally, ten times or more, "Father thou art harmony, harmonize my error stricken dear one". Affirm till feeling comes "God has heard and He has answered". - Sri Sri Paramahansa Yogananda 'Where there is light.'

Bringing with her life-sustaining blessing and giving life to the lifeless, the Divine Dawn imparts her brilliant lustre to the world. The cosmic energy grows in space unbounded. The friend of mankind lies within the lap of nature's laws. The cosmic energy is the generator of the universe. It remains ever illumined by its own radiance. It provides sustenance for its beloved progeny.- *The Holy Veda*

Song/Prayer – Blissful Mother

Spiritually born child of Mother, I aspire wholeheartedly.

May my mind become radiantly pure.

With this mind of purity, I meditate.
Upon the mystic seed sound 'OM MAOM'.
Entrusted to me by my Cosmic Mother.
O childish mind, meditate this way.
Merging ever more deeply with Her reality.
Death and life are simply Her play.

ॐॐॐॐॐ

Suppression is harmful. Do not hold the thoughts. Do constructive efforts to get over it. Self-control is beneficial. Replace wrong thoughts by right thoughts. Do not dwell on evil. It hurts gravely. Change thoughts and actions. Fill mind with wisdom. Engage in constructive activities. - Sri Sri Paramahansa Yogananda 'Where there is light.'

The place of divine forces is in superior mysterious locations. The flames of mighty cosmic energy descend. Agani the Cosmic Fire was discovered by resolute seeker from the lotus-leaf lake after deep contemplation. The cosmic energy and cosmic radiation leave us unharmed when they pass by our dwellings. O mighty wind, inflict no pain upon us. the divine melody-knowledge with uniform light spreads over the whole world. pious Devotees expand their field of knowledge. The refreshing glow of Divine Consciousness sends forth each busy man to his pursuit. SHE knows no delay. - *The Holy Veda*

Song/Prayer-

O mind! Pay clear attention.
To the root of your own being.
The path of original source is ecstatic love.
Intensely love your most intimate companion.
Direct all tender feelings.
Toward the Mother of Universe.
Who is pure awareness.
Contemplate deeply.
Discover non-duality.
there is only Mother Reality.

My Mother, source of creativity, expresses fully through all creatures.
Moving about subtly, secretly and blissfully.
Within Her own essentiality.

ॐॐॐॐॐ

Wrath springs only from thwarted desires. Do not expect anything from others, so their actions cannot be in opposition to wishes of mine. Think of all the good things about the person who has hurt you and of all the goodness of your life. Do not take notice of the insults people give you. - Sri Sri Paramahansa Yogananda 'Where there is light.'

This immortal nature of Universe takes its place in the hearts of mortal humans and it also blesses them in all their sacred aspirations, with its spiritual radiance, reflecting by intense love and knowing all secrets of wisdom. It shines extensively. The divine light of cosmic. Intelligence which has golden radiance and a sweet voice, descends from heaven to inspire us thrice at our assemblies. O Lord of Divine Light accept our praises to fulfill our aspirations. - *The Holy Vedas*

Song/Prayer-

O wavering mind! Awaken your upward-flowing awareness.
Comprehend Her! She moves with graceful power through the body.
She dwells as the primal lotus of conscious energy.
And also as the thousand - petal blossom complete enlightenment.
She is none other than primordial bliss.
This great swan ever swimming.
Through the lotus jungle of the subtle body.
Gaze intently into the blazing heart of joy.
And perceive my Blissful Mother.
Matrix of all phenomena.

ॐॐॐॐॐ

Have only love in heart for others. See the good in all. Hold the consciousness of good. That will establish good in ourselves. The way to make people good is to see good in them. Do not nag them. Remain calm, serene and always in command of yourself. Try to concentrate to behold God. Do not hate. Do not poison system physically and emotionally. It will become easy to get along with all. - Sri Sri Paramahansa Yogananda 'Where there is light.'

Listen to the melodious music of the divine poet. He plays upon the flute of love; the notes soar to high heaven and reach the distant stars and dance on the raging waves of the sea. The earth, the sea, the sky, the stars are all woven together by the soft strings of divine music. Its vibrations echo through the corridors of time in the endless canopy of the sky. - *The Holy Vedas*

Song/Prayer -

O Mother of Universe! The vision of Thee, Mother Kali.

Kindles the fire of unitive wisdom.

Burning down conventional barriers.

Pervading minds and worlds with light.

Reavealing her exalted beauty full of love.

As universal flower garden.

Where lovers of Mother merge with Mother Reality.

Experiencing the single task of non-duality.

Universe is full of Mother's love Bliss.

Being lover of Mother! I Sing Jai MaaKali , Jai Maa Kali in love bliss.

ॐॐॐॐॐ

Cleanse mind of all adverse criticism of others. Correct lovingly a receptive person. Do not force correction. Do not hold critical thoughts even while remaining silent. Thoughts are more effective than words. The human mind is the most powerful broadcasting machine. Broadcast constantly positive thoughts with love which will have an effect on others. Others will also respond to thoughts with love. Pray to God to put His power behind efforts. Beloved God help me to help my dear one. Lord be with him. Bless me to do my part. Be in deep communion with God. - Sri Sri Paramahansa Yogananda 'Where there is light.'

O the stream of conscious divine, we offer presentation with adoration and praises. Acknowledge that and place us under your kind care. We take shelter under you as a traveler takes refuge under a tree. O Beautiful spiritual stream of divine light, by your blessings we get both kind of nourishment, physical and superamental. Be considerate to us. Friend of the vital breaths, bestow riches on us when we are sincere in devotion. - *The Holy Vedas*

Song/Prayer -

My beloved Mother! As an ardent lover, I long only to gaze upon Thee, my Mother.

Why I will close my eyes? Will thou counter in meditation?

Mother of wisdom, let thy child, thy lover gaze upon Thee in relative world.

Mother of loving child! I cry out to Thee when my countless egocentric impulses invade me.

My lamp of devotion is constantly in danger by wind of selfish desires.

Mother! Mother! Protect thy child, me.

Bless thy child, me to sing with joy Ma! Ma! Ma!

Bless me always within light, O Mother.

Always returning home to light, when physical eyes close for the last time.

Darkness will dissolve into light and light into Thee, my Mother.

ॐॐॐॐॐ

Love must be sincere. It must come from heart. Love is magical. Do not look for the effects. Give love and forget. Do not expect anything. Then there will be magical result. Overcome evil with the power of divine love - Supreme love of God. Jesus showed us the real nature of God. By forgiveness the universe is held together. - Sri Sri Paramahansa Yogananda 'Where there is light.'

The auspicious stream of divine light may bestow spiritual fortune upon us. People of Divine vision may glorify us. Seekers of truth may glorify us. He (the Lord) has set high constellations above us. They are visible at night and disappear by day. His laws remain always unviolated. By His command, the moon during night moves on its splendour. Cosmic luminaries of equal splendour, the sun, the dwarf - stars and the giant-stars, sons of Mother Infinity be pleased by our invocations. Purify us by showers of effulgence. They abandon none. They are irreproachable and unassailable. - *The Holy Veda*

Song/Prayer

Mother of Universe! Thine eternal love abides in every soul.

Mother, thou direct the entire drama of relativity.

Thine children are lost in thy relative world.

Thou alone can awaken me fully as to the essence of thine reality.

The courageous lover tastes the bliss of Mother's love.

Mother! Thou art the intimate companion of the soul.

I plunge into union with my loving Mother.

Mother's love seizes me totally.

Mother's child sings madly 'My delusion is gone, gone, utterly gone.

In blazing fire of love, relativity of world gone.

ॐॐॐॐॐ

God is constantly forgiving us even though He knows all our wicked thoughts. Great souls are in tune with Him. They give that same love. Learn to be sympathetic. Have genuine feelings for others. Hatred accomplishes nothing. Love rewards. Conquer by love, not by might. Hatred begets hatred. Lord Jesus, "Father, forgive them, for they know not what they do" at the time of being brutally crucified. He could have destroyed with a look, yet forgiven.

- Sri Sri Paramahansa Yogananda 'Where there is light.'

The cosmic pair of day and night comes to cherish our noble deeds. The golden rays of the sun lit up the path of action. O Man, awake from the slumber. Darkness of the night is over. May each dawn lead us from triumph to triumph in the long journey of life. O Lord of solar systems free us from every bond. O Lord of cosmic light and bliss, may we partake thy bounty. O Heaven and Earth, may wc livc through your blessings. – *The Holy Veda*

Song/Prayer

Mother Dear! Thou art loving and kind to me, thy child.

Thou have given me the boat of thy name to sail the stormy water of worldliness.

With the heavy treasure of thy name, I make efforts to sail the boat of thy name.

I cry Ma, Ma when the boat of thy name face storms of worldliness.

Mother wisdom, save thy child, bless thy child to sail the boat of thy name.

Cutting away both subjectively and objectively.

With thy flashing sword of non-duality.

Bless me to sing thy glorious and love songs of my soul.

ॐॐॐॐॐ

Affirm. I will try to please everyone by kind, considerate actions, ever striving to remove any misunderstanding knowingly or unknowingly caused by me. Today I forgive all those who have ever offended me. I give my love to all thirsty hearts; both to those who love me and those who do not love me. - Sri Sri Paramahansa Yogananda 'Where there is light.'

In Him, rest the vitality of both organic and inorganic worlds. All shower blessings on us. Water, pure, faultless, sweet essence of the earth is the first beverage of the Lord. O Divine water sustains us. We, devotees of Nature's bounty share your joy today. Unsoiled by dust the clouds are shining. They are invested with great strength and virile energies. The clouds come with tremendous speed and the brilliant ones shed the rains. This Divine elixir mixed with sweet celestial waters may be given to the soul to infuse vigour and heroism.

- *The Holy Veda*

Song/Prayer

I live in the mysterious kingdom of merciful Mother Kali.

I am Her child.

I am Her direct representative.

O Death! Recognize me, know me, don't terrify me.
I am Her loving child.
My Mother Kali is my Supreme beloved.
My life's essence is Her love.
I am the eternal companion and child of Ma Kali.
I am filled with courage and love.
I will return to my Mother's home at Her sweet will.
Smiling, hand in hand of Ma Kali, I will return to my home.
O Death! Do your job elsewhere, my sovereign is My Mother Kali.

ॐॐॐॐॐ

Love permeates every part of creation. Love is the divine power of attraction in creation that harmonizes, unites and binds together. Live in tune with attractive force of love that achieves harmony with nature and fellow beings. They are attracted to blissful reunion with God. Divine love is without condition without boundary and without change. The flux of human heart is gone forever at the transfixing touch of pure love. - Sri Sri Paramahansa Yogananda 'Where there is light.'

Knowledge, jnana is the light of the sun. Sun is older than the earth. Space has no dimensions. See unity in diversity. Behold one Divine Form appearing in multi forms. Immense is His vastness, unparalleled is His glory. All the countless earths, suns and planets which are seen and which are beyond our perceptions exist and His command. Kindled in various forms, the perennial flame is one, sprinkling the world with golden beams at dawn. Painting the evening clouds with changing colours, the sun is one. - *The Holy Veda*

Song/Prayer -

Mother Tara! Sings calling me my child! Courage! Courage! Be courageous!
Sail with me! Sail with me in the ship of your life.
In the deep, stormy ocean of delusion.
Board the transcendental vessel of your Mother Tara.

That brings your soul to the truth, Mother's reality.

Unfurl the bright sail Ma Tara, Ma Tara, Ma Tara.

Ply with vigor the oars of contemplation.

Sing the songs of love of soul for Ma Tara, Ma Tara.

Merge in bliss union with Ma Tara.

ॐॐॐॐॐ

Lover of God cannot wilfullyhurt anyone. Love God without reservation. He fills your heart with His unconditional love for all. Be not centred in the consciousness of I, me and mine. Discover the omnipresent God who resides in you and all other beings. All souls are reflection of one God. We are part of one spirit. True meaning of Religion is to know God and realise that He is the Self and that He exists equally and impartially in all beings. Then one will be able to love others as your own self. - Sri Sri Paramahansa Yogananda 'Where there is light.'

O Mother of Divine Powers, the life force of the earth may shine forth exalted. Bestow reward on us for our devotion. Make us eminent among the people. These stars, sons of Mother Infinity are of huge dimensions, unparalleled, provided with super brilliance, radiating out as if from innumerable eyes appearas if beholding from their innermost places both our vices and our virtues. - *The Holy Veda*

Song/Prayer -

Ma Tara! Thou are truly the exalted one

The essence of awareness.

Thou are the radiant truth.

Mother of Universe! Consider what thou bestow on me.

My mind wanders at random from morning to night.

For livelihood, delicious food and so on even at times of prayers and contemplation.

Mother Tara! In thy Motherly affection, bestow the vision.

Allow my consciousness to be absorbed in thy vision of thine Reality.

Affectionately and lovingly bless me to plunge into deep thought of thine.

Bless me to realize thy love and be in thy love.

In love bliss, let me cry Ma! Ma! Ma!

Daughter of mystic mountain! My Mother let us dance in love trance.

ॐॐॐॐॐ

Immerse in the love of Divine God in the consciousness. There will be no deception, no narrowness of caste or creed, and no boundaries of any kind. One will commune with all nature. One will love all equally. Compassion towards all beings is necessary for divine realization. God Himself is ever flowing with compassion. Feel the suffering of others. - Sri Sri Paramahansa Yogananda 'Where there is light.'

In this creation three regions terrestrial, inter-spatial and celestial are held in balance. Three divine realms pertaining to body, mind and spirit (soul) are provided with three eternal functions - physical mental and transcendental sons of mother infinity, the dwarf stars, the sun and the giant stars are excellent and great since they further the eternal law (of the Lord). The stream of spiritual awareness, limitless, shining, issuing forth from the ocean of cosmic intelligence comes onward with a tempestuous roar. - *The Holy Vedas*

Song/Prayer

Mother! Mother! Mother!

Thine dream-play universe is sheer delight.

Souls caught in the seriousness of thine drama are constantly running, looking for release.

The egocentric bind themselves mindlessly repeating, this is I, that is mine.

But, souls who know their boundless nature are free and happy under every condition.

Mother release me from thy dream-play.

Plunge me into the ocean of thy love.

ॐॐॐॐॐ

Remember always, 'I am Spirit' I am the soul. A soul is made in God's image. The soul is immutable unqualified image of God. The soul impersonates both man and woman. Realize divine potential. God is both infinite wisdom and infinite feeling. God manifested Himself in creation. God gave His wisdom a form in the father and He gave His feeling a form in the mother. Both father and mother have fatherly wisdom and motherly tenderness of God. They have to perfect these endowments. The divine man develops both the fatherly and motherly qualities in Himself. - Sri Sri Paramahansa Yogananda 'Where there is light.'

May the solar systems, the Mother Infinity, the most loving sun, waters, and the fire divine be extolled. They are being glorified by us. May they ever cherish us with blessings. Thy guardian of the world may accept the elixir of our devotion. May He who augments the plants, waters and rules the whole earth with His divine magnanimity give us shelter, all sorts of felicity and desired light at three seasons.

- *The Holy Veda*

Song/ Prayer -

Joy and sorrow are simply Mother Kali's play.
Sow seeds of selflessness.
Reap a harvest of insight.
The principle of action and its fruit is incontrovertible.
Sing Ma Kali, Ma Kali, Ma Kali .
Breath becomes pure and selfless.
Practice Her contemplation.
Cut time down with the sword of non-duality.
Think clearly and kindly.

- By Dr. H.P. Kanoria based on combination of own feelings and other poems.

ॐॐॐॐॐ

God manifested man and woman to help each other in developing divine qualities of perfect reason and feeling. Each should strive towards a balance by learning from one another through friendship and understanding. Each one should strive for an inner balance of both reason and feeling and so become a 'whole' personality, a perfected human being. Commune with God to bring about the harmony and balance of these two qualities within. - Sri Sri Paramahansa Yogananda 'Where there is light.'

The brilliant stars, sons of Mother Infinity are upholders of all gravitational bodies, movable or apparently stationary. They are the protectors of the universe balancing the equilibrium. They are provident in acts, dispeller of darkness, true to eternal law and acquit nature's debts. The divine cosmic embraces the entire cosmic creation for providing protection. Man crowns Him (God) along with their offerings and hymns. Possessed of golden flames he distinguishes himself in both regions of universe. - *Holy Veda*

Song/Prayer-

Mother Kali! I have become a beast of burden, bridled, saddled.

Ridden by senses, passions and mental faculties.

Each rider wants to take a different way.

How I can reach evolutionary goal,

Conscious union with Her reality.

With folded hands, I sing Ma Kali, Ma Kali with tears rolling.

Mother loving, do not let the ocean of thy love dry by world diversion.

ॐॐॐॐॐ

Great saints have ideal masculine and feminine qualities – reasons and feelings. Jesus and Paramhansa Ramakrishna were like that. Attain perfect reason and feeling of equilibrium. Strive to see the reflection of God in women and realize her spiritual nature. In pure love there is complete harmony in body, mind and soul. It results in a perfect unity. - Sri Sri Paramahansa Yogananda 'Where there is light.'

May we prosper, invigorated by Thy cosmic laws which are generous, diverse in form, but with similar functions. The earth is potent. The sky takes whatever shape it desires. The Mother earth receives water from the father sky who nourishes all living beings. May we humbly bow to thee, O Supreme Lord. At thy command moves the mighty wheel of time. Thou art eternal and beyond eternity.

- *The Holy Veda*

Song/ Prayer

Mother of Universe, thou alone know the fathom of thy judgement

I await thy order, I am free from diversion

My palms touch constantly in prayer to thee

I repeat day and night thine power name Ma Kali, Ma Kali

I sing in love trance thy mystic name Ma Kali, Ma Tara, Ma Tara

Mother I do not have strength to bear thy examination

My mind is lacking purity and clarity

My soul refuge is my Mother's love and my Baba Shiva's love

ॐॐॐॐॐ

We have come to earth to learn to develop pure and unconditional love between parent and children, husband and wife, friend and friend. In marriage two persons unite with their lives to help each other toward divine realization and unconditional friendship and love. Catalytic power of love changes the selfishness, bad temper and bad behaviour into patience and understanding. Eliminate these poisons and purify your nature. - Sri Sri Paramahansa Yogananda 'Where there is light.'

He is the prime source of contemplation and divine light. He is the center of cosmic orbit. He is the piercing intellect. He is the wellwisher of all. All behold Him. He gives the earth to noble men. Rain to the mortals who till the soil. He sets free the roaring water. The cosmic powers obey His order. Through His love He demolishes all strongholds of evils for His devotees. He destroys all malicious forces. He helps His dear devotees who obey Him. The divine powers abide by His order. Principal energies are based on Him. He destroys evil forces. As the vulnerable Lord, He rules over all . - *The Holy Veda*

Song/Prayer-

My loving Mother! Thou art my sole refuge.

My mind is lacking purity and clarity.

I will not stand thy examination.

With melting heart, I cry out Ma Kali! Ma Kali! Ma Kali!

Only to merge with Thee.

Permit me to draw my final breath.

My entire being is shining with Thy Name.

Ma Kali! Ma Kali! Ma Kali! Om Baba Shiva! Om Baba Shiva!

ॐॐॐॐॐ

Wish spirituality for each other's soul unfoldment which brings out the divine qualities of understanding, patience, thoughtfulness and love. Don't force spiritual growth. Your love and goodness will inspire all loved ones. Do not have lack of courtesy, suspiciousness, insulting speech on acts, argument before others or anger. Attain spiritual goals by study, effort and self discipline. - Sri Sri Paramahansa Yogananda 'Where there is light.'

He covers the frail body and mind with His loving care, His blissful divine love to clothe human being with eternal joy. He, the cosmic observe grants, ample strength for living, kindness of all, divine powers, compassion for victorious onward journey of life. O men, open the eyes and behold. He is before us. All things, He transcends in greatness and majesty that exist. He is the teacher of truth. Illuminate spreading knowledge of His far and wide. Adored by all worlds, He cherishes them with tender care. - *The Holy Vedas*

Song/Prayer -

My Loving Mother! I am Thy child, I fear none.

I live in the bliss love of Her non-duality.

My beloved father Lord Shiva transcends every limited conception and transaction.

There is no disharmony or injustice.

There is no division, no separation.

There is no religious obligations.

Constantly remember Her inwardly.

Eternally breathing Ma Kali, Ma Kali, Ma Kali.

ॐॐॐॐॐ

Develop similarity of interest - intellectual, social, environmental and enlightenment. Learn to control emotions. Nurture high ideals and have the wine of God's inspiration. Use kind words and create a new happiness in the family. - Sri Sri Paramahansa Yogananda 'Where there is light.'

God blesses a human being with a life of a hundred years. Reap full benefit of this God's gift by keeping the body and mind healthy and fit. He strikes with deadly weapons the big exploiters as the lightning strikes the furious clouds. - *The Holy Vedas*

Song/Prayer -

I am the mad child of Divine Mother Kali.

I cherish one's consuming desire to have delight of Her boundless love.

And give this boundless love of Ma Kali freely to all beings.

O Ma Kali, drama of my life was composed and acted out in the blazing summer field of destiny.

Loving Mother! Mother! Now, please bring thy little child home through the fragrant cool of evening.

Cradled in thine loving arms, lost in thy gaze, disappearing in thy love.

ॐॐॐॐॐ

God's loving cosmic intelligence permeates every atom of creation. In a family's temple all family members together offer deep devotion unto God and unite their soul forever in ever joyous cosmic consciousness. The more we meditate together, the deeper our love for one another will grow. - Sri SriParamahansaYogananda 'Where there is light.' He moves the cosmic forces of vitality and wealth of the luminaries and all celestial powers. He sustains the cosmic sources of water and light. He is the centre of energy; light and life give by the Sun, Air, Fire and all other beneficial cosmic forces. He is the mother and restorer of wealth. He knows all that is worth knowing and expressing. The divine powers function with His instructions. He

possesses all domains. His hymns are chanted at all places. - *The Holy Vedas*

Song/Prayer -

With the Mother of Universe, I have a serious grievance to settle.

My all protecting Mother! Even I apparently awake.

The house of my mind and body is ransacked by robbers' my countless egocentric impulses.

Everyday, every moment of my resolve to repeat thy name as the most powerful defense.

But forget my good intention just as the intruders arrive.

In thy playfulness thou elude my willful grasp.

Thou bestow no power of inward prayer upon thy child.

So thou receive not consistent devotion from me.

I no longer regard this as my fault.

Only what thou give me, I am return to Thee.

ॐॐॐॐॐ

Friendship is the purest form of God's love. Ideal friendship destroys the partitions of ego consciousness. The treasure of friendship is the richest possession. It goes beyond their life. All true friends will meet again in the home of the Father for real love is never lost. Spiritual friendship perfects each one. - Sri Sri Paramahansa Yogananda 'Where there is light.'

O Enlightened Men! Through His power all the creatures take breath, eat, see and hear. Even all do not know that all dwell is His love, He is in all and all are in Him. When He speaks, His words bring joy. He grants powers to men whom he favours. He makes them divine, the seer and men of perfection. - *The Holy Vedas*

Song/Prayer -

O Mother of Universe! Fame and infamy, good and bad tastes of life.

All phenomena are thine graceful play.

O Mother! Lead us in Thine wisdom and love way.

Mother! Thou have placed a dream in every mind.
Free us from egocentricity, Awaken us to Thy love.
Awakening from this dark dream, we cry with tears of contrition.
Simply continue to intone Ma! Ma! Ma!
We taste the honey of Her mercy, Her love.

ॐॐॐॐॐ

Develop the quality of unselfishness and thinking of others. This is magnet. Behave divinely. Be spiritual to be pure and unselfish. Be useful. Cheer a friend in distress, advice him in trouble. Be helpful. Regardless of differences in opinion, have mutual respect and trust. Establish friendship with God. This is a lasting relation. - Sri Sri Paramahansa Yogananda 'Where there is light.'

He stretches the bow of the defender of cosmic life, so that His arrows may pierce the malicious powers. He rouses the fury in the hearts of people to battle against evils. He penetrates the heaven and earth so that none violates His eternal laws. He breathes like the wind pervading all regions. He goes beyond the heavens, beyond the limits of this vast earth. He is invincible. None can deny Him. - *The Holy Vedas*

Song/Prayer -

Awake! Awake! into profound longing of Mother Kali.
Just imbue entire being with Ma Kali, Ma Kali, Ma Kali.
Counting only Ma Kali,MaKali,Ma Kali.
Be joyful and carefree.
Be lost in Mother's innate Bliss.
Behold Radha, Krishna and Kali are one reality.
Love flows through the lovely eyes of Krishna.
Dance in love ecstasy chanting Hare Krishna, Hare Krishna, Hare Rama, Hare Rama.
Mahaprabhu Chaitanya dances in love Bliss 'Hari Bole, Hari Bole, Krishna! Krishna!.

ॐॐॐॐॐ

It is wrong to speak the truth which hurts a friend or someone. In the name of truthfulness, do not announce the weakness of a friend. Be protective about other's personal faults, so long as they harm no one else. Speak privately. Awaken His wisdom and will power. Tell him about the harmful effects of drinks privately. Feel cooperation and empathy from inside not only from outside. Have the willingness to cooperate for good. - Sri Sri Paramahansa Yogananda 'Where there is light.'

He is the possessor of all riches. He is the leader among equals. The Supreme Knowledge is His soul. A friend of man is dear to His heart. His heart is free from sorrow. His heart has capacity of a sea, a dwelling place for all beloved and friendly. He is a terror to the wicked. The wicked are stunned to see Him. He upholds the moisture shedding, cosmic ocean. He upholds the effulgent region in the abode of the eternal order. Being the preserver of eternity, He created all the regions of the Universe. - *The Holy Vedas*

Song/Prayer -

Ma Kali's dancing energy and Baba Shiva's pure tranquility.

Simply one essence of awareness.

Ma Kali emerges into form and action in response to every prayer and longing.

Ma Kali overflows with compassion.

Her lovers who are simple, overflowing their hearts with Her pure love and non-dual wisdom.

Repeat Her name with every heartbeat, every breath.

Universe becomes a radiant garden of bliss.

Each Atom singing Ma Tara, Ma Tara, Ma Tara.

Her human lovers become the absolute, singing Ma Tara, Ma Tara

Merged in bliss beneath Her flashing feet.

Now only Ma Tara remains.

ॐॐॐॐॐ

Be not sarcastic to a friend. Encourage him. Do not agree with him when he is wrong. Be true, be sincere, be spiritual. Encourage him to be spiritual. Be sincere. Sweeten relationship with good manners and thoughtfulness. Then friendship becomes truly wonderful and enduring. Inner and outer sweetness fosters the growth of friendship. - Sri Sri Paramahansa Yogananda 'Where there is light.'

He is potent eternal law. Neither Arya or Non-Arya can break His power by no means. The four corners of the world pay homage to Him. The waves of the ocean rise in obedience to Him. Within these, O enlightened man, He place heaven and earth. Inside our heart He places celestial luminaries, wisdom and strength. Develop harmony with all and enjoy life in full. - *The Holy Vedas*

Song/Prayer -

Lovers of mother long to play.

In eternal companionship with Divinity and to merge completely with Divine Reality.

This mirror mind and rainbow body are Her marvelous play.

Through the transparent medium of Her elements.

After death, Her dancing elements flow on and simply mother remains.

We will be in the end what we were in the beginning.

Clear bubbles forming and dissolving in the stream of timeless wisdom.

ॐॐॐॐॐ

Friendship/togetherness is noble, fruitful, holy, when separate souls march in difference yet in harmony, agreeing and disagreeing, glowingly improving diversely but nurturing each in the soil of measureless love in the seeking of soul progress together smoothing the way for each other. Anchor love in God's love. Be with God. That inspires true friendship/togetherness. - Sri Sri Paramahansa Yogananda 'Where there is light.'

God pervades the worlds. He bears many a lapse of ours. He helps the pious in countless ways. He does the welfare of Godly devotees. He works unceasingly. He guides His devotees as Sun regulates seasons. He is the observer of the truth and dispeller of evil forces. He is eternal and omniscient. He carries His devotees across the turbulent sea of life. - *The Holy Vedas*

Song/Prayer -

O Mother of Universe thou art infinite, thine splendour manifest.

Mother thou feed the boundless expanse of creatures from thine own rich abundance.

The Mother of the Universe treats with tenderness every manifest spark of Her own infinite life.

Only ecstatic love and selfless meditation offer to the Mother Goddess of wisdom.

External forms of worship and propitiation are bribes.

She will never accept without love.

ॐॐॐॐॐ

The river of divine friendship broadens as it flows onward, powerful and truthful, eventually merging in the oceanic presence of God. Try to perfect friendship with a few souls. Give unconditional friendship to them. Then, heart will be ready to give perfect friendship to all. God and great ones give friendship to every being irrespective of personality. Divine love is the magnet that draws all goodness. Radiate love and good will to all. - Sri SriParamahansaYogananda 'Where there is light.' Offer reverence to the Lord of Destiny who with His sharp edge of justice severs the bondage of life and death, liberates us from it and then delivers us to the God of death (Yama), who hands us over back to destiny. Thus the cycle of life and death continues till ultimate liberation is achieved. - *The Holy Vedas*

Song/Prayer -

Mother Tara is the liberator of those who

travel through temporal existence.

Compassionate Mother Tara, take responsibility for Her lover.

Mother purify the intentions of my heart,

so clever enemy egocentric passion and compulsion,

can no longer laugh at me and deride me.

I live with the hope of touching my forehead the wisdom feet of Ma Kali.

My loving Mother, I turn to Thee only with tears flowing in love.

Mother, thine one glance will blend me completely with Thee.

I remain with Mother, Mother remain with me.

ॐॐॐॐॐ

God is the purpose of life. God is Happiness. God is bliss. He is love. He is joy that will never go away from the soul. Acquire that happiness. Cultivate the joy of love of God. Joy in God's love is ever lasting. Find this joy within. In God one will tap the reservoir of perennial,unending bliss. Feel the joy in communion with God. The joy of God is boundless, unceasing all the time new. Be in consciousness of Him. By His grace one will understand what one wants to understand - Sri Sri Paramahansa Yogananda 'Where there is light.'

Offer reverence to Him, the most exalted Supreme Lord. He has made the wind as the life of creation, the rays of light as its eyes, the directions of space as the organs of hearing. Reverence is to the mighty one. Reverence sustains earth and heaven. Offer reverence to Nature's bounties. Reverence overwhelms all evil. Offer penance in the form of reverence for sins which might have been committed over in life. - *The Holy Vedas*

Song/Prayer

Hum with every breath Mother's powerful Mantra.

Om Ma Kali Ma, Om Ma Kali Ma, Om Ma Kali Ma.

These sacred sounds crystallizes in the subtle body.

Diverting the current of conscious energy.

Even in the deepest contemplation.

Various exalted heavenly beings, including Brahma Lord of creation.

Have failed to penetrate Her radiant mystery.

Shiva alone has abandoned His being.

Beneath Her dancing red soled feet.

Merging with Her entirely, Shiva is lost! Lost in Mother.

Sing songs of non-duality, with intense devotion.

Powerful mantra Om Ma Kali Ma would empower to taste and see Her.

ॐॐॐॐॐ

Sit in silence of deep meditation, joy bubbles up from within, roused by no outer stimulus. The joy of meditation is overwhelming. Go into the silence of true meditation to have real joy. Drop every unnecessary activity. Meditate and try to know God. Day and night be in His/Her divine consciousness. Economize time. Realise the value of immortal time that God has given us. Do not while away time in idleness or gossips. - Sri Sri Paramahansa Yogananda 'Where there is light.'

We offer reverence to that Supreme Lord, who is bliss incarnate, peace incarnate, reverence to Him who bestows bliss and peace. Reverence to Him who is benign, evermore benign (kindly, mild). We offer obeisance to Thee. O Lord Supreme the ordainer. Reverence to Thy fierce form of punitive power. Obeisance to Thy divine bow and arrow by which thou destroyest the wicked. Reverence to thy mighty arms that support the pious and assail the evil minded. - *Holy Vedas*

Song/Prayer -

Mother of Universe, thou reside deep within my secret heart.

Mysterious Mother Kali, how can I say, you are distant from me?

Mother thou manifest so elusively.

O Mother Goddess of cosmic illusion.

O Mahamaya Ma disguising thine clear light with countless masks.

Mother! Thou assume contrasting roles to harmonize with every calling of worship, prayer and meditation.

Mother! Thou cannot continue to allude thy lover.

Thy lover knows thine surprising forms.

All express the single essence of awareness.

And ignite thy love with joy-bliss.

ॐॐॐॐॐ

We do not have time for God because of Maya, the net of cosmic delusion that entangles us in mundane interests and makes us forget the Lord. Find time for God. First duty is to God. Then take care of all other duties. First, in the morning give time to God. Meditate. Sing songs of love of Him. Our needs are few, while our wants can be limitless. In order to find freedom and Bliss, minister only needs. Stop creating limitless wants. Stop pursuing false happiness. - Sri Sri Paramahansa Yogananda 'Where there is light.'

Offer reverence to Nature's bounties to old and the young. Speak with force at our command the glory of all Divine Powers. We may not overlook any of them however big or small. The Supreme Lord is omnipresent like space and Eternal like His word. All nature's bounties have their repose in Him. Know the Divine Principle. Come close to the Lord. - *The Holy Vedas*

Song/Prayer – Blissful Mother

Ma! Ma! Ma!

Take responsibility of mine.

I surrender to thy lotus feet.

O Loving Wisdom Mother.

Composed of consciousness, my heart awakens to thy truth.

Like a flower naturally blossoming.

Mother loving! Please reveal thine transparent presence.

Within lotus heart of mine.

As open space, forever shining.

Jai Ma! Jai Ma! Jai Ma!

ॐॐॐॐॐ

Have faith in God. Love Him. He knows our need. He chooses better things for us. Do not tell Him our want/need. He does not give what is not good for us. He sees that His impulsive children do not plunge into the flames of fire, wrong or excessive desires. He tries to protect us from being burnt. He answers our prayers differently not according to our wishes. Our perfect prayers led by wisdom infused with spirituality and love are being responded. - Sri Sri Paramahansa Yogananda 'Where there is light.'

Know the truth that God is one. He possesses the Supreme power. He is the one - The One Alone. In Him all divine powers become the One Alone. He is Brahma, the Supreme Lord of all. He is the ultimate power, protector of all beings. The perennial divine flame is one. That alone is kindled in various forms. The Sun is one and one alone, gives us warmth and life. It grows in vibrant colours. The dawn is one, one alone, that beautifies the face of the universe with its multicolouredlustre. - *The Holy Vedas*

Song/Prayer -

O wonderful Mother Mahamaya.
With thy dream power thou projects the momentary universe.
Thou art eternally mad with wisdom bliss.
But, thou have driven us mad with habitual diversion.
Lost within thine magic projection.
We cannot recognize each other as strands of one consciousness.
Due to ironic twist in Ma Kali's play.
We, Her children are unable to see Mother as She is.
Through Her boundless grace.
Every suffering vanishes with tearful eyes in love.
Just chant JayMa Kali, JayMa Kali, JayMa Kali.

ॐॐॐॐॐ

Trust more in God. Believe that he will maintain us. He anticipates our every need. He sustains us. Depend on His will. Sometimes God denies our little prayers because He intends to bestow on us a better gift. Trust more in God. Love Him with intensity. All the necessities of life become unnecessary. In the consciousness of God, we become more healthy, more joyous, more bountiful in every way. Do not seek little things. Make life simple. - Sri Sri Paramahansa Yogananda 'Where there is light.'

The Supreme Reality has been styled by various names by the learned seers. His bodily forms are innumerable. Millions are in His million. He is one and one forever remaineth alone. He is the Supreme in the worlds. He is the One Lord of all holy service. His glory is truly great. Really, He is One. - *The Holy Vedas*

Song/Prayer -

O Mother Gracious! Drive me out of my mind.

What is the use of esoteric knowledge or philosophical discrimination?

Mother! Transform me totally with the intoxicating wine of thine allembracing love.

Mother Mystic! Mother of Mystery, Thou imbues the hearts of thy lovers with mystery.

My loving Mother! Immerse me irretrievably in the stormy ocean of thine pure love, pure love, pure love

ॐॐॐॐॐ

Be nearer to God and goal. Concentrate. Be not victim of circumstances and bad habits. Blame no one but yourself for your troubles. Make up mind to control circumstances according to law. Adjust accordingly. Learn to lead a controlled existence. Master every moment of life. Do not permit life to cheat. Good habits make life happy. Follow a simple diet, do exercise, meditate daily at least either morning or evening/night. Feel His presence. Have thoughts of God. Have Divine aspirations. - Sri Sri Paramahansa Yogananda 'Where there is light.'

The Glorious Lord sustains the creation in perfect order. He is void of form, dwelleth in and out of everything with form and shape. He is free from lapses, faults and impurities. He transcends all the bodily facilities. Being divine poet, He is genius. He manifests maintaining peace and harmony. He is the creator and controller. All the enlightened souls attain immortal bliss in Him. They reach the loftiest goal, the ultimate salvation - liberation. - *The Holy Vedas*

Song/Prayer – Blissful Mother

O Mother ! Thine lovers appear to live in madhouse.

Some are laughing with thine freedom.

Some weep tears of thine tenderness and love.

Some dance whirling with thine love bliss.

Thine lover, Gautama, Moses, Jesus, Nanak, Ramakrishna, Chaitanya and Meera are lost in the rapture of Thine pure love.

Loving Mother! Grant me companionship with thy mad lovers.

Mother! This child of thine sings Om Ma Kali Ma Om.

Om Ma Kali Ma Om, Om Ma Tara Ma Om.

ॐॐॐॐॐ

Joy lies in constantly thinking of God. Have constant longing for Him. Then mind will never wander away. Greatest affliction of body, mind and soul will not take consciousness from the living presence of God. Live, think and feel God all the time. Remain in the castle of His presence. The great spirit of God will be behind speech, thoughts, will and love of heart. Think and feel. He is always near us. Lord Krishna said in Geeta. "He who perceives me everywhere and beholds everything in me never loseth sight of me, nor do I ever lose sight of him". The Lord never fails us. - Sri Sri Paramahansa Yogananda 'Where there is light.'

He is the Lord of cosmic energy. He is the progenitor of all that is eternal and immortal. He freely moveth hither and thither, above or below with an eye on all dimensions and directions. He fashioneth the Universe. He possessed the multifaceted knowledge. He supported and sustaineth everything. He seeth all and is exalted above all. In Him, the soul enjoys bliss. He accomplisheth for the souls things which yield happiness. He, the Supreme Being is to be worshiped. - *The Holy Vedas*

Song/Prayer

Mother of Universe! None can fathom thy mystery.

Thine eternal play of love with love.

Thine divine love madness makes thy lovers made in thy love.

Thy love madness infill thy made lovers with bliss.

Thy lovers dance, clap and sing Jay Ma Kali Ma.

Jay Ma Kali Ma, Jay Ma Kali, Jay Ma Kali.

Thy lovers become madly wealthy with the infinite treasure of thy love.

ॐॐॐॐॐ

God is visible in the mighty manifested universe. God is everything. Creation which appears solid and real is the thought of God frozen into physical forms. Condition the mind to this realization in little ways each day. See a beautiful sun set. Think it is God's painting in the sky. The love in my heart is God. The blood in my body is God. - Sri Sri Paramahansa Yogananda 'Where there is light.'

God is omnipresent and all powerful. He rules over all the three regions - earth, mid-region and the celestial. He is beyond the knowledge of mankind. He preserves the indomitable universe. He sustains and protects the sanctity of all vital functions that keep constancy of universal life. Seek Him everywhere. All is within His reach. He knows all the things. He is full of wisdom. He determines what ought to be done. He is the only recourse. All powers are vested in Him. He fulfills all our aspirations. He is the source of all our nourishment and vigour, intelligence and strength. - *The Holy Vedas*

Song/Prayer -

Most compassionate Mother Kali!

Mother Gracious! Free me from six enemies, ego and senses.

They have kept constant company with me.

Troubling me, never allowing me to act selflessly.

Always drawing me to duality.

With resolution, I am taking refuge at thy lotus feet, O Mother.

Mother! Purify me in the fire of thy love.

Bless me to cry in thy love trance every moment.

Thou art my Mother, I am thy child.

Mother only takes care of child.
With fearful eyes, I lay at thy lotus feet.

ॐॐॐॐॐ

Do everything with the consciousness of God. Not only when meditating, but also working. Anchor thoughts in Him. Do work to please God. Unite all activity with Him. Both meditation and right activity are essential. Think of God while performing duties honestly in this world. Be mentally united with Him. Work for God not self. Doing things for God is very satisfying and enjoying. Meditation helps works. Balance meditation and work. Do not become lazy with meditation only. - Sri Sri Paramahansa Yogananda 'Where there is light.'

He is an all pervading, unchanging Supreme Being. He is the purest of pure. He is there in the hearts of holy men, women and children. He permeates all eternal laws. He manifests throughout the Universe - the seas, the earth and the mountains. He is life's force. He inspires sacred words. He is the dear chief in the household. He manifests every form. He is to be identified with all nature's richness. His manifestation is seen everywhere in creation. He moves in forms by His creative charm. His Divine energy is the life force which animates all created things. - *The Holy Vedas*

Song/Prayer -

Mother! Thou alone fulfill my soul's most secret yearning.
Transcendent desire for union constantly burn in my heart.
Mother Gracious! Sweep away my separate self by thy illumination.
With every breath I confess the ultimate realization of thee.
Ma! Ma! Ma! Must feel my desperate longing for thee.
In love trance, I cry Ma! Ma! Ma!

ॐॐॐॐॐ

Know the God through activity. Persistently, selflessly perform every action with love - inspired thoughts of God that He will come and He is watching. Think of Him before performing the action and after finishing it. Must work.Let God work through you. Constantly think of Him. Whisper your love to God. Be in contact with Him in the mad rush of present day life. - Sri SriParamahansaYogananda 'Where there is light.'

The Only Path - I realise the presence of the Almighty Lord, the Universal Entity, the one who is self-illuminated and radiant like the Sun. He is beyond all darkness, with this realisation, now I fear not even death. I proclaim, this is the path, the only path to salvation to the goal of life, the eternal bliss. He is the omniscient, the creator, invested with dynamic energy. His eyes are all-seeing. He sustains everything - the heaven and earth. - *The Holy Vedas*

Song/Prayer -

My Mother of the Universe, I have a serious quarrel with Thee.

Thou have overwhelmed me with the responsibility for family.

Formless meditation on thee is too much demanding.

As a child of thine I can simply cry with tears Ma, Ma, Ma.

The practice of selfless giving is superior.

Love/Service is the noble path.

Remember even Mother Radha, lover of divine love incarnate bears gifts.

When visiting Her beloved Krishna.

Her priceless blue jewel of love ecstasy.

Mother! Mother! I offer thee my love.

I cry Ma! Ma! Ma! Bestow me upon thy love.

Thy love settles all disputes with Thee.

ॐॐॐॐॐ

Develop the habit of mental whispering to God. Have God constantly in the mind irrespective of what you are doing. Transmute petty desires into one great desire for God. Night and day, night and day look for Him. There cannot be an excuse for not thinking of God. Day and night roll in the background of mind God! God! God! Inwardly say O God! O Krishna! O Ma Kali! manifest to me. God is in the heart and everywhere. Every thought sets up a particular subtle vibration. When we mentally utter the word of God and keep on repeating that thought within, it sets up a vibration that invokes the presence of God. - Sri Sri Paramahansa Yogananda 'Where there is light.'

The whole universe in His Kingdom. He alone ruleth over us. He alone controls and directs our five cognizant senses. He is the sovereign of the universe. He sustains the tree's stem (the universe). Its branches spread downward, its roots rest high above. None can ignore Him or Ventures to displease Him. The obstructions cannot threaten His glory, neither those who tyrannize nor those whose minds are bent upon wrong doing. - *The Holy Vedas*

Song/Prayer -

My loving Mother! My entire life has now become thine.

Immerse in Thine own secret contemplation.

Mother's Fire of love has purified all dross from the gold of consciousness.

My only desire is to shape my human temple from this golden energy.

O Blissful Mother, adore my life with thine priceless gems.

Compassion, beauty, clarity, intensity, love

To thee alone, my blissful Mother, the Universe belongs.

ॐॐॐॐॐ

Bring the wandering mind from the maze of myriad worldly thoughts to indwelling God in the heart. He is ever with us. Just remember Him. He talks with us. See Him/Her in every flower/everything. God is bliss Himself. True joy eludes the man who forsakes God. Make God friend. Cultivate His acquaintance. Establish relationship as mother, father or friend. Establish the relationship of Mother with Mother Kali. - Sri Sri Paramahansa Yogananda 'Where there is light.'

God rescues good human impulses. He causes the Spiritual Elixir to flow forcefully - love, truth, benevolence, austerity, contentment, generosity and knowledge. He protects the virtuous. He is the wise surveyor. He is law giving Lord. One becomes prosperous whom divine powers take in their own arms. One overcomes all obstructions. One is defended from the malignant. - *The Holy Veda*

Song/Prayer -

Mother of Universe! All is thy dynamic play.

Bless me to have the crest - jewel of illumination.

Bear on my forehead the radiance of thine pure love alone.

Thou art the Absolute Reality.

Thou art the absolute love.

O Majestic Mother Kali! Thou art living mystery.

Thou sweep away every difficulty.

Goddess of wealth! Thou avoid every display of wealth and power.

Thou resemble thine own consort Shiva.

Lord Shiva lives only on the crushed hemp leaves of transcendent knowing.

Mother tells me to live in simplicity and austerity.

Amidst abundance of prosperity.

ॐॐॐॐॐ

God is a loving, compassionate, heavenly Father. He is the infinite receptacle of all love and goodness. God is eternal Bliss, love, wisdom and joy. He is both personal and impersonal. He manifests Himself whatever He pleases for the welfare of creation / Universe. Christian sees Christ. A Hindu beholds Krishna or Divine Mother and so on. In impersonal turn, a devotee sees an infinite light or hears the wondrous sound of Aum. An enlightened man feels that bliss, in which every other aspect of divinity – love, wisdom, immortality – is full, contained. - Paramhansa Sri Sri Yogananda Where there is light

His devotee is never vanquished. His devotees easily gain the best treasures of the world. One is also rewarded with brave offspring like oneself. Lord is the most glorious and all wise bearing in His hand all might. He abides and delegates His strength to the true seekers. The sages realised Him through deep meditation and sincere devotion. He is the resplendent Lord. He created the fast moving Universe. He drives away the dark evil forces. He snatches off the riches of the malicious like a hunter striking his prey. - *The Holy Veda*

Song/Prayer

Mother of Universe! Thy lovers shine with inward illumination.

The subtle bodies of pure lovers are adorned invisibly.

By the beauty of inward renunciation.

The realization of non-duality.

Great Mother! Through thy inconceivable will alone.

My soul incarnated upon this earth.

Thou give me experience after experience.

But, by thy grace and love, I cry in love Ma Kali, Ma Kali, Ma Kali.

Courageously, I make efforts to elude thy mirage of thy illusion (Maya).

ॐॐॐॐॐ

Seek God for His own sake. Feel Him as Bliss, welling up from your infinite depths. Do not yearn for visions, spiritual phenomena or thrilling experiences. God responds to the devotees every effort, every devotional call. Learn to recognize Him as the quiet, inner peace. This peace is the first proof of God's presence within. Realise that He is guiding you to take right decision in life. Feel His strength empowering you to overcome bad habits and nurture spiritual qualities. Know Him as ever-increasing joy and love that surges deep within, overflowing into your everyday life and relationship. - Sri Sri Paramahansa Yogananda 'Where there is light.'

O God! The Beloved

O most revered and resplendent,

And loving adorable Lord;

Surely thou bestow on thy devotees - lovers

All the attributes that vest in thee

May thy love fill our bodies and souls.

Thou alone fill ours empty life

Turning it into an ocean of fullness

Let us dedicate the best in us at thy feet.

And surrender our ego in thy service.

O Lord of material and spiritual powers,

Thou art powerful and kind as kinsmen.

We solicit friendship and affection from thee

Desirous of possessing wisdom.

We have recourse to thee for full protection.

Let me be with thee, face to face, O my beloved.

ॐॐॐॐॐ

God is present right on the throne of peace within us. Find Him there first. We will find Him in all the noble pursuits of life, in true friends, in the beauty of nature, in good books, in good thoughts and in noble aspirations. Realize Him as peace existing in the universal harmony of all things. Feel peace in meditation, the closer to God. He moves nearer and nearer in deep meditation. - Sri Sri Paramahansa Yogananda 'Where there is light.'

O God! The Beloved

O Lord! Keep me worthy of Thy love ever,

In my dreams or awake I converse with Thee and pray,

Let me be with Thee, face to face, O my beloved,

O God, let my cup of happiness be filled by thy love alone.

Whenever, I search my heart in my dreams or awake.

I encounter and converse with Thee.

Myheart fill with Thy love.

We pray with all humility for the purity of Thy resplendent glory.

Thy flame in our heart has the soul of Thy omniscient aurora, the source of all conscience.

We pray to Thee, thy progenitor of all that exists with heart full of love.

O Radiant Self, bless that my virtues and deeds conform to Thy wishes.

May love for Thee above the selfish ego rise.

Bless me with a vision to transcend the barriers of 'thine and mine'.

Let there be neither me nor mine, only Thou and Thine.

ॐॐॐॐॐ

God does answer our prayers through His laws after He becomes absolutely sure of His devotee/lover. The Lord of Universe is so humble that He does not speak. He influences the devotee to use own free will to choose or reject Him. Once you know Him, you will love Him. To know Him, one has to have unconditional love and faith. He is listening to all our prayers. He manifests His presence. Be close to Him. He will be nearer and nearer. - Sri Sri Paramahansa Yogananda 'Where there is light.'

God Krishna, the Beloved.

The Supreme Lord is too nearer, to be abandoned.

Too close to be witnessed.

Behold nature's splendour and the Lord's Divine poetry.

Both are beyond decay and death.

O God, be thou are Savior.

Looking after and showing mercy to the worshipers.

Friend, Father, Fatherliest of fathers.

Who for the loving worshiper provides all comforts.

These offerings have been made by us with adoration.

May the Goddess of speech be pleased with each of our prayers.

Under Thy protection, thou most beloved!

May we approach thee for shelter.

Supported by Thee, O God! May we answer all who defy us.

Thou art ours and we are thine.

ॐॐॐॐॐ

My Dear Children,

Be earnest in prayers to God by persistence and regularity. Cleanse mind of all negation, such as fear, worry, anger and then fill it with thoughts of love, service and joyous expectation. In sanctum of heart, enshrine one power, one joy, one peace - God. Desire Him only. Be not satisfied with anything else. Have God as first in the heart. Be with Him, no matter if sleep is lost. He will come positively. Ruler of creation will come forth to reveal Himself. He talks to His true lovers and plays hide and seek with them. He grants every wish of His lover. - Sri Sri Paramahansa Yogananda 'Where there is light.'

Thou draw thy lover/devotee/friend like a cow for milking.

Wake up God, move Him for the gift of His bounty.

O Effulgent One, Thou hast made the sun ageless, star to mount the sky conferring light on men.

Thou O Effulgent One art the people's light.

Best and dearest art thou by our side.

I am the devotee, feel thirsty even in the midst of deep water.

O blissful Lord! Have mercy.

Slake my thirst, bless me with happiness and contentment.

ॐॐॐॐॐ

Coax God with steady and unceasing zeal. Have an immense thirst for the Divine. Do not give undue importance to anything else - the tests of the world or the tests of the body - then He will come. Have the resolute desire for God. God responds to earnest calls - prayers. Be like a naughty child who is not confronted by anything except the mother's presence. He cries till mother does not come. Cry for God. Earnestly sing songs of heart. - Sri Sri Paramahansa Yogananda 'Where there is light.'

Adoration - The Lord - God - Krishna.

O Adorable Supreme Lord!

Thou art the protector of the unprotected.

Cosmic sacrifice of the creation.

May Thy blessing from all sides assuredly reach the seeker of truth.

O Resplendent Lord, the wielder of adamantine justice.

Thou art the coordinator of all elements.

At thy command all cosmic energies are harnessed.

To the richly - decorated canopy of the universe.

Thy come speedily to our help everywhere.

Great art Thou God, greater than the greatest, beyond measure.

Thou art boundless, much beyond the celestial space.

Surely, Thou art the source of all greatness.

ॐॐॐॐॐ

Have ever increasing love for God. Feel the ever increasing thrill of joy bursting in whole body and heart. Thrill of joy continues to increase even after meditation. Joy is response of God. In Him find the love of all hearts. In Him find completeness. He is the nearest of the near, the dearest of the dear. Love Him as a miser love's money and as an ardent lover his sweetheart (SantTulsidas) and as a drowning person loves breath. When one yearns for God with intensity, He comes. - Paramhansa Sri Sri Yoganandaji where there is light Adoration of God.

Infinite are thy powers and capacity to draw and discharge like oceans.

Thou protectest the entire creation by thy radiance.

Like the ocean thou collectest and like the sun rays thou disperseth.

O Omniscient God, thy glory enlightens the celestial, terrestrial and all other regions of the Universe.

The man whom thou protectest in the internal and external conflicts become free from all vices and attains eternal wisdom.

ॐॐॐॐॐ

God wants our sincere love. He is like a little child who wants Mother's love. The child refuses to accept any gift except the Mother. Cry to Him, O God, I love thee. He comes running like the mother runs hearing the cry of the child. God will not tell us that He desires our love. God who created us yearns for our love. He wants us to give our love spontaneously. God does not possess our love unless we give. God has something to attain: our love. Give love and be happy. - Sri Sri Paramahansa Yogananda 'Where there is light.'

Adoration of God -

O all wise and all seeing God.

Direct the ignorant worshipper and help him to revert to acts.

Which will reclaim him.

Always thou protectest in times of conflict.

Those who are feeble but tread the path of truth against those who are strong but tumble on the wrong path.

O adorable God!

Thou lightest up mortal man to superb immortality by providing sustenance.

Thou bestow happiness and sustenance on the wise.

In both the lives.

The present and the one to come.

ॐॐॐॐॐ

Experience love in communion with God in meditation. Millions of thrills pass through the heart. When one feels His divine love, one can give that pure love to others. Feel a particle of divine love. Divine love gives great joy. It is over powering. Attune to God. Our perception will be limitless pervading everywhere in the oceanic flow of the Divine Presence. When the spirit is known - and when we know ourselves as Spirit, there is no land or sea, no earth or sky – all is He. The melting of everything in spirit is a state no one can describe. A great bliss is felt – eternal fullness of joy, knowledge and love. - Sri Sri Paramahansa Yogananda 'Where there is light.'

Prayer to God- Lord Krishna

Nature's beauty is an art of Thine.

Let us feel the touch of God's invisible hands in everything beautiful.

By the first touch of his hand, rivers throb and ripple.

When He smiles the sun shines, the moon glimmers, the stars twinkle, the flowers bloom.

By the first rays of the rising sun, the Universe is stirred.

The shining gold is sprinkled on the smiling buds of rose; the fragrant air is filled with sweet melodies of singing birds.

The dawn is the dream of God's creative fancy.

ॐॐॐॐॐ

Realize God is greater than all His gifts. Then find Him. The love of God, the love of the spirit lead the devotee on and on in the eternal realms. That love will never be taken away from the heart. It shall burn there and its fire shall find the great magnetism of the spirit that draws others unto one and attracts whatsoever one truly needs or desires. All questions shall be answered through God not through man. He is. He is. Like gentle Zephyrs, His love comes over the soul. It goes on increasing. God calls on. - Sri Sri Paramahansa Yogananda 'Where there is light.'

Prayer to God- Lord Krishna

Adorable Supreme Lord.

Thou art so gracious to us that we feel.

Thou art our father, our life giver and we are thy close kinsmen.

Invincible as thou art.

Thou love brave people.

Defender as thou art of the pious.

So things most prized speed unto thee in hundreds, why in thousands.

Thou art the Supreme Being of Spiritual knowledge.

O Lord of spiritual wisdom! Listen to us with Thy graces and in the place of worship.

ॐॐॐॐॐ

Human being has come on earth solely to learn to know God, he is here for no other reason. This is the true message of God to all those who seek and love Him. He tells of that great life where there is only ineffable happiness that will never grow stale, happiness always new. It is worthwhile to seek God. Sincerely seek Him and find Him surely. Love Him. Yearn to enter His kingdom. Sincerely wish in heart to know Him and find Him. Have an increasing desire for Him day and night. He acknowledges our love by fulfilling His promise throughout eternity. One will know joy and happiness unending. All is light, all is joy, all is peace, all is love. He is all. Find Him in the temple of each thought and activity. Finding Him in within, one finds Him in all and in all conditions. O Lord Bless me. - Sri Sri Paramahansa Yogananda 'Where there is light.'

Creative Fancy of God

O God! I bow down to thee just like a son.

I bow down to great thee, thou grant happiness to me.

With thy excellent guidance Thou leadest and protectest me.

No danger would overtake me.

I offer my offering to thee.

Thou doest humble the wrath of a violent man.

Supreme O Lord Supreme, thou art the greatest.

ॐॐॐॐॐ

God is one. Truth is His name. He is the Creator, complete in everything beyond fear and beyond hate, beyond time and beyond birth. He is the light. By His grace we worship Him. - Guru Nanak.

Creative Fancy of God-

O Supreme Creator!

None can break thy dispensations.

Even the wild beasts roaming in the desert in search of water are refreshed by the thirst allaying rivers which thou hast endowed.

Woods are there for birds to feed on.

With great reverence I proclaim the truth that whatever exists that by thy blessing.

That thou art the master of all this Universe, of all the wealth that is in Heaven or on earth.

O Divine Creator, surely first thou greatest immortality.

To the highly elevated man, dedicated to learning and devotion.

Thereafter, thou completely shieldest him with thy protection and continuously showerest thy blessings on him.

None can ever obstruct or deviate thee from thy way.

O sustainer of the Whole world!

Thy touch is widely visible over the extent of the earth and the magnitude of the heaven.

ॐॐॐॐॐ

Have faith in ourselves. Have faith to do great work. Be strong and have faith. Everything is bound to follow. Faith, sympathy, fiery faith, fiery sympathy! Faith in ourselves, faith in God – this is the secret of greatness. Faith is one of the potent factors of humanity. Be steady, and above all be pure and be sincere to the backbone. Have faith in destiny. It is the greatest help. Feel the presence of one God or one pervading consciousness everywhere. - Swami Vivekananda.

Soul – the restless swan -

Life is perennial search for truth.

The restless swan – the human soul is on the journey infinite to find the truth.

For thousands of years he is flying and flying with his wings outstretched

And the will to reach the unscaled heights of heaven, higher and ever higher.

The restless soul-swan is on the journey infinite.

He has all the blessings of the mighty God, his piercing eyes perceive all the universe below,

Yet he knows no rest, no peace an keeps flying higher and ever higher.

The restless soul swan is on the journey infinite. - *The Holy Veda*

ॐॐॐॐॐ

Prayer

The Restless Human Being – Swan

O God, Thou raisest Thy devotees to the highest level.

Just as the sun riseth above the vast clouds.

They are provided dwellings filled with all comforts.

The more they rise in their levels,

The more Thou fillest their hearts with devotion.

And the more they are in possession of thy love.

The more they obey thy command.

O inspirer of benevolent deeds!

The divine powers honour thee.

As the benefactor of all.

Thou art the inspirer of men and mankind.

All the cosmic forces adore thee, O Lord!

The cosmic fire, abiding in mysterious darkness.

Let the immortal adorable divine preserve us with His protection, afford us all provisions.

O doer of great deeds, performer of cosmic sacrifice!

Thou knowest the paths and ways.

And also how to travel and function with speed.

Wheresoever and upon Whomsoever Thy kindness is directed.

Thou makest him eminent and givest uncommon vigour.

And in his heart thou makest thine own abode.

- *The Holy Vedas*

ॐॐॐॐॐ

Prayer

The Restless Human Being – Swan

Thou blesseth this adorance, O Self-Sustaining Lord!

Thou art heartily appreciated!

That we succeed in retaining what we have earned.

And are able to acquire more through thy grace.

Thou art divine amongst mortal men and art Preserver of their sacred deeds, Therefore we worship thee in every benevolent task.

Thou art the same in any place.

Thou art the Supreme Lord.

Amid all the people of creation.

In fray and fight we call on thee.

O Lord, Thou bestowest upon the true seeker the joys of attainment, A body free of desires,

A mind pure and virtuous and an intellectual sharp and discriminate.

We humble invoked thee, from far off places .

And be sought thee to protect us everywhere.

And emancipate us from decay and death.

Our invocations are listened to.

And from all directions, thy blissful benedictions are showered on us.

O Lord of cosmic light and energy!

Thou thyself bindest thyself to cosmic orders.

- *The Holy Vedas*

ॐॐॐॐॐ

Arjun to Lord Krishna - Should he renounce work or work with devotion?

Krishna - Work with devotion than renunciation of work, work with devotion in consciousnesses of Lord Krishna and in the knowledge that everything in existence belongs to Lord Krishna. Work for the welfare of Krishna's creation. Do not desire the fruits of action/activities. Free from the bondage of duality, one is liberated even doing activities in the material world. All actions must be done in the service of Krishna i.e humanity. Engage in activities in Krishna's consciousness than to be a Sanayasi - monk. With control of mind and senses work with devotion in consciousness of Soul and Krishna. He lives in consciousness of Krishna's love. He works for all. His mind becomes controlled as he is engaged in activities for Krishna and His creation. His senses are controlled as he is in consciousness of Krishna. Know and realise that one is not doing anything at all. One is aloof of all activities. One is doing as desired by Krishna. One is engaged is the loving transcendental service of Krishna. Krishna's conscious person is always free even though he appears to be engaged in a affairs of senses. Perform duties without attachment and in exception of results and surrendering to Lord Krishna. Work with devotion but free from ego with Krishna in all activities. Be in union with Krishna. Krishna is the Supreme Absolute Truth. There is no duality. While engaging in work, mentally renounce the results and remember Krishna.

- Chapter V - Bhagwad Gita

Invocation – Blissful Lord Krishna – God

O Lord Krishna! I approach thee with reverential homage.

Through sublime thoughts and noble deeds day and night.

As thy earnest seeker, I pursue the ultimate salvation and union with thee.

O Beloved Lord! Support me firmly at every step forward.

Thy loving care and guidance enlighten my path.

I ascend from one summit to a higher one .

Thou bestow me with Divine blessings.

With bent head and folded hands.

Every hour of day and night.

Surrendering all at thy Divine feet.

I pray to Thee my beloved Lord.

O Lord! Bless and guide me on the path to self-revelation and union Bliss with thee.

O Supreme Lord! Speed me on with pure and exalted love .

Bestow upon me thy priceless blessings and love.

And bestow upon me wealth abundance.

To enable me to tide over all the ills of life.

Bless me with charming eloquence, good fortune and fair name.

- *The Holy Vedas*

ॐॐॐॐॐ

Invocation Prayer Blissful Lord Krishna - Go

O Lord! Come, Come, towards me,

Bring along with thee thy divine power.

Come, O Universal Divine Power!

Hear my invocations and be established in my heart.

Unite me with thee, O Lord Divine.

As rivers unite with the ocean.

I do not drift to unfertile lands in search of fertile things.

I dwell, live and love each other well.

At the break of the day, I invoke the Lord Supreme

Lord of cosmic light and plasma

The pair of twin divines

The lord of riches and nourishment

Lord of bliss and vitality

I sing sacred hymns with intense devotion.

With nature's bounties, partake in the sparkling glory of the supreme Lord.

Friends! Let us with one accord offer reverence and oblation to the Lord.

ॐॐॐॐॐ

Dedicate our life to God, who gives life's breath, power and vigour. His cosmic arms embrace the whole universe. He never harms us. Hear the songs of His glory echoing in the thundering ocean waves. Look at the reflection of His grandeur in the snow clad mountains.

Dedication to God Supreme - Lord Krishna.

To Lord Supreme! God! Lord Krishna we dedicate our life Thee.

Thou art is the giver of life's breath, power and vigour

Whose command all the Divine Powers obey.

To Thee we dedicate our life thoudwelleth the universe.

To Thee, to Thee alone.

Thine grandeur is reflected in the snow clad mountains.

Thine songs of glory are echoed by the thundering ocean waves.

Thine cosmic arms embrace the whole universe.

We dedicate our life and offer obeisance to Thee.

The Creator of Universe never harms us.

Thoumaketh the universe and observeth the norms.

Thourealeseth the powerful and crystal waters.

We dedicate our life to Thee alone.

O Father of all creations, thou embracest all.

Thou granteth the wishes of our prayers.

We dedicate our life to Thee alone, none but Thee.

We pray to Thee in love again and again.

We sing sweet songs of love for Thee.

ॐॐॐॐॐ

God gives bounteous gifts of His divine wisdom and wealth to His devotees/lovers spontaneously. All powers of existence are given to who are involved in benevolent work. Have full and firm faith in God. With faith, trust and love in God one conquers adverse circumstances. One, who renders selfless service to mankind and loves God, attains oneness with God.

Prayer - God's promise

O God, Thou are all in all.

Thou give the power of existence to help those who are benevolent.

Thou give bounteous gifts of wisdom and wealth.

As spontaneously as ripe fruit drops from a loaded branch.

Thou extend Thy helping hands to those who surrender to Thee in full faith and love.

A firm faith in Thee is the only ray of hope that penetrates this gloom of fear and ignorance.

With faith, trust and love in Thee

One invariably adverse circumstances.

With firm faith and love in Thee, one emerges the winner, rich with bounty in the struggle of life.

O Beloved God! Thou take those who dedicate life to service of Thee, in Thy loving fold.

Thy devotees/lovers are blessed with supreme celestial powers.

Thy devotees bask happily in the sunshine of Thy love.

O dear God! Bless me/us with Thy faith and love.

ॐॐॐॐॐ

God's assure and promise

O blissful Lord, thou assure

That God assures and promise

That thou are ever our fast and true friend.

When we are ever awake in thy love.

When we seek Thee through heart love songs.

When we, wisely and innocently remain engrossed in selfless service to mankind.

We attain oneness with Thee when we offer oblation to Thee in soul love.

We are blessed with the privilege of bringing up brave, fearless children.

O the blissful God!

Thou abide within the heart and the soul of every human being.

With this firm faith and a sublime contented smile,

We find enough strength to surmount and bear the greatest tragedies.

The dark clouds of sorrows never overshadow us

When our mind remain in perpetual love devotion of Thee.

O Resplendent Lord! Thy devotee/lover become humbed workers philanthropist.

Thou shower on Him thy bounty more and ever more.

Prayer

Mind is the source of all wisdom.

It has to perform God-assigned tasks like a good charioteer

May it guide Noble firm resolve

Mind as the light of lights.

The only source of all wisdom.

Whether I am asleep or awake.

It travels too far, wanders to far off places.

By this mind assiduous and intellectual person.

Perform then God assigned tasks.

The spirit that lies in all creatures.

Make me to resolve firm on what is noble.

Mind is the source of highest knowledge.

The source of wisdom, the source of the power of memory.

The immortal flame of consciousness within all living beings.

Without which no action whatever is performed.

O God! Bless us to resolve to make our mind noble.

Mind, which abides in the heart.

Most swift and vigorous.

O God! Bless me to resolve my minds noble.

Mind, the immortal spirit comprehend the world.

All the past and present.

By which all the benevolent works are promoted and conducted through seven sense organs.

Mind imbibes and holds the teaching of scriptures-Holy Vedas.

Like spokes in the nave of a chariot wheel.

In which all thoughts of living world, lie interwoven.

I resolve to make my mind noble.

ॐॐॐॐॐ

Pray to Lord for His blessing of prosperity, lustre of fame, vital elements, happy life, peace, wisdom, performer of benevolent deeds, bliss union with Thee.

Invoke Blessing of Lord.

O Lord of Resplendence, bless us with prosperity,

And lustre of fame and magnificent majesty,

So that we may shine like the blazing sun in the sky.

O Cosmic vital physician, the mightiest of the mighty.

Wielder of adamantine justice.

Carry us safely beyond danger.

And cure sickness of the body and the mind.

O Divine Architect of Creation, the Dexterous Doer.

The Possessor of Wisdom, the Observer of truth.

Bestow on us necessary things for our preservation.

O wise sages, engaged in service of Lord make us joyful.

O Supreme virtuous Lord! Bless us to be sinless in Thy judgement.

Thou showest mercy even to the sinner.

Bless us to obey the commandments of Mother Eternity.

May she preserve us with Her blessing.

O the Divine Architect with His ever moving Cosmic Chariot.

Continue giving us wealth, wisdom and happiness.

O Glorious Lord! Giver of nourishing food.

Bless us with happy life, peace and prosperity.

ॐॐॐॐॐ

Pray to Lord for the well disciplined wealth of wisdom, vigour, excellent posterity, spirit of invincible fullness, infinite happiness, agreeable wealth for the service of others and creative endeavour.

Invoke Blessing of Lord - God

O Lord Superascient, bless unto master

The well-disciplined wealth of wisdom and vigour.

Bestow on us excellent posterity.

Listen to our invocations through divine hymns.

O Mother of Riches grant us prosperity.

O the Adorable and Resplendent Lord prop us.

O Spirit of Invincible fullness

Bestow all prosperity upon us.

O All wise Lord destroy the demoniac forces in us.

Grant infinite happiness

And most agreeable wealth for the service of others.

O Supreme Lord, invest the universe with thy undecayings plendour and brilliance.

Bless that our prosperity lead us to peace.

The social discipline lead us to harmony.

The intellectual pursuits result in sublimity.

The aim of our riches is harmony varied in all nature and society.

May the varied systems of law and order

Result in all around peace, progress and prosperity.

ॐॐॐॐॐ

Pray to God for creative endeavor, ambassador of peace, productivity, sustenance, harmony, charming appearance and victorious with divine power.

Invoke Blessing of God-Lord

O God! Thou manifestest Thy glory in firmanent.

Waters, rocks, forests and plants of the earth.

O self-effulgent Lord of the cosmic world.

Bless us with creative endeavor and in charge of sustenance.

Bless us to have peace and harmony.

Let the wide earth provide all provisions and be productive.

Let the mountain inspire peace and reverence.

Let the pious invocations of nature's bounties secure us peace.

The fire with splendour of flame provides peace.

The cosmic light and bliss and the divine twins secure peace.

Let the impetuous wind give our body and mind peaceful sustenance.

Let the heaven and earth be helpful to our happiness.

The mid-space be for our happiness.

The hearts and forest trees provide us health and charming appearance.

O Lord, thy divine powers favour us with all felicity.

ॐॐॐॐॐ

Pray to the Divine Radiant Lord to provide nourishing water, gentle wind, inspiration, divine speech, holy thoughts, humbleness, graciousness, large heartedness and peacefulness.

Invoke Blessing of Lord - God

Let the sun with extensive radiance rise for peace.

Let the rivers provide us with nourishing waters and make our fields fertile.

Mother Infinity, through holy observance bring us peace and happiness.

O the Divine Refulgent Lord! the saviour bless us for our peace.

O Radiant Lord provide inspiration to us.

O Sovereign Lord of the Universe bless us with happiness and peace.

May the cloud inspire us to attain harmony.

May the universal bounties bring us abundance and peace.

May the sages and priest assist us at our sacred works.

Bless us to be gracious, the liberal and the large hearted givers.

Bless us to have holy thoughts and divine speech.

Bless us with heavenly powers and eternal truths.

May the eternal truths contribute to our thoughts and actions.

May the virtuous men of experience and wisdom confer peace and progress on us.

O Divine Lord! With one foot thou measured the entire universe.

Bless us with peaceful, harmonious existence with love for Thee.

Let the entire nature provide us with abundance.

O Supreme Lord! Endow me today with the Divine vision

That the enlightened and realised ancient sages enjoy.

ॐॐॐॐॐ

Pray to Supreme Creator to establish Himself in our heart, to disperse ill thoughts, to see thy spiritual radiance, to serve humanity, to engage in the welfare of mankind, to grant spiritual strength, to receive worldly joys, to give divine vision and to lead to virtuous path.

Divine Light Command/Guidance

O Supreme God! Establish Thyself in the innermost chamber of our heart.

Let the smoke of ill thoughts be dispersed.

Enable us to see Thy spiritual radiance.

Inspire us to devote our life to the service of humanity.

O Gracious Lord! Inspire us to work for the welfare of mankind.

O Magnificent Lord! Grant us spiritual strength and purity.

In love, we rest all our life in the clasp of Thy everlasting loving arms.

And earn the right to be the recipients of worldly joys.

O Beloved Lord! Grant us wisdom to enjoy Thy blessings.

Bless us to be law - abiding devotees and protector of Nature.

O Resplendent Lord! Bless us with divine vision, vibrant spirit, name and fame.

Bless us to learn lessons from Nature's theme and Nature's harmony.

And live within the realms of thy Divine Order.

O God Almighty! Lead our minds towards the virtuous path.

O Lord of Universe,

Bless that our speech be eloquent, vigorous and faultless.

ॐॐॐॐॐ

Pray Lord to give insight to follow the righteous path, spiritual knowledge, rigorous discipline, guide to immortal bliss and enlightenment.

Divine light/command/guidance

O Resplendent Effulgent Lord!

Give us insights to follow the righteous path.

Traversed by the sages and seers.

We submit to Thee, O Lord.

Let thy kindly light guide us to immortal bliss.

Take us to the realm of spiritual heights

Enlighten our mind by the luminous sun of wisdom.

O Lord! Lead us on the path of virtue for physical and spiritual wealth.

Keep us away from sinful acts which make us stray.

Bless us that we ever remain in uttering Thy love songs and prayers.

Let the luminous Sun and Divine Self-refulgent Gods shower thy grace on us.

O Lord of Strength! Save us from the nescience - illusion, Maya of world.

- *The Holy Vedas*

ॐॐॐॐॐ

Pray to God for his protection, grace and love. O God! Bless us to imbibe with generosity and loving kindness.

Prayer –

Protection, grace, love, generosity

O God! We seek thy protection, grace, love, generosity.

Thou rule the universe, thou command waves and clouds.

Let all the fierce forces be merged to us.

Let no evil and untowered befall us

And we all prosper always.

O Supreme Lord! Bless us to appreciate the benevolent wisdom of the divine powers.

Help us to imbibe generosity and loving kindness.

Bless us to rejoice with abundance of thine bounteous glory.

Help us to be contented and filled with peace and love.

Bless us to hear resolutely with our ears what is good?

Bless us to see with our eyes what is good?

Bless us to enjoy the divinely ordained term of our life

With firm limbs and healthy body and full satisfaction of mind.

In the service of Thee, O my loving Lord.

O illustrious Blissful lord!

Thou be considerate to us and accept our homage.

O gracious Lord! Be Thou our champion in all solemnity.

Bless us with Thine graces and love.

ॐॐॐॐॐ

Pray to Lord for his rainbow of compassion, strength, vigour, discipline, harmony of mind, intellect and body.

Prayer for his rainbow of compassion

O omnipresent Lord! Shower on us thy torrential bliss.

O Lord of Cosmic powers! Thou givest without asking.

Bless us with rainbow of thy compassion.

O Supreme Lord! Give us fiery spirit, strength and vigour.

Give us discipline, conquering might and thy love.

O God! Bless that the faculties of mind, intellect and body function in harmony to perfect fulfilment.

O Lord! Thou art the protector and giver of sustenance.

Protect us from ferocious animal instincts.

And blind forces that seek to destroy us.

O Adorable Lord! Keep us away from wicked and voracious.

O God! Bless us with thy love and attributes.

O Supreme Lord! Come to help us in our struggles for Thy love.

Where the flashing arrows of passion are hurled all around.

Make us triumphant in our inner conflicts through thy grace.

ॐॐॐॐॐ

Work and live happily. Achieve immortal fame. Have complete satisfaction and all offer to Lord in gratitude of His blessing and grace.

Surrender to God in gratitude of His blessing and grace

O My God! I work with devotion as an act of offering to Thee.

I live happily with satisfaction and achieve immortal fame.

All, I offer to Thee in gratitude of thy blessing and grace.

Life is like nectar - honey of the flower.

When I work with devotion in sacrifice and in service to Thee.

Bless me that the sacred flame of divine fire shine brightly in my soul.

O Omniscient Lord! Guard me from the malignant.

O Lord preserve me from sin and the wicked.

O Adorable Lord! Guide and rule my vigour and speech aright.

O Mighty God! Thou art rescuer and saviour.

O Master of All Knowledge! Guard me from evil in every possible way.

Keep away from me who are intolerent and jealous.

I invoke Mother Divine, Mother Infinity to bless me and shower Her grace.

O Sovereign Lord! Liberate me from my animal passions.

ॐॐॐॐॐ

Lord is near us. He is within our heart. We cannot abandon Him. Behold the nature splendour and His Divine poetry. Pray to Lord to overcome inner feelings of enmity to become pure and pious to overcome all obstacles and to live a glorious life.

Surrender to God

O Supreme Lord! Thou art too near me.

Never to be abandoned, Thou art witness.

Behold Thee in nature's splendour.

Behold Thine Divine's poetry, beyond decay and death.

O Virtuous Lord! Bless us to pass into the world of virtue.

In thy mighty arms, we seek fearless shelter.

O Lord of Universe! Grant us freedom from depression, misery and insecurity.

Grant us strength to overcome inner feelings of enmity and bad.

O Lord Supreme, Embodiment of all that is vast and benevolent.

Be Thou ever merciful to us.

Bless us with incessant protective bounties.

O Lord of the vast Universe!

Grant us strength to enjoy thy divinity and bounties.

Bless us that we become pure and pious.

And gather divine lustre, like cosmic luminaries.

Bless us that we overcome all obstacles.

And live a glorious life.

O God! The protector! protect our all limbs and bodies.

Bestow on us intellectual brilliance.

Bless us to spread Thy message of Divine aspirations.

Give us Thy loving refuge and strength to do noble deeds.

Bless us to live a life of self-respect without being a burden to anyone.

Bless us to be trees, not creepers.

ॐॐॐॐॐ

Pray merciful God for forgiveness of immersed totally in our affairs and if committed any sin knowingly and unknowingly.

Forgiveness

O Merciful God! Forgive us for totally remaining in our own affairs.

Forgive us for any sin committed knowingly or unknowingly.

Cares are eating inside us, O Lord shower thy mercy on us.

Be merciful and compassionate to us.

Do not let the wicked violent powers harm us.

O Lord! Help us to overcome to commit any sin.

O Lord! Carry us across the turbulent river of adversities.

To err is human, we are full of desires.

Forgive us for our blunders, errors and defaults.

All pervading merciful Lord! Be thou not displeased with us and abandon us.

O Invincible Lord! Bless us to approach Thee with our devotion and love.

O Virtuous Lord! Forgive us for wrong as our hard environment betrays us.

O Lord of Justice! Mercy- Mercy-Mercy.

It is the vice of intoxication of ego and wrath.

O Savior! Liberate us from the cycle of birth and rebirth.

Liberate us to the union of thy love bliss.

O God! Thou art the ultimate source of conscious life.

Thou art the Supreme Entity.

Thou art that Aum.

Thou art the face of Truth.

Thou shines in the sun.

ॐॐॐॐॐ

O Lord! In the eyes of thine, no one is big or small. All are alike. All are recipients of thy love and blessings for prosperity.

Divine Justice

O Lord of justice, sitting on the pinnacle of cosmos.

Sustainer of the universe.

With full faith we seek thy divine justice.

Let thy devotees, honest and virtuous have thy gracious blessings.

O Effulgent Lord! Be thou with us for our progress and prosperity.

Carry us through all troubles as a boat carries accross the river against all hurdles.

Those who incite sinful acts, loses thy favour and fellow brothers.

Bless us to enjoy wealth of our own efforts and share with less fortunate.

Bless us not to go astray from the right path and piety.

Bless us not to merely indulge in sensual pleasures.

O Lord! Drive away all perils with Thy conquering might.

Let those who hurt us, be the victim of their own designs.

O Effulgent Lord! Consume all our evils with thy strong flames.

Through Thy fear the evil forces come under control.

O Adorable Lord! Shine upon all beings.

And burn the roots of their vices.

O Cosmic God! Bless us with physical and spiritual power.

Let thy strength and divine justice for the pious people.

ॐॐॐॐॐ

Pray. May the Divine speech that perfect our understanding and divine knowledge and all satisfying divine culture be with us at our faultless yajna and worship and protect us for our welfare.

Prayer for Mother Saraswati - Divine Speech – Divine understandingly Divine knowledge

May the divine speech, Mother Saraswati.

The fountain head of all faculties (mental & spiritual).

The purifier and bestower of true union.

The recompenser of worship.

Be the source of inspiration and accomplishment.

For all our benevolent acts.

Mother sets in motion all the energies of the soul and intellect.

Mother imparts deep knowledge to all who are seeker of truth.

It is from Thee that the vast ocean of scriptures spring up.

It is because of Thee that the universe is full of life.

Through Thee indeed, the imperishable God unfolds Himself.

And from Thee, verily, the whole universe draws its sustenance.

Four are the definite grades of speech.

The learned and wise know them.

Common men speak the fourth grade of speech.

O Divine Mother of Speech.

Thou art source of delight.

Thou bestowest all good things.

Thou art the container of wealth.

Thou art the distributor of riches, the giver of good fortune.

ॐॐॐॐॐ

Pray Mother Saraswati - to perfect our understanding, divine knowledge, divine culture, keep our speech, sweet, gentle, meaningful, loving and divine.

Prayer for Mother Saraswati

May the Divine Mother Saraswati perfect our understanding and divine

knowledge.

May all divine culture be with us at our worship.

And protect us for our welfare.

The Divine sages discovered this light of truth.

The Vedas present truth in crystal clear form.

God created speech Divine Mother.

Even living creatures of all species utter it.

May most gracious and eternal life-giving Mother Saraswati.

Impart extensive knowledge to us.

O Mother of Speech, humans utter first most excellent and pure word.

And they discover love

The secret hidden deep in their hearts.

They discover the essence of language with wisdom.

All start acknowledging love and friendship.

And their talk retains the sentiments expressed through it.

O Mother Saraswati! Reveal the deeper meaning of divine words.

Give us ability to understand the deeper meaning of divine words.

O Mother Saraswati!

Keep our speech sweet, gentle, meaningful, loving and divine.

- *The Holy Vedas*

ॐॐॐॐॐ

God is always near us. He is not far. Just remember Him. Cry for Him, as cry for Mother in childhood. He suddenly showers His blessing to our prayers which is good for us ultimately. We do not know which prayer of ours is good.

Sudden showers of Blessing

God is just near and behind us.

He suddenly showers His blessing to our intent prayers.

Feel not that our prayers do not reach Him.

We seek the assurance of safety,

The clouds of gloomy fears are swept in a moment.

Soul bathed in celestial joy.

The choicest gifts are showered from all directions.

And we are lost in complete bliss.

O Lord Divine! We invoke Thee.

With loving heart and deep faith.

May we sense thy loving beckoning!

In this mutual love, we proceed and progress with Thy Divine Blessings.

Under Thy direct inspiration may

We never go against Thy directions embeded in our conscience.

Spirit Supreme voices speak truth pointing to Him, the Creator.

We pray to the Supreme Lord to be with us.

We pray to grant us peace.

By making us pure and virtuous.

Sing the songs of celestial love.

The mighty celestial powers grant us peace.

ॐॐॐॐॐ

Pray to Lord to bless us to sing songs of celestial love, to stay in our hearts and souls forever, to feel His presence within forever, to be courageous to hear the inner voice.

Sing the song of celestial love

Sing the songs of celestial love.

The Divine fountain of eternal grace and joy enter our souls.

O the Blissful Lord stay in our hearts and souls forever!

O Blissful Lord pluck the strings of our inner souls with Thy celestial fingers.

Bless us to feel thine own presence within forever.

Bless us with a divine voice to sing songs of love to Thee.

Bless us to move courageously and never engrossed in futile imagination.

Bless us to understand wise words and understand others.

Bless us to chant hymns harmonized by the heart and mind.

Bless us to perform sacred deeds.

Bless us that inner voices lead to thee-divine bliss.

We the sons of immortal spirit listen to thine divine words.

O Lord of Resplendence! Sharpen our intellects.

And wake up our thoughts and spirits.

So that we may overcome illusion of world.

Bless us to speak beneficent words

To kin and aliens alike to all.

ॐॐॐॐॐ

Pray to Lord to bless us to be on the path of austerity with dedication, diligence and perseverance and be worthy of being loved by Him and all.

Eternity

This wheel of eternal time, knows no decay.

Perpetually revolves around.

Truth, infallible laws, consecration, austerity, prayer and sacrifice, these uphold the earth.

May Mother Earth, the mistress of our past and future confer prosperity on us.

Teach us, O Radiant Lord.

To follow the path of ascetic austerity with dedication, diligence and perseverance.

Bless us that we be worthy of being loved by preceptors, Thee and all.

Enable us to live the full span of life.

Enjoying bright intellect.

The ever true principles of cosmic order alone.

Sustain the balance of Mother Earth.

Observe and follow the path of virtue.

That lead to eternal happiness which is sought by enlightened sages.

- *The Holy Vedas*

ॐॐॐॐॐ

Pure light is the prime element of creation. Sing in praise the eternal cosmic order. Glorify eternal truth. Practice truth in action. Infinite are the powers of eternal laws. Abide by these laws. The contemplation dispels all sorrows.

Eternity

Fire Divine, Pure Light Agni manifests itself as the prime element of creation.

A person knowing the eternal laws of fire flourishes.

With fervent devotion I sing in praise of the eternal cosmic order.

Designed to continue from eternity to eternity.

O Lord! Enable us to understand its wondrous design.

Help us to know why the cow yields rich, sweet and pure white milk.

Glorify eternal truth and practice truth in action.

Cling fast to Eternal Truth to attain ultimate truth itself.

The strength of Eternal Order is far-reaching.

It brings wisdom to those who pursue it.

Earth and heaven owe their existence to Ritu eternally.

And the Supreme powers yield their treasure contents.

In perfect obedience to the Lord of Eternal Existence.

Infinite are the powers of eternal laws.

Abiding by these ends all afflictions.

The contemplation on eternal existence dispels all sorrows.

Even an understanding of these laws is illuminating and purifying to living beings.

The eternal message impresses and inspires even the unheading ears.

- *The Holy Vedas*

ॐॐॐॐॐ

Pray for realisation of God and live in His proximity, the ultimate aim of life's pilgrimage. Offer all to blissful Lord and live in the eternal consciousness of eternal joy. Serve those who need help. Lord is mighty and magnificent.

Eternity

O Eternity! Enable us to realise God who keeps us in state of eternal joy.

Inspire us to experience fulfilment of our aspirations.

O Lord! Bless us

That we realise the fulfilment of our aspiration in the eternal joy of Thy proximity.

Eternal joy is the ultimate aim of life's pilgrimage.

O men of Godly nature!

Partake of His Divinity and experience the joy of ecstasy.

Let us offer all at the feet of the Blissful Lord to obtain His blessings.

To live in the consciousness of eternal joy.

Mother Nature descends towards the one who suffers for others,

And those who deserve help.

Then She sets mind towards the Supreme.

O mighty and magnificent Lord!

Thy vastness and glory unparalleled.

Hundreds of earths, suns and planets exist under Thy command.

All the worlds, existent or non-existent,

Born or unborn are just a fraction of Thy limitless being.

Around Thee move all the planets of the universe.

- Based on The Holy Veda

ॐॐॐॐॐ

Divine love cleans the heart of all. The soul then is pure and free of fear, sorrows and ignorance. Divine love is unceasing fountain of life force. It fills the mind with serene thoughts and emotions. It lifts the soul on the stream of spiritual ecstasy to the highest.

Elixir of Divine Love- Soma of Divine Love

The Elixir of Divine Love, cleanses the heart of all.

Unwanted and undesirable tendencies.

The soul then is free of fear, sorrow and ignorance.

Thus liberated, full of divine faith and spiritual joy.

The brave soul discovers God in all His splendorous forms.

This exhilarating ambrosia inspires.

Deep reverence in the heart of all sincere lovers.

And fills their bodies with pure serene thoughts and emotions.

Divine love sings only of the glory of His divine splendour.

Every grain of this vast Universe dance with joy.

It is this unceasing fountain of life-force which, like a benevolent power, shines.

Through the golden rays of the sun.

And guide us like a true friend.

On the path of righteousness.

Some spread joyous bliss through pure knowledge.

And uplifts the soul on the stream of spiritual ecstasy to the highest.

ॐॐॐॐॐ

The law of eternal existence is firm and resistless for the good of living beings. By the grace of order of eternity it showers gifts on God - loving devotees. It becomes the soul - force of all righteous thoughts and actions. It enables the loving devotees to win the battle of life.

The Elixir of Divine Love – Soma of Divine Love

The elixir of spiritual light and divine love has wings to fly.

It flies to settle in all the material elements of the earth

Joined to the melody of divine music.

It flows swiftly like the waves of a river.

Again, it continues to flow on its journey.

Like a warrior marching with his brave associates,

Eager to win the battle of life.

The law of eternal existence is firm

And resistless for the good of living beings.

The eternal order assumes infinite and beauteous forms.

Because of eternity men, hope for long-lasting food.

The Vedas enshrine eternal truths within themselves.

By the grace of the order of eternity.

It showers gifts on God-loving devotees with speed.

It allows its voice to be heard by all.

It flows towards all virtuous thoughts and blesses them.

It becomes the soul-force of all righteous thoughts and actions.

It protects and disperses all divine knowledge

For the benefit of the entire Universe.

ॐॐॐॐॐ

God is omnipotent and omnipresent. He is within and beyond all. Go deep to know Him. He is dispeller of suffering and all pervading. He is the cord of unity. Pursuit the spiritual knowledge with meditation, intuition and vision. Partake in material gains also for contribution to continuity.

Meditation, Vision, Wisdom, Intellect

He who goes deeper and perceives the string inside the string .

The thin binding separate life forces with cord of unity.

He knows truly omnipotent and omnipresent God.

Who is within and beyond all formulated entities of the vast Universe

In different colours, forms, shapes and words.

Penetrate deeper to know the ultimate truth.

Know the secret of the conscious soul pervading all.

Achieve equanimity.

Be rewarded by God with institutional insight and eternal glory.

O Supreme Lord! Grant us that vision that makes us divine.

O Supreme God! Thou art self - existent, Omniscient All - Bliss.

Thou art source of life, the dispeller of suffering and all pervading.

We medite on the mast glory of the Supreme God.

O God! lead us to noble works.

O God! Bless us to involve in pursuit of spiritual knowledge.

We partake in material gains for contribution to the continuity.

We are neither engrossed in spiritual knowledge nor in material gains.

Knowledge of eternal truth leads to eternal peace and bliss.

ॐॐॐॐॐ

Opious devotees! Meditate on Om

Walk on Divine Path for greater wisdom and divine glory. God escorts and is a constant companion to those who work hard. He showers the joy of His blessings. Supreme God assigns specific work to everyone. Respond to His command. Meditate on Him. Worship Him in all His manifestations.

Meditation, Vision, Wisdom, Intellect

O Light Divine, the mind preserves thee.

To give light to the sense-organs and vital systems.

Born out of the eternal law.

Walk the divine path for greater wisdom and divine glory.

God escorts me.

He is a constant companion.

To those who are inspired to work hard.

On them does He constantly shower the joy of His Blessings.

Devotee energies to noble and beneficial works.

The Supreme - God assigns specific work to everyone.

It is His pleasure that all of us respond to His commands.

Meditate on the excellent and adorable glory of Lord.

Which is ever existent, ever conscious and ever blissful.

And imbibe the attribute of the Divine creator

Who is all sustaining and victorious.

May He stimulate our vision and mental powers.

Constant and deep meditation reveal the divine worship of the Supreme Lord.

Sharpen the intellect like the sharp blade of steel for success and happy life.

Vow to live by truth and truth alone, dedicating life to God.

O Lord, teach us to worship Thee in all Thy manifestations.

May my immortal soul blend with the Universal soul.

ॐॐॐॐॐ

Know we are the messengers of the Divine Will. Make mind and intellect with Divine Vision. Enhance the discriminative power of intellect. Fill the heart with most ennobling thoughts. By yoga and meditation rise from the material earth to have union and perennial bliss with the Lord. Live in complete harmony with Mother Nature and be blessed by God's reassuring love.

Mother Nature

Live in complete harmony with Mother Nature.

Experience the grace of God in the splendour of the Universe.

Be blessed by God's reassuring love.

The sweet dawn will sweeten soul.

The dazzling mid-day will set heart applaud.

And the serene music of soul guides towards peace and prosperity.

And after the day's task is over, sleep in the lap of Mother Nature.

All the duties will be favourable.

Know that we are the messengers of the Divine Will.

Make mind imbued with Divine Vision.

Enhance the discriminative power of intellect

Instillthe spirit of invincible valourin the body.

Achieve knowledge, power and beauty by means of yoga and meditation.

Be blessed by eternal light, might and sight.

Fill the heart with most ennobling thoughts.

Divine guidance of Vedas give everlasting peace and prosperity.

By dint of yoga, rise from the material earth.

Have union with the Supreme and have perennial bliss.

ॐॐॐॐॐ

The string of the invisible thread bids the separate life forces with cord of unity. Know the ultimate reality and realize the Supreme Lord. He is within and in all entities. The cosmos is created by means of toil by patience and perseverance the invisible thread. Knowledge protects us.

May body and mind work in harmony.

Mother Nature- The Supreme Lord

Know the first vital string.

Binding all the things formed in shape, colour and words.

Know only the physical form of the Universe, that very little.
Go deeper and perceive the string,
The invisible thread inside mind and actions is in unison.
The thin web, binding separate life forces with cords of unity.
Know the ultimate reality and realize the Supreme Lord.
He is within and beyond all formulated entities.
Of the vast Universe, know the whole truth.
The cosmos is created by means of toil, patience and perseverance.
Understood through knowledge and being vested with truth.
Stay firmly.
Thy knowledge protects us from the wrath of sin.
Lift us aloft to spiritual heights.
Bless us with divine vision at morning.
At noon of the day, at evening, at night.
Bless us that seeds of intelligence ever flourish.
In the warmth of thy love.
As plants flourish bathed in the rays of the rising sun.
May our body and mind work in harmony.
May mind and actions be in unison.
The gracious Lord of the Universe has assembled body and mind.
To work together in complete coordination.

ॐॐॐॐॐ

Sharpen the intellect and enrich mind with brighter vision to lead a blissful life, for protection and progress. Acquire and enhance treasure of wisdom to discriminate between truth and falsehood. Perform virtuous deeds. Act and perform deeds of superb quality in the spirit of dedication.

Blissful Life – Supreme Lord
In order to lead a blissful life,

Sharpen the intellect and enrich mind with brighter vision.

In order to protect yourself and make progress in life

Enhance the treasure of wisdom and vision.

Acquire and develop wisdom,

Through discriminating between truth and falsehood.

Perform virtuous deeds.

Live life according to the precepts and wisdom of the Vedas/scriptures.

Act and perform deeds of superb quality in the spirit of dedication.

Intellect and faith are two dependable oars.

That bears the wise men safely.

Across the tumultuous ocean of life.

O Supreme Lord!

Thou art ever existent.

Ever conscious, ever blissful.

We remember thee, we meditate on Thee.

Thy most adorable glory.

May thou guide, and inspire our intellect.

On the path of higher divinity.

Enable us to discriminate between truth and falsehood.

ॐॐॐॐॐ

Turn mind and heart towards the Love of God, the source of all light. Unite with His love. His love is immortal bliss. Be immortal in the eternal bliss of love. Streams of good deeds will flow on and on.

Immortality

Let my mind turn towards the love of,

The Resplendent Lord, the source of all light.

Speed fast, then, O mind.

And unite with the source of eternal bliss.

Lead me onto that sate of eternal light.

The light that shows the way to,

Perpetual, undecaying and immortal bliss.

May my heart turn towards the love of Lord,

Speed fast, then, O mind.

And unite with the source of eternal bliss,

Make me immortal in that world.

Where love of the Lord,

And His supreme purity hold sovereign sway.

Before which the heavens themselves are but a prison-house.

Where the streams of good deeds flow on and on.

Speed fast, then, O mind,

And unite with the source of eternal bliss.

Make me immortal in that state of eternal bliss.

Which is more luminous than heavens.

Where reigns absolute freedom of movement and action.

The dwellers whereof are endowed with eternal light.

Speed fast, then, O mind,

And unite with the source of eternal bliss.

- Dr. H P Kanoria

Based on The Holy Vedas

ॐॐॐॐॐ

O Lord! Liberate over souls from shadows of birth and death. Put an end to all physical desires. Bless me to partake in nectar of immortal love. Unite me with the source of eternal Bliss.

Eternal Love Bliss

O Lord! Liberate our souls.

From the shadows of birth and death.

Put an end to all physical desires of the maligned body.

Bless me to partake the nectar of immortal love.

Make me immortal in the immortal love.

Which forever abounds in joy.

Which is the home of happiness and ecstatic Bliss.

Where all things longed for are attained and all wishes are fulfilled.

Speed fast, then, O mind.

And unite with the source of eternal Bliss.

Man's paradise is on earth.

This living world is the beloved place of all.

It has the blessing of Nature's bounties.

Live in a lovely spirit of unity amidst diversity.

Protect Mother Earth, work for welfare of creation.

Death is imperative, when destiny calls.

Fear not, Trust Him, Be full of love and divine Bliss.

ॐॐॐॐॐ

Mother Divine is granter of eternal glory. Surrender and dedicate completely. Be full of love and divine Bliss. Turn the mind and heart towards Mother Divine. Every noble aspiration find fulfilment.

Eternal Love Bliss Mother Divine

Worship the Mother of three realms.

She is the granter of eternal glory.

May Mother separate our souls from bodies, a step to absolute liberation.

May Mother release our soul from the bondage of mortallives.

As the ripened melon is separated from its stem.

We are child of immortality.

Complete surrender and dedication lead to gain immortality.

Be full of love and divine bliss.

There are wise men who are full of love and divine Bliss.

Turn the mind and heart towards the Mother.

Every noble aspirations find fulfillment.

And happiness is gained never to be lost.

All things longed for are attained

And all wishes are fulfilled.

Blessed by Mother Divine, may we live a full span of life with joy.

Unite with the source of eternal bliss.

Speed mind and heart towards love and eternal love.

ॐॐॐॐॐ

Every mortal body is enlivened by the soul in accordance with its previous actions (Karma) ceaselessly taking birth and rebirth. Exhilarated by spiritual bliss, the powerful soul controls the venomous baser tendencies. It destroys the vice of petty mindedness, greed and malice.

Human Soul

Two birds (God and Soul), with their beauteous wings.

Associate in intimacy, perch on the same tree.

Of them, soul, tastes its fruits, the other God. The God enjoys without tasting,

Every mortal body is enlivened by the immortal soul.

In accordance with its previous actions (Karma).

The immortal soul associated with the mortal body ceaselessly takes birth and rebirth.

According to its own actions,

The soul is free from the body.

The resplendent self, the foremost, as soon as it is born excelleth all other faculties.

Owing to the supremacy of its strength.

The duality of body and mind functions well.

The resplendent self makes the trembling body firm.

Tranquillizes the agitated senses.

Keeps the celestial mental realm upright.

Exhilarated by sweet spiritual bliss.

The soul controls the venomous baser tendencies.

The delicious streams of this bliss begins to flow.

As birds fly towards their nests.

The powerful soul destroys the vice of petty mindedness, greed and malice.

ॐॐॐॐॐ

Spiritualize the soul. Then, the powerful soul casts off evil desires and evil tendencies. It sharpens the will power and subdues the baser impulses. Along with the soul, invoke the Lord for glory, diligence and fearlessness. Let our inner strength be awaken.

Human Soul

Exhilarated by sweet spiritual bliss,

The powerful soul casts off

The cloud of blind and dark impulses and evil thoughts.

The stream of wisdom flow to overcome all obstacles.

It accumulates the strength in three virtuous directions.

Physical, mental and spiritual.

It sharpen will-power and subdue the baser impulses.

The strong soul, the wielder of powerful spiritual power.

Becometh the sovereign of all.

That is movable and immovable of impulses and emotions.

He becometh monarch of all men.

Then all activities are centred within Him.

As the circumference comprehendeth the spokes of a wheel.

The spiritualized soul conquers adversaries.

With its swift and forceful disintegrating power.

It destroys the central living place of blind instincts.

It dismantles the resting place of these evil impulses.

And thereupon rejoices in His Victory.

Along with our soul, we invoke Thee, O Lord.

For glory, diligence and fearlessness.

Let our inner strength

Also carry with it the idea of progress

And vigorous leadership

To do away with our evil desires.

ॐॐॐॐॐ

With Divine love make the soul strong. Divinely blessed overpowers the wicked and perverted thoughts. By the subtle strength, disciplines the hundreds of strong holds of capricious instincts. Like rivers flow to ocean, the soul merges with Lord.

Human Soul

When the soul is strong,

No baser impulses like sensuous thoughts,

Passions or any sort of temptations can harm us.

The triumph of the soul in the context.

Becomes full and final over the wicked impulses.

O Divinely Blessed Soul, unaided and alone.

Thou over powerest the wicked and perverted thoughts.

With Thy sharp intellect and makest way for reverential ones.

Thou by Thy subtle strength disciplinest hundreds of strongholds of capricious instincts.

While surrounded by earnest and simple thoughts.

O blessed soul, thou reignest supreme over the wayward senses.

By thy resolute strength, thou overcomest all deluding devilish temptations.

Thy divinity surpasseth all others in strength.

Glorious light of inner consciousness appears.

This heavenly light keeps the adversities far away.

Thou rulest even those who are superior.

O Inner Self, thy clear and loud voice becomes the oars of the boat of our life.

Guide us to the safe shores through the stormy sea of life avoiding all calamities.

As the rivers fill up the ocean,

Human soul with divine happiness offers itself to Lord.

ॐॐॐॐॐ

Live in tune with the universal soul-God. Creation is the image of the creator. Every particle of human body is a symbol of universal existence. Let there be no distance, no distinction. Cast off the separate ego and merge in the universal unity. Live in tune with the universal soul-God. Let this be final craving and prayer.

Commune with Universal Soul

I live in tune with the universal soul-God.

Let this be final craving which I cherish.

Let this be my last prayer.

Cast off my separate ego and merge in the universal entity.

Let there be no distance, no distinction.

Every particle of human body is a symbol of universal existence.

Creation is the image of creator.

The experience of unity is the fulfillment of human endeavors.

ॐॐॐॐॐ

The human body is temple of God. The radiant soul within the body gives impetus to the wheel of intellect. Kindle light of awareness within to get true light. The body and mind resign to the soul. Keep the mind clean at all time. It controls the vital organs. It saves from the inner conflicts by remembering, concentrating and meditating. Kindle the love for God. The soul sips the elixir of spiritual joy - elixir of joy of God's love. A person achieves glorious success.

Inner Flame

The human body is temple of God.

The radiant soul within the body gives impetus to the wheel of the intellect.

Even the self-sustaining powers of intellect,

And mind bow before the potent self.

And the body resigns to the soul.

As the soul shares its vigour with all other faculties.

These faculties offer reverence to the soul.

The soul sips the elixir of spiritual joy.

Given to it by God.

The soul gives protection to the humble.

Flickering and erring human mind.

And makes the person worthy of achieving glorious success.

By remembering, concentrating and meditating.

Kindle the love for God.

Enjoy the elixir of love of God - inner soul

ॐॐॐॐॐ

The human body is temple of God. The radiant soul within the body gives impetus to the wheel of intellect. Kindle light of awareness within to get true light. The body and mind resign to the soul. Keep the mind clean at all time. It controls the vital organs. It saves from the inner conflicts by remembering, concentrating and meditating. Kindle the love for God. The soul sips the elixir of spiritual joy - elixir of joy of God's love. A person achieves glorious success.

Inner Flame

The human body is temple of God.

The radiant soul within the body gives impetus to the wheel of the intellect.

Even the self-sustaining powers of intellect,

And mind bow before the potent self.

And the body resigns to the soul.

As the soul shares its vigour with all other faculties.

These faculties offer reverence to the soul.

The soul sips the elixir of spiritual joy.

Given to it by God.

The soul gives protection to the humble.

Flickering and erring human mind.

And makes the person worthy of achieving glorious success.

By remembering, concentrating and meditating.

Kindle the love for God.

Enjoy the elixir of love of God - inner soul

ॐॐॐॐॐ

O Divine Men Awake! Awake! God blesses those who keep themselves awake. Divine forces help them in all their noble deeds. God assures them all success. Be not lethargic and morbid. Work hard for benevolent cause. Become brave and strong. God helps to conquer all adversaries. Awake the spirit of generosity.

Awakening

Awake, Divine people, Awake.

He who keeps awake is blessed by the Lord.

He alone is befriended by the Divine forces who keeps vigilant.

In all his noble deeds God assures him success.

God helps only those who work hard with vigour and courage.

Worthy of the Lord's assocation are not those who are lethargic and sleepy.

None ever comes to the aid of one who is morbid and fatalistic.

The Lord defend and favours.

Only those who work hard.

And work for a benevolent cause.

Those who perform benevolent works.

Become brave and strong.

And thier minds and bodies.

Become free from sin and disease.

God helps them to conquer their adversaries.

Like an angry lion.

Driving away a herd of elelphants.

Awake the spirit of generosity.

Be not miser in giving charity.

ॐॐॐॐॐ

Awake O Man! Awake! Be self-sufficient to architect own destiny. Realise the virtues of self-reliance and self-sacrifice. Be inspired by the wisdom of seers and follow their instructions with full faith. Acquire happiness through the cultivation of virtuous qualities and through joy of devotion - worship. Keep away the evils of anger at all stages. Speak sweetly. Resolve along with leaders to keep a strict vigil over the safety of mother land.

Awakening

Be self-sufficient, O Man!

Be not slave to any outside help.

Listen to such words that enable to conquer inner foes.

Be so illustrious that all approach you for guidance.

Be self sufficient to architect own destiny.

Realise the virtues of self-reliance and self-sacrifice.

Be inspired by the wisdom of seers which are true and effective.

Follow their instructions with full faith.

Along with leaders of Nation

Resolve to keep a strict vigil over the safety of our motherland.

Acquire happiness through the joy of worship – devotion and work hard with devotion.

And the cultivation of virtuous qualities.

A true devotee is always soft in speech.

And considerate towards others.

Keep away from the evils of violent anger at all stages of life.

O God! Bless us with divine fragrance.

And purify our speech.

Bless us to speak sweetly.

ॐॐॐॐॐ

Have faith in God. For profound contentment put in best efforts. Do beneficial works for society honestly. Keep mind under control. Patiently search for inner vision. Fill mind and heart with joy of love of God.

Virtuous Awakening Thoughts and Noble Deeds

Have faith in God.

Put in best efforts to be blessed with profound contentment.

Do beneficial works for society honestly.

Work honestly and patiently

To have sure and inevitable gains for true desires.

Wise men attain salvation through their own patient search

And inner vision and adherence to the knowledge acquired.

Call back the mind which goes for away

So to keep under control.

Mind goes far away to all that occurred in the past

And will occur in future.

Call it back.

Keep under control.

O Lord! Fill our hearts and minds with thy love, joy and sweetness.

May it flow like a stream of honey.

O Lord of Creation! Purify our vision to behold truth.

Let Aum be the word, the undiminishing experience of divine light and joy.

Remain in our hearts for all time to come.

ॐॐॐॐॐ

Stand firm and erect. Build body strong like a rock. Strengthen body and mind to perform all duties. Have a piercing intellect. Accept ever true ideals of life. Infuse all the virtues of universe. Offer reverence to parents. Have faith in self and God.

Awakening Virtuous Thoughts and Noble Deeds

Stand firm and erect, build body strong like a rock.
And strengthen body and mind to perform all duties.
And fulfill your responsibilities gaining prosperity and riches.
Surely live, strong and sturdy warding off all evils.
Remain far away from the fire of sin, which consumes.
God blesses the liberal and pious devotees.
Remain free of debt of any kind throughout the life.
To fall is not our nature.
Have a piercing intellect to avoid pitfalls.
Resolve to discard all the false values.
And accept ever-true ideals of life.
Offer reverence to saints and parents.
Treat them with respect.
Have faith that you are invincible.
Possess the strength of an unconquerable hero.
Recognize own inherent power
To infuse all the virtues of universe.
Never speak harsh words.
Let it not escape from lips.
Let the sublime aura of pure joy embrace us in its fold of intense love forever.

ॐॐॐॐॐ

Find the eternal objects of quest within soul. Turn the gaze inward. Realise the bright light of faith. With joy, find the soul of Universe, the eternal object of quest. Behold the light divine guiding towards eternal joy. Have always noble thoughts in mind. Remember and pray to God.

Awakening Realisation

Find the eternal object of quest within soul.

Not to search in ignorance and groping in helplessness.

Turn gaze inward, realise the bright light of faith.

The lasting truth is shining around.

With rapturous joy, find the soul of Universe, the eternal object of quest.

Find the object of search within own heart.

Inner vision is illuminated by this new realisation.

Resolve with courage to crush the deceitful.

Overcome violent urges with firmness as those are enemies.

Through rigorous discipline and strict austerity.

Burn the passionate desires.

Always have noble thoughts in mind.

Never express bitter words.

Get rid of jealousy from heart and eschew violence.

Rise above material desires.

To the divine path of spiritual experience.

And behold the light divine, guiding towards eternal joy.

O God! Help us to be ever on the divine path

With faith and love in Thee

ॐॐॐॐॐ

Supreme Being is the architect of the universe. He is omnipotent, omniscient & omnipresent. First oceans were created, thereafter, the solid mass-earth. Mortal man takes birth depending on his good or evil deeds. Through realization he gets released from the cycle of births and deaths. Supreme Being Himself is never born.

The Universe

The dynamic universe is the result of intensive divine fervour, application of the mind – force to matter

The Supreme being is the architect of the Universe.

He is omnipotent, omniscient, omnipresent and also dazzling brilliant

First the oceans were created.

Thereafter the solid land mass was formed.

The Supreme Being chiseled the planetary system in as great a variety forms.

Mortal man takes birth depending upon his good or evil and sinful deeds.

Through his intuitive perception and realization.

He gets release on from the ever revolving cycle of births and deaths.

He conquers fear of suffering and unhappiness of all kinds.

The Supreme Being himself is never born.

The intellectual seers, engaged in deep contemplation upon God.

Intuitively perceive the entire creation

ॐॐॐॐॐ

The wisdom of God united with energies manages the whole universe. He controls the immortal wheel of universe. In Him all are well placed. All these elements enjoy themselves at His very approach. In Him all divine cosmic powers become one. He watches all creatures. He is the Lord of all.

The Universe

The all-controlling immortal wheel of the universe is revolving in infinite space.

The wisdom of God, united with energy manages the whole universe.

On this energy rest and depend all regions and planets.

In the very infinite are well placed, the mind, the vital breath and the name.

All these elements enjoy themselves.

At His very approach.

In the self-same Infinite are fully established.

The austerity, the grandeur, the vast universe and the Vedic

He is the Lord of all.

In Him all divine cosmic powers become one.

He is the Father of all hymns and praises.

Messenger of all Divines.

He purifieth all regions and watcheth all creatures.

In Him all deities become one and only one.

The sun, the eye of the universe is divinely placed.

The whole of the universe is stained in the omnipresent and omnipotent God.

We see Him in various forms.

He brings to light, all these worlds pervading the vast sky.

ॐॐॐॐॐ

The Universe – Offer sincere and obeisance with unswerving Devotion to the Supreme Entity. He causes the creation of all earth, water, fire, sun, moon and constellations. Meditate and offer prayers. Have understanding, experiences and realization to discipline conscious mind and faculties. Follow the path of devotion to be able to control the physical energies and have liberation.

The Universe

We offer our sincere homage and obeisance with unswerving devotion to the Supreme Entity.

The Omniscient Illuminated Being causes the creation of all matters

Comprising the earth, water, fire, the sun, moon and constellations that display cosmic energies.

Upon Him all intellectual devotees meditate and offer their prayers.

He, the Supreme Being is their guide and mentor.

The Exalted Being was the most only powerful force

Before the creation of divine substance and the radiant universe.

Man realizes liberation only by understanding and experiencing this sublime i=universal existence.

Having realized Brahman (Supreme Being) they advocate path of devotion as a means of liberation/salvation.

These enlightened intellectual Blessed with the intuitive perception of

Brahman

Are able to control the elemental physical energies

As well as to discipline their conscious mind and faculties.

ॐॐॐॐॐ

Sun, moon and galaxies proclaim His existence. Realizing His powers, we pray, "Guide and inspire us to attain sublime Bliss. Bless us with everlasting peace, happiness in every way and nectar of thy love forever.

The Universe

The Outer Space illuminated with suns

Galaxies proclaims His cosmic existence.

With the strength of His Divine fervour the universe is created.

The most powerful object in creation is the Sun.

The most radiant possession of the Universe is the Earth.

Spiritual and material splendours symbolize the two principal attributes of the Supreme Being.

Realizing His power we pray.

O Supreme Being, inspire us and guide us to attain Sublime Bliss.

Bless us to progress in every respect in this Universe.

Bless us with everlasting peace and happiness in every way.

Bless us to be on path of thy righteousness and devotion.

Bless us with the nectar of thy love forever.

ॐॐॐॐॐ

Truth, Eternal Order, Austerity, Prayers and Devotion uphold the Mother Earth which gives us in abundance plenty types of plants bearing fruits, herbal medicine, finest harvest, waters and varieties of treasures. Never Sleeping Cosmic Power protects Mother Earth.

Mother Earth

Truth, Eternal Order, that is great and stern.

Consecration, Austerity, Prayer and Devotion.

Uphold the Mother Earth.

The Earth has many heights, slopes and unconfined plains.

In the Earth lies the sea, the rivers and other waters.

In her food and cornfields have come to be.

The Earth bears plants of various healing powers.

May she provide vast space for us.

May she confer on us the finest of her harvest.

May she give us cattle and crops.

May she give us magnificence and lustre.

The Earth bears all sustaining, treasure-beraing places.

The Earth bears the sacred Universal fire.

May the Supreme Lord and talented sages

Give us spiritual wealth and wealth.

Never sleeping cosmic powers protect Mother Earth without erring.

May Mother Earth pour on us riches in many turns

And endow us with lustre.

ॐॐॐॐॐ

O Mother Earth! Purify us from all sides, make us shine forth with righteousness and truth. Let there be love and devotion and no hatred. May we, through long life, be active, vigilant and serve Thee with devotion.

Mother Earth

O Mother Earth! Purify us from all sides.

The Earth is our mother, we are Her children.

Infinite space is our father, may we have plenty.

Mother of all plants,

Firm Earth is upheld by Eternal Law.

May She be ever beneficent and gracious on us.

O Mother Earth, make us shine forth with righteousness and truth.

Let there be love and devotion and no hatred.

The fragrance that rises from Thee, O Mother Earth.

That plants and waters carry and is shred by solar rays.

Make us sweet with that, may there be all devotion.

O Mother Earth, let thy bosom be free from sickness and decay.

May we, through long life, be active, vigilant

And serve Thee with devotion.

ॐॐॐॐॐ

Mother Earth contains rivers common to all, snow clad mountains, woods, black/brown mountains and fire. May Mother Earth gives us bounty to live long. Let Her radiance units us all and sharpen us bright.

The Mother Earth

The Mother Earth contains rivers common to all.

Moving on all sides, flowing day and night.

May Mother Earth pour on us riches in many forms

And endow us with lustre.

O Mother Earth! Thou are pleasant with snow clad mountains.

Thou art pleasant with woods, brown/black, multicoloured mountains.

The Supreme Lord protects Thee.

There lies the fire in Thee.

There is a fire within all.

The same fire burns in the heavens.

Men kindle this fire that bears the oblation.
May Mother Earth sharpen us bright.
May she give us breath and life.
May she make us long-lived.
Let thy fragrance make us sweet.
Let thy radiance unite us with these.
Our obeisance to gold-breasted Earth.

ॐॐॐॐॐ

The Mother Earth grows strong with spiritual might. Seven sages, World Building Seers, Enlightened people pray and praise the Supreme Lord and Mother Earth with austerity and oblations. May Her all seasons pour their abundance on us. May Mother Earth grant us wealth to live with comfort.

The Mother Earth

The Patient Mother Earth grows strong through spiritual might.
She bearest power in plenty and our share of food.
We cleanse ourselves, which that purify us.
May all regions be pleasant for us to tread upon.
Rising or sitting standing or walking, we never totter on Mother Earth.
As we look on Thee from around with the Sun as a friend.
May not our vision fail.
May we not injure Thy vitals or Thy heart.
May thy all seasons - summer, spirng, autumn, winter.
Pour their abundance on us.
Seven sages, world-building seers, enlightened people praise the Lord of Universe with verses from Vedas.
With austerity and oblation, they worship the Lord Supreme and Mother Earth.
May the gracious Lord gives us the task and come to lead the way.
May Mother Earth grant us wealth to live with comfort.

Mother Earth's bounties, treasures, food grains, plants, forests and animals uphold us to live in grace and splendour. May Mother Earth give us loving kindness, sweetness to speak sweetly free from ego, intellect and milk of Her nectar Blessing. With joyous speed and unity we shall protect Mother Earth by all means. We shall save Her from Global Warming, by living in simplicity and austerity and not to waste.

Mother Earth

May Mother Earth's bounties uphold us in grace and splendour.

Mother Earth gives us food grains on which to live.

Mother Earth bears treasures at many places.

Bounteous Mother gives us gems, gold and other treasures.

May Mother give us loving kindness free from ego.

Mother Earth gives provisions to wild animals and birds.

Mother Earth is canopied by rain.

May she establish us with bliss in every home.

With joyous speed, she protects forest, trees and plants.

Heaven, Earth and Mid - Air have given us this wide space.

And all cosmic powers together have endowed us with intellect.

We speak in praise of Her everywhere.

May what we speak, we speak with sweetness.

Peaceful, sweet - smelling, gracious Earth,

Filled with milk, bearing nectar in Her breast.

May she give us with the milk Her blessing.

We invoke all - supporting Mother Earth for Her Blessing.

ॐॐॐॐॐ

Waters & Rivers - Knowingly or unknowingly, foolishly or impudently we may not violate the laws of nature. Water is useful for upkeep of body and contains medicaments. O Rivers! flow with restraints for the benefit of all.

Water & Rivers

Water contains all disease dispelling medicaments.

Useful for the upkeep of the body, so that we may live long.

To enjoy the bright Sun.

By their proper use become wiser.

May we not violate the laws of Nature.

Knowingly or unknowingly, foolishly or impudently.

O powerful waters take away whatever wrong or deficient in us.

Some water collects together to flow as rivers into the ocean.

Down from the lap of mountains.

O Rivers, let all flow with restraint and stay within limits for the benefit of all.

ॐॐॐॐॐ

Water & Rivers - The Divine water, the purifiers never violate the sacred laws of Lord. Water and rivers irrigate the lands providing life giving food to us. Refreshing divine elixir water flowing through rivers and tributaries make us fresh and delightful. Should not waste water nor make it dirty.

Water & Rivers

The Divine water, the purifiers never violate the sacred laws of Resplendent Lord.

Rejoicing in this innate nature, pursue the paths of Nature's forces.

We offer our tribute to rivers rich in affection and love.

The lands fed by thee provide immense food.

Thou irrigate the banks on both sides carrying the water of tributaries.

The water is the sovereign remedy.

It is for the Resplendent Lord, that this blissful,

Refreshing divine elixir is flowing in hundreds and thousands of rivulets.

Making everything clean, lovely and delightful.

And it is for Him that fountains burst.

Into sweet melodies.

In the solitary region of green valleys.

And the confluence of the rivers.

The sages obtain.

Divine intuition.

ॐॐॐॐॐ

Entreat God to reside in our hearts and make our body His temple. He gives us bounty of harvest for our righteous actions. Let us speak sweetly free of ego. Dedicate all at His lotus feet.

Supreme Lord - God

May God come and reside in our hearts.

May our body be the temple of God!

May He feed freely upon the harvest of our actions.

May we reap the harvest of our life and dedicate all at His feet.

May we ever remain His true children.

Lord is full of sweetness.

He creates all things full of sweetness.

May our words be full of sweetness.

ॐॐॐॐॐ

Motherland - Love and protect Motherland. Work hard with devotion and righteousness to create and generate wealth for our countrymen speaking different dialects, having different religions, following different profession and worship Motherland as we worship God. Swami Vivekananda said, "Very dust of Motherland India is holy to me".

Motherland

Let us work with devotion for the glory of the Motherland.

Let us work hard for our countrymen speaking different dialects.

Let us give due respect to the faith and aspirations of the people.

Countless are the resources of Mother Earth.

From Motherland flow the rivers of wealth in hundreds of srteams.

Motherland gives bounty of food, herbs, plants and space.

From time eternal, Motherland is giving life to Her children.

We owe debts to Her.

Let us sacrifice our lives for the protection of Motherland.

Let us have loyalty to Motherland irrespective of religions.

Let us worship Motherland as we worship God.

Let us work hard with devotion and righteousness.

Let us create and generate wealth for prosperity and happiness of all.

Let us protect Motherland from enemies and global warming.

Let us worship Motherland as we Worship God.

ॐॐॐॐॐ

The Cosmic energy is great. Let us live in the limit of eternal law, rejoice in all the moods of nature and experience the unseen divine glory manifested in various forms. May the Divine forces not allow us to err.

The One Source - The Lord

Great is the energy of the cosmic forces.

May the Divine not allow us to err.

Let us live in limit of eternal law.

The medicinal herbs of the motherland make us healthy and happy.

Rejoice in all the moods of nature.

Experience the unseen divine glory manifested in various forms.

Spring is the season of flowers and scented breeze which gladdens the hearts.

Summer follows and has a beauty of its own.

The rain with its dark clouds and dazzling flashes bathes the entire earth with its splendour.

Autumn and winter too possess their peculiar charm and beauty.

God has set the sun in the midst of heaven.

It attracts rain water and pours it down.

It protects us thoroughly.

It pervades lights.

O Lord! Grant us happiness in creation with children.

May we enjoy thine unassailedprotection.

ॐॐॐॐॐ

God is the cherisher of all benevolent thoughts and deeds. He is the Lord. Before Him we all bow. The Earth is filled with the milk of eternal laws. Vayu is the chief element pervading space. Vayu is born of Agani. The solar system and the galaxy of stars move as if woven in a string. The enlightened souls see the invisible, the Creator behind the creation.

One Source - The Lord

Great is the one source of energy of the cosmic forces.

Our desires fly about in many places.

The Earth is filled with the milk of eternal law.

Only He who knows the secret of the visible.

The science of creation.

May glimpse the invisible, the Creator behind the creation.

Vayu is the chief element pervading space.

The solar system and the galaxy of stars move as if in a string, woven by this vayu.

Vayu is born of Agani and gives out lustre.

Heat waves affected space, the sun became effulgent.

Sun and Moon shed light on Earth creating motion and natural stability.

In spite the atomic friction there is a uniformity of motion and affinity.

He is the Lord, before whom we all bow.

The powers of celestial and terrestrial regions.

He is the cherisher of all benevolent thoughts and deeds.

ॐॐॐॐॐ

God is the sovereign ruler of the Universe. He is the Divine observer. He seeth all in the Universe and beyond Universe. He measureth everything. He has given us Will power to live happily.

One Source - The Lord God

Being Sovereign Ruler of the Universe.

He is the Divine Observer.

He seeth all that lies between heaven and earth.

And beyond them.

Even the twinkling of the eyes He counteth.

As a dicer counter his dice.

He seeth and measureth everything.

He hast given us Will power to exercise to live happily.

He hast given several kind of plenty herbal plants as medicines.

- The Holy Vedas

ॐॐॐॐॐ

Offer reverence to the Supreme Creator, who gave us waters, river, the Sun, the moon, galaxy of stars and bounties in Nature. Sun moves with Divine Rays and shines and causes to shine. The Sun beholding good and evil acts of mortal manifest their intentions.

The Sun

We offer gratitude to the waters flowing in the rivers.

Kissed by the sun rays.

As we offer reverance to the Supreme Creator.

The wheels of the Sun have two functions.

One imparts knowledge, the other destroys evil.

The Sun shines and causes to shine.

By dint of eternal cosmic law, He illuminates the morning.

He moves with Divine Rays, yoked by eternal order.

He furnishes human being with such nerve-centres that make them feel joyous.

The Sun, beholding good and evil acts of mortals manifest their intentions.

O Sun, on Thy coming, All living beings are awakened.

And the winged birds flock around from the boundaries of skies to greet Thee.

ॐॐॐॐॐ

The Sun is the divine leader in the solar system. He spreads His immortal all benefiting lights to all. He is the source of creativity. May the Sun endow us with energy, instill vigour in our souls and liberate us.

The Sun

The Sun divine has diffused golden lustre in the sky.

The Sun divine the leaders of all in the solar system.

Spreads his immortal, all-benefiting light.

Being the eye of all nature's bounties.

He becomes the source of creativity and makes all regions visible.

The Sun is the soul of the world, be it static or moving.

May the Sun promptly favour us with its protection.

May the rivers, the clouds, herbs and vegetation give us happiness.

May the Sun Divine stretch forth His golden arms to us.

And inspire us like an eloquent orator.

May the Sun, endowed with energy provide nourishment to all.

May the radiant Sun instill vigour in our souls.

May the rising Sun liberate us from the bondage of birth and death.

ॐॐॐॐॐ

The Golden Rays beings of the dawn fill one's life with Divine lustre. It rouses up the people. Birds fly forth. Human being rise to work and earn their sustenance. Sages sing the hymns of welcome. May Divine forces continue to shower abundance, affection and blessing on all.

The Golden Dawn

The Golden Rays of the dawn fill one's life with Divine lustre.

For Divine Dawn the sages sing the hymns of welcome.

The lovely Dawn rouses up the people.

Makes the paths easy to tread and goes forward.

She opens paths to a happy life.

As praised by all, she shines with every blessing.

O Divine dawn, when the birds fly forth from their nests.

Human beings must rise to work and earn their sustenance.

The glow of divine in the east and moves westward.

May the dawns come to bless our worship.

May the dawns bring divine grace and prosperity.

May the auspicious dawn brighten our path.

And grant us wealth, vitality, wisdom and valiant prosperity.

May she come with all abundance and affection.

And associated divine forces continue to shower blessing upon us.

- *The Holy Vedas*

ॐॐॐॐॐ

God has given us emotional heart and logical mind. Give prominence to intellect over emotion. Neither be swayed by emotion nor be carried away by logic. Obtain inspiration from heart and guidance from reasons. Develop intellect by spirituality.

Harmony, Intellect and Emotion

Give prominence to intellect over emotions.
God has housed emotional heart and logical mind in one body.
Do not be swayed by emotions, nor be carried by mere logic.
Obtain inspiration from the heart.
But guidance from the brain

And go ahead with steady steps.

The place of reason is higher than the place of heart.

Try to develop intellect on the same principle

Which enlightened and inspired seers followed.

May all the divine and material forces be merciful and benevolent to us.

May peace itself bestow eternal joy on us.

- *The Holy Vedas*

ॐॐॐॐॐ

O Citizens of the world! Live in harmony and concord. Be organised and cooperative. Make resolution with one mind. Perform duties righteously and honestly. Have faith in God. You will not falter. He will help us.

Cooperation, Action, Harmony

O Citizens of the world!

Live in harmony and concord.

Be organised and cooperative.

Speak with one voice

Make your resolutions with one mind.

Like ancient seers, leaders, preceptors perform your duties righteously.

Similarly you will not falter to execute your duties.

- *The Holy Vedas*

ॐॐॐॐॐ

Perform duty and leave the rest to God. Have deep faith in His justice. In the dark whirlpool of turbulent stream of life only all powerful God may carry us across the ocean of troubles. Only He can navigate our lives to the shore of divine fulfilment. Dedicate all thoughts and desires to God with full faith and love. He will bless through His divine mercy and love.

Cooperation, Action, Harmony

Perform duty and leave the rest to God.

Have deep faith in His justice.

The world is torn by strife, enmities and rivalries.

In this dark whirlpool of turbulent stream of life.

Only all-powerful God may carry us across the ocean of troubles.

Only He can navigate our lives to the shore of divine fulfillment.

The waves of the stormy life will become calm at His nod.

Dedicate all thoughts and desires to God with full faith.

Only He can bless to conquer troubles through His Divine Mercy.

- The Holy Vedas

ॐॐॐॐॐ

Do duty ever unswervingly as do the sun and the moon. Serve humanity without demanding the price of service. Be benevolent, kind, self-sacrificing, detached and adjustable. Surrender all and serve the humanity and creation like the sun and moon.

Duty

May we ever unswervingly follow the path of duty as do the sun and the moon.

May we always serve humanity without demanding the price of our service.

May we ever be benevolent, kind, self-sacrificing, detached and adjustable.

May we surrender all and serve humanity like the sun and the moon.

ॐॐॐॐॐ

May our minds and hearts work in unison for one supreme goal and common ideal. May our innermost aspirations be perfectly harmonious and welded into strong fellowship and unity. May we realise that nobody is higher or lower by birth, so to work together for well being of all.

Prayer for the social consciousness - welfare of the people

O God! May our prayer be one and the same

May we belong to one fraternity

May our minds move in accord

May our hearts work in unison for one supreme goal

May we inspired by a common ideal

May we sing thy praises in congregation

May our innermost aspirations be perfectly harmonious

May our heart beat in unison

May absolute concord reign in our minds

May we all be welded into strong fellowship and unity.

May we enjoy the wealth as one

May we dedicate our lives to eradicate the evils of society

May we strive at all times for the well being of the people

May we realise that in mankind nobody is higher or lower

May we toil along the path of progress by diligently exploiting natural resources

- *The Holy Vedas*

ॐॐॐॐॐ

May we utilize our earned and inherited wealth for noble deeds, to create wealth for generation of wealth in the service of all with combined energies and diverse skills. May we realise that we are children of Supreme Being (God) and no one is small or big by birth and no one is feeble. All are truly great. All have strength to fight for noble and righteous cause.

Prayers for consciousness of welfare of all

May we utilize our wealth for noble deeds.

May we not hoard wealth.

May we use earned and inherited wealth for creating and generating wealth.

May farmers grow food for all.

May teachers impart knowledge than that of being a silent saint.

May all members of a family and society have a common objective.

May their hearts beat as one and their minds think alike.

May with their combined energies and diverse skills accomplish their objectives satisfactorily.

May all love and respect each other.

No one is small no one is big.

Not one is a feeble child, all are truly great.

May All have strength to fight for noble and righteous causes.

May all work hard for welfare of creation.

- *The Holy Vedas*

ॐॐॐॐॐ

O citizens of the world! Live in harmony and concord. With cooperation, faith, devotion and unity perform duties righteously. There is accurate regulation of actions and reactions. One reaps what one sows. Share food and bounty of Mother Earth. No one is higher or lower by birth. Help all. God blesses all who have noble missions and actions.

Prayers for consciousness of welfare of family, society, nation and the world

O citizens of the world ! Live in harmony and concord.

Be organised and co-operative.

Speak with one voice.

Make resolution with one mind.

Perform duties righteously with devotion and faith.

There is no flaw, no reservation in the law of Karma (action).

It is an exact and accurate regulation of actions and reactions.

One reaps what one sows.

Share food and bounty of Mother Earth.

All be united and work hard with devotion for progress and welfare of all.

Have courage in espousing great cause.

Lead and guide the wayward struggling masses.

Help the poor, weak, hungry, deficient and old.

Live in concord and harmony with all.

The Supreme being (God) blesses all

Who have noble missions and actions

- *The Holy Vedas*

ॐॐॐॐॐ

God hath given us ample riches and supreme strength. Feel not that our soul is hollow. Crave not for more. Set our minds and hearts on definite righteous objectives. Faith, love in God with healthy body, mind, soul and hard work with devotion will enable us to achieve desired goals.

Happiness and Welfare

The Supreme Lord hath given ample riches to us.

Still we feel our soul is hollow, we crave for more.

God hath given us supreme strength.

Still we feel weak and emaciated.

Let the stream of God's love flow in our soul.

Let the streams of God's love flow in our veins to face the adversaries of life.

Let we have the calm confidence in God's love.

Let we set our heart on a definite objective.

Let we work hard with devotion and righteousness with blessing of God.

Let we keep our mind and body in perfect condition.

Faith, Love in God with healthy body, mind, soul and hard work.

Shall enable us to achieve desired goal.

- *The Holy Vedas*

ॐॐॐॐॐ

God has bound mankind together towards one objective to work with devotion, righteousness, mutual accord and love for the welfare of all and creation. Share the fruits. Let no one be hungry. Share wealth with the needy and deserving. Ignite fire of virtues, respect and service to elders, divine qualities and love for God.

Happiness and welfare

Almighty God calls on His children
O Children ! I bind you together towards one objective.
The welfare of human beings and creation
Toil together with mutual love and goodwill.
Accomplish work with mutual accord in pursuit of mission.
Engage in working together with devotion and righteousness.
Share the fruits, let no one be hungry.
Carefully observe the ways of virtuousness and righteousness.
Vigorously follow the path that leads to happiness.
Be enlightened to dwell in sweet blissfulness.
All are bonded in brotherhood and sisterhood.
Share wealth with those who deserve and need
And seek love of God, the most precious treasure of human birth.
Carry forward the torch of virtues.
Live upto expectations of elders, sages, saints and God.
O leaders, imbibe divine attributes.
Be hardworking with honesty and devotion.
Have moral strength to proclaim truth fearlessly.
Spread the message of divinity on earth.
Ignite the fire of virtues, hard working sharing divinity on earth.

- *The Holy Vedas*

ॐॐॐॐॐ

God is in the solitary channel of heart. Surrender all thoughts and deeds to Him. Feel fortified by His presence in the conscious realisation. Bear all the pleasures and pains with calm confidence. Live in the spirit of sacrifice with constant hard work and virtuous deeds.

Happiness & Welfare

O Supreme Lord ! Thou art in the solitary chambers of my heart.

Unto thy hands I surrender all my thoughts and deeds.

By the blessing I become pure and strong to face all the situations in life.

I remain fortified by thy presence in my conscious realisation.

I bear all the pleasures and pains with calm confidence.

I live in the spirit of sacrifice with constant hard work and virtuous deeds.

- *The Holy Vedas*

ॐॐॐॐॐ

All virtues and evils have entered human body. The Soul within the mortal body is called Brahman. The soul is desireless, serene, immortal and self-existent. The soul fears no one, not even death. Engage in beneficial pursuits. Affirm I am perfect. My entire being is perfect. I am at peace.

Human Being - Children of God

When God, Divine Architect planned and fashioned the human body

All the virtues and evils entered the mortal frame and made it their home.

The soul walled within the mortal body is called Brahman.

The soul is desireless, serene, immortal and self existent.

Youthful Supreme soul fears no one, not even death.

The body is an unfailing instrument.

Engaged in beneficial pursuits.

Affirm, I am perfect.

Perfect is my mind.

Perfect are mine eyes, perfect are mine ears, perfect is my breath

Perfect is my entire being.

At peace with myself am I.

- The Holy Vedas

ॐॐॐॐॐ

O human beings! Awake, Arise, Resolve to take the banner of truth in firm hands. Remain ever active with honest efforts even in old age with grace. Be brave like a lion/lioness with gentle heart. Elevate soul to the highest peak of spiritual joy.

Human Beings - Children of God

O Children ! Live full span of life.

Welcome the old age with grace.

Remain ever active with honest efforts.

Ascend day by day higher and higher summits of eternal glory and bliss.

Awake, arise, resolve.

And take the banner of truth in firm hands.

March forward and annihilate.

Those who are evil spirited.

O soul, be brave like a lion and a lioness.

And strike down foes.

Resolve to elevate soul to the highest peak of spiritual joy.

- The Holy Vedas

ॐॐॐॐॐ

God calls 'O Divine Children! Awake,Arise and march ahead with courage facing troubles bravely. While offering love and respect do constant hard work with diligence and devotion for welfare of humanity and creation'.

Human Beings - Children of God

Godcalls ! O Children !Come, March ahead with courage

Face troubles bravely.

No obstacles can check your progress.

While you are on right path.

Be wakeful, O godly brave children!.

Throw your weapons at the violent and cruel.

Achieve objectives through own efforts.

I help those who help themselves

And work hard under divine guidance.

I leave here those who are not progressive and benevolent.

Ye enlightened children ! Uplift the fallen and degraded.

Uplift those who have sinned to begin life anew.

Remember, offering love and respect alone are not enough.

Constant hard work and diligence are essential for success.

Then alone I shower my blessing upon them.

Awake, Arise O Divine Children with rise of glorious Sun with love but without ego.

Full of zest and zeal progress on the path of glory.

Remember ! I abide within the inner self of all human beings.

ॐॐॐॐॐ

Find delight in hard work with devotion and righteousness. God is the giver. Share fruits of hard work. Be noble. Perform noble deeds diligently. Be happy. Make others happy. Have hearts full of generosity, kindness and love. Arise, Awake, work at the knocking of dawn Enlightened the souls with divine words. Enjoy riches sharing with all.

Human Beings - Children of God

O adorable Supreme Father God.

Grant us wisdom.

That we find delight in hard work with devotion and righteousness.

Enjoy the fruits that bear sharing under thy guardianship.
And with thy blessing, thou art the giver of all.
May through our nobility and noble deeds.
Earn happiness and make others happy.
May our hearts be full of generosity, kindness and love.
May we lead life on the ideals and in spirit of sacrifice.
May we share thy spiritual knowledge and experience.
O Supreme Father ! May our souls' speed be of tempest and brightness.
May souls be so bright to enlighten the whole Universe.
May we awake, arise at the knocking of dawn.
May we enjoy riches sharing with all through patience, perseverance and thy grace.
May we work diligently at all times with devotional righteousness.
Following the path of self sacrifice may we render service to humanity.

ॐॐॐॐॐ

Human Beings - Children of God

Godcalls ! O Children.
Realise, All in One, One in All.
Behave with others as you would with yourself.
Look upon all the livings as your bosom friends.
Know that in all of them reside one universal soul.
All are but a part of that universal soul.
Believe all are your soul mates, love all alike.
Awaken the divine qualities of forgiveness, compassion and service.
That will make you lovable in the eyes of all.
Withdraw from all strife and struggles of life.
Harbor no enmity for anyone in your heart.
Fear no one, have sublime peace.

Experience intense joy.

Feel secure under God's infinite shelter.

- The Holy Vedas

ॐॐॐॐॐ

God calls O Children! Brighten the intellect for doing divine duties. Never lose sight of earthly duties. Unfold the hidden truths. Be brave to overcome evils with daring courage. Realize own inner strength. Fear no one. Be steady. Have wings of virtues and vitality. Let nothing destroy character.

God's call to His Children

Let not the wings of soul take you so high.

That you lose the sight of earthly duties.

Attain fortitude and firmness.

By obeying the commands of God, never defy them.

Brighten intellect for doing divine duties.

And unfolding the hidden truth.

Be brave and overcome evils.

With daring courage.

Realise own inner strength, fear no one.

Be steady and strong.

O brave! Advance speedily crush the violent forces of enemy.

Have the speed that of a tempest and strength that of a wild horse.

Overpowers the adversaries with a heroic spirit.

Have wings of virtues and vitality.

Establish yourself on the surface of the earth.

Fill the firmament with your radiance.

Cover the sphere with your lustre.

Spread effulgence in all directions.

Let nothing destroy your character.

- The Holy Vedas

ॐॐॐॐॐ

God calls O Children! Rise up. Sink not. Be brave, invincible, resolute and steadfast to progress. Glow like the radiant sun. Move forward with firm steps. Fear not. Human life is like a turbulent stream. Be brave to step into it to smoothly cross over it. A stream of eternal life will flow.

God's commandments to His Children

O Children! Rise up, sink not and cast away the bonds.

Fear not, Be not frustrated.

Shine like the flames of a blazing fire.

Glow like the radiant sun.

Human life is like a turbulent stream.

Be brave to step into it to smoothly cross over it.

O human soul! Gather your strength.

A stream of eternal life flows.

Move forward with firm steps.

Cross over the realm of eternal glory.

Live with a heroic spirit till ripe old age.

Be equipped with strong will-power.

The Brave are invincible.

Be brave, invincible, resolute and steadfast to win.

God guides His children to the radiant light of wisdom and to solemn peace.

Be secure under your Universal Father's infinite shelter.

- The Holy Vedas

ॐॐॐॐॐ

God calls O Children! Cultivate strength of will power. An idle mind is an easy prey to evil thoughts. Get rid of the feelings of inferiority, superiority, envy, greed, anger and other evil impulses. Be friendly and live in harmony and peace. Be virtuous, righteous, hardworking, helpful, gentle, humble with strength and love alone. Fix heart and mind on God.

God's commandments to His children

Know that an idle mind is an easy prey to evil thoughts.

Engage in the process of self-realization.

Evil desires are automatically consumed and destroyed.

Cultivate the strength of will power.

To conquer the passionate urges of the sense organs.

Dispel the deep dark curtain of ignorance.

Destroy the voracious instinct of greed.

Get rid of the feelings of envy, inferiority, superiority, greed and other evil impulses.

Cast off anger from your heart like an arrow from the bow.

Be friendly and live together in harmony.

Reform, if failed either sap or destroy wicked persons + + +

Who torture righteous, good, honest persons.

Invoke the blessing of God on those who either harm you or the good people.

Have firm determination to subdue or destroy all evils.

Your vigour is your strength, manifest own divinity

Dispel ignorance through patience and perseverance.

Be virtuous, righteous, hard working, helpful, gentle, humble

With strength, lovable and praying or prayful.

Be then blessed with good health, happiness and good fortune.

- Based on the Holy Vedas

ॐॐॐॐॐ

Behold God. See the Divine Light in the heart and center of two eyes. Compass the mind towards Him. Comprehend Him. Speak to Him with heart's language. Feel His presence. Be fearless to carve your own path. Do not have craving for material gains and fame.

Spiritual Discipline/ Prayer

Behold Him, Be eager to know Him.

See the Divine Light placed in the heart and centre of two eyes.

Compass the mind towards Him.

Comprehend Him, speak to Him with heart's language.

Be fearless to carve out own path.

Ask one who knows it.

Feel His presence and see Him.

Feel He has acceoted your heart's songs.

Feel that I am full of spirit and bliss.

Material gains do not tempt me.

Neither I have craving for fame nor it attracts me.

I am aware of divine qualities and brilliance.

- Based on the Holy Vedas

ॐॐॐॐॐ

O God, Our Father, Mother, bless us to find the sure way of truth, obtain humility, become intelligent and wise to traverse worldly path easily and live perpetually in a state of evevrlasting spiritual esctasy.

Spiritual Discipline/Prayer

O Gracious Lord!

Bless us to find out the sure way of truth.

May through resolute will we obtain consecration.

May we obtain humility by consecration.

May we obtain reverence and faith through humility.

May by faith we obtain the knowledge of truth.

Bless us to be intelligent and wise to traverse worldly path easily.

Bless us to feel around us an unwavering flame of eternal light.

Protecting us from all adversities.

O Lord! Bless us to live perpetually in a state of everlasting spiritual ecstasy. *- Based on the Holy Vedas*

ॐॐॐॐॐ

O God, our Father! Bless us to know the true nature of soul and virtues of earth and divinity. Bless us to be free from clutches of material world and be in the domain of unlimited ocean of eternal glory. May we shine with spirituality like the glowing Sun.

Spiritual Prayer

O Lord! Bless us to resolve.

To dedicate our life to the service of mankind.

And uplift them to divinity.

Bless us to know the true nature of soul.

And identify ourselves with it completely.

O Lord! Thou art the Supreme being beyond the limits of darkness.

O Lord! Bless us to uphold the true virtues of earth and divinity.

May our spiritual teachers takes us in the inmost fold of their loving hearts.

As a mother embraces her child.

With austere life, learning and hardwork we serve all and respect cosmic powers.

Bless us to be free from the clutches of material world.

Bless us to be in the domain of unlimited ocean of eternal glory.

May our soul for knowledge be eternal.

May we shine with spirituality like the glowing Sun.

- *Based on the Holy Vedas*

ॐॐॐॐॐ

Attain liberation through discriminative power, devotion, love and total surrender while marching on the path of righteousness for work.

Bondage & liberation

In the realization of spiritual bliss.

The human soul is released from bondage of physical sphere

And rises above celestial realm.

Becoming one with Brahman.

With freedom absolute.

Be free from self-inflicted bondages.

Through discriminative power attain liberation.

Through total surrender, devotion and love have union with Brahman.

Free from desires and temptations march on the path of righteousness.

Offer reverence to God and crave for His tender love.

May virtuous Lord free us from successive bond and tie.

May Mother Eternity and Supreme Lord give us motherly love.

- Based on the Holy Vedas

ॐॐॐॐॐ

Have creative intellect. Work with diligence and devotion. Be resolute with virtues of Supreme Lord. Look on all with friendly eyes and harmony. Inspire people to perform duty with dedication.

An Enlightened Being/Spiritual Being

Have creative intellect.

Dedicate life to Godly work.

Work with diligence and devotion.

Inspire people to perform duty with dedication.

Free of desires and full of devotional love.

Attain highest glory and everlasting peace.

Be resolute with the virtues of Supreme Lord.

Look on all with friendly eyes and harmony.

Experience complete harmony with all.

- Based on the Holy Vedas

ॐॐॐॐॐ

All living beings are a apart of the Universal soul. Be friendly. Love all. Hate no one. Feel and affirm that of being trustee of wealth. Be enriched by love of all. Perform all acts with devotion, wisdom and righteousness with meditating mind and love. Be noblest of all and loving Child of God.

An Enlightened Being

All human beings are children of God.

All living beings are manifestation of God.

Love all intensely conceiving a part of Universal soul.

Do not look down on anyone.

No one is lower or higher.

Never hate anyone.

Never fall victim of hatred, grief or sorrow.

Too much wealth makes one greedy.

Feel and affirm that of being trustee of wealth.

Create and generate wealth for welfare of God's creation.

Flow with the stream of love for all and happiness.

Be enriched by love of all.

Perform all acts with devotion and full wisdom.

With submission and glorious vision of God.

Pray for God's love and release of all bondages.

With meditating mind and heart full of love.

Be noblest of all.

Have glorious success and humble fame.

- Based on the Holy Vedas

ॐॐॐॐॐ

O Lord of the entire universe. We offer reverence to Thee. Thou art the sovereign of the world and cosmos. Thou rule the past, present and future. Around thee all the planets of the universe move. Thou command the world existent or non-existent. Thou art the absolute Bliss. To thy glory we sing the songs of soul.

Reverence to the Supreme Lord

To Him, the most exalted Lord offer reverence.

To Him, who rules the past, the present and the future.

Who presides over the entire universe.

Who is the overall sovereign of the world and the cosmos.

Who is above the reach at the time of death.

Who is immutable and absolute Bliss.

Who is immense in vastness.

Whose glory is unparalleled.

Around whom all the planets of the universe move.

Who commands all the world, existent or non-existent.

To Him in most reverence, we bow again and again.

To His glory we sing the songs of love of soul.

- Based on the Holy Vedas

ॐॐॐॐॐ

Divine words of sages are full of wisdom. They beat through all obstacles. These words draw themselves to God. These divine words highlight every aspect of God. They provide us unmingled bliss and fulfill all our desires. These divine words spring us constantly into our divine awareness.

Divine Words

Great streams of divine words flow out.

From the minds of sages.

Surging with the high waves of wisdom.

They beat through all obstacles.

The divine words draw themselves to God.

These solemn words highlight every aspect of God.

Three Vedas are packed with all radiant wisdom.

They provide us a store of rare excellence of unmingled bliss.

He who fulfills all our desires.

Spring us constantly into our divine awareness.

So much that He voices aloud His presence.

- Based on the Holy Vedas

ॐॐॐॐॐ

The Fire Divine rises and spreads over all worlds establishing our relation with nature's forces. The fire of penance purifies the soul just as the flame of fire purifies gold. Make the journey of life in the spirit of dedication. Our noble works prosper in the spirit of dedication. Pray to God to enable us to understand the threads of warp and weft of His creation and surrender to His will.

Fire Divine

The Fire Divine rises and spreads over all worlds.

Establish our relation with Nature's forces.

The fire of penance purifies the soul.

Just as the flame of fire purifies gold.

The pure soul alone is worthy of exaltation.

The Ahuti or oblations for yajna rise into space.

Get mingled with air and beautify the atmosphere.

They soar to the rays of the sun.

Therefore they bring rain for our betterment.

May our journey of life be made in the spirit of dedication.

May our life prosper in the spirit of dedication.

May all our noble works prosper in the spirit of dedication.

O Lord! Enable us to conduct our life yajna in the spirit of dedication.

O Lord! Enable us to understand the threads of warp and weft of Thy creation.

O Lord! Give us strength to surrender our will at the altar of thy will.

- Based on the Holy Vedas

ॐॐॐॐॐ

God calls, O Children! Adapt Dharma (Righteousness), Artha (Wealth), Kama (Family) and Moksha (Liberation). When married as husband and wife, live happily with love and affection to each other. Be considerate to each other. Beget noble, brave children, have noble and brave grand and great grand children. Be wise and benevolent. Never go against inner voice of soul. Develop intellect to control mind by devotion and prayers. Both live blissful lives. Have magnanimous hearts and common mission.

Family Life - Wedded Man & Woman

God calls, O Children!

Adapt Dharma (Righteousness), Artha (Wealth), Kama (Family) and Moksha (Liberation).

O man and women when married as husband and wife.

Look at each other with love and affection.

Live together happily without malice with one spirit.

Be considerate and affectionate towards each other.

Live joyously in home with children, grand children and great grand children.

Follow the path of duty, justice, love and spirituality.

Beget noble and brave children.

Both be wise, benevolent and live to inspire all with blissful life.

Never go against inner voice of soul.

Develop intellect by devotion and prayers.

Be respectful with love to elders and loveable to youngers.

Be respectful with love to in-laws of each one and family.

Have magnanimous hearts.

March ahead and progress with common aim and goal.

- Based on the Holy Vedas

ॐॐॐॐॐ

God calls, O Wedded Man! Be virtuous. Be master of habits not slave. Be free from vice of addiction. Be courageous. Be respectful and dutiful to parents, in-laws, seniors and family. Be serviceable, lovable, humble and gentle to all. Perform marital duties with love. Obey God assigned duties. Pray to God for a happy family life and wedded bliss. Work hard with devotion and righteousness selflessly and fearlessly.

Family Life – Wedded Man

O Wedded Man! Be virtuous. Be master of habits not slave.

Be free from vices of addiction.

With the courage and conviction follow the path of Dharma.

Remain respectful and dutiful to parents, in-laws, seniors and family.

Be serviceable, lovable, humble and gentle to children and all.

Perform marital duties with love, strength, humour and valour.

Obey God - assigned duties and be happy.

Pray to Lord for a happy family life, wedded bliss and joy to all.

- *Based on the Holy Vedas*

ॐॐॐॐॐ

Family Life - O Wedded Woman

O Wedded Woman! Unite and become the guiding light of this new family.

Endowed with Dharma (righteousness), intelligence, understanding and love.

Care and respect for all the members of the family.

Share their joys and sorrows.

Attend to the well being of all.

Bring happiness and prosperity to this house.

Be free from greed, selfishness, ego, possessiveness, me and mine.

Speak and behave with harmony and sweetness.

Be all unanimous and of one accord.

Be not separated from one another;

Talk to each one sweet words with love.

Serve and hold in high esteem parents and elders.

Serve, share and love youngers with intelligence and understanding.

With love share food and other things.

Treat all children equally with your children.

Be honest and loyal to the husband and family.

Have positive thoughts and vibrations.

Never pay heed to negative opinions against in-laws and family.

Treat in-laws as own parents.

Treat family members as own brothers & sisters and children.

Perform household duties while progressing in career.

Be courageous, generous and benevolent.

Achieve Bliss and Admiration.

The Supreme Lord by His mystical powers blesses both.

With sublime love, prosperity, health, happiness and humble fame.

- Based on the Holy Vedas

ॐॐॐॐॐ

Family Life – Parents of girls & man

Realize that parents of the wedded woman/girl part with their beloved daughter.

They had nurtured her with all care and love.

Parents of married men should treat the wedded woman with respect, care and love.

Treat her like own daughter.

Never find fault in her.

Give positive vibrations and suggestions with love.

Know and realize that new comer will take time to adjust in new environment.

Never criticize her and her parents.

Keep her happy to keep son happy.

Do not load on her all household works.

Give time to her and son to enjoy their lives.

O parents of girl do not interfere in the life of daughter.

Do not feed her mind with negative thoughts about in-laws.

Advise her to treat husband's parents as own parents.

Advise her to treat husband's family as own.

Advise her to treat husband's family children as her own – God gifted.

She brings happiness and prosperity to both houses.

With happiness she will beget noble children and honour all.

- Based on the Holy Vedas

ॐॐॐॐॐ

God calls O Children!

Become instruments of my will.

Be firmly established in the world.

Earn honestly by honest hard work and share generously.

Be on the path of own inner wisdom and law.

Never gamble, never be addict, never be selfish.

Never waste, never be proud of wealth.

Be wise in using wealth.

Goddess of Wealth, Mother Lakshmi does not stay in home of addict & unvirtuous person.

Know that the wheels of the wealth-chariot are ever rolling.

Riches come today to one, tomorrow to another.

O Children! Have the habit of working hard honestly with vigour and vitality.

The law of Providence is such that the wealth earned through evil means is scattered away.

The wealth earned through pious means flourishes.

Be virtuous, Inspire, Aspire others to be virtuous.

- Based on the Holy Vedas

ॐॐॐॐॐ

God Calls O Children!

Be efficient with spiritual lustre.

Earn wealth by hard work with honesty.

Do not exploit others.

Be on the path of righteousness.

Have the counsel with own inner wisdom.

Never gamble, never be addict; be content.

Enjoy the wealth earned by honest means while sharing with needy.

O Children! I then bestow the best treasureson such children.

I bless such children with peace and joy.

Such righteous, benevolent children never suffer a setback.

Even in days of adversity, sorrow does not touch them.

Truthful, hard working, honest, righteous, benevolent children never suffer.

They are blessed to create wealth for generating wealth for welfare.

- Based on the Holy Vedas

ॐॐॐॐॐ

God Calls, O Leaders!

O Leader! Realise that the people have elected you.

Be just and merciful, be just and firm.

Be strong, just, wise, honest and spiritual.

Like a lion drive away all evil forces by being strengthened by people.

Be formidable and firm like a rock.

Follow the path of duty.

Be trustee of wealth and nature of the nation.

Engage the people in hard work with honesty and righteousness.

Be not engaged in populist measures squandering the wealth of the nation.

Do not tax the people heavily.

Do not create an army of idle people.

Trust the children of the nation and help them to create wealth.

Never create/conflict based on caste, religion, lower and upper, rich and poor.

Never create/conflict among minority and majority.

Promote unity in diversity.

Protect merchants, warriors, artisans and all who build Nation.

Protect women, children and senior citizens.

Live like a saint, not only appear like a saint.

Work hard, be fearless, be spiritual and believe in the essence of all religions.

Have uniform laws for all the people.

While being on the spiritual path promote spirituality and unity in diversity.

- Based on the Holy Vedas

ॐॐॐॐॐ

God's Manifestation

God Calls O Children!

God Calls O Children!

All living beings are my manifestation.

I am seated in the heart of all.

There is no caste by birth, no lower or upper, all are divine.

O Brahmins (scholars), be not proud of either knowledge or worship.

Impart knowledge to all, allow worship to all, love all, hate none.

O Warriors (kshatrias), with bold spirit resort the land, wealth, possession of the righteous people and the nation.

Be soft in temperament, never torture people after winning.

Have the spirit of spirituality, empathy, humility and love.

Restore the wealth of the people and their family members.

Honour all women even enemies;

Mother Infinity grants success.

O Artisans! Skilled in constructive works, do useful works.

Develop technology for the welfare and prosperity of the people.

O (Vyasa) Businessmen! Engage in creating wealth and generating wealth for welfare of all.

Be honest and righteous in dealings, never exploit.

Be gentle, humble, hardworking, honest , cooperative and serviceful.

Be trustee of wealth and use wealth in the spirit of generosity.

- Based on the Holy Vedas

ॐॐॐॐॐ

The Holy Veda

Prayer for Motherland & Humanity

Prayers to Supreme Lord for Nation and humanity

O Supreme Lord, let eminent scholars

Possessing of spiritual knowledge be born in our Nation

Let us be brave, kind hearted.

Let righteous warriors and statesman be born in our nation

Let there be plentiful cows giving plentiful milk

Let there be virtuous woman and valorous man

May clouds shower rains as much as required

May the soft blowing breeze refresh and revitalize us

The treasure of immortal joy lies hidden within divine cloud

O divine cloud! Bestow on us a little of immortal joy

May there be plenty of fruits bearing trees

May there be medicinal herbs conducive to health

May the Lord of the field be sweet to us

May the Lord nourishes us, our cows, bulls, horses and all being

O farmers plough the fields happily to live on harvest yourselves and all Honour farmers.

Pray Mother Divine to give farmers with plenty yield year after year

May She grants prosperity to farmers

To make us to live healthy and happily.

Let all live with joy, harmony and peace
Let all follow their own respective religion.
Let no one hate others religions.
Let not try to convert others in own religion.
Have faith all in one and one in all.

ॐॐॐॐॐ

Mother Cows

The Mother cows have come and brought us good fortunes
May Mother cows yield milk for worship and nourishing us
May Supreme Lord protects the cows, bulls, ...
May God increase wealth for everwho keep and protect them
May the wicked do not injure them and rob them
May they never be led to slaughtering house.

Glimpses of Previous Confluence

2010

2011

Glimpses of Previous Confluence

2012

2012

Glimpses of Previous Confluence

2013

2014

Glimpses of Previous Confluence

2015 New Delhi

Glimpses of Previous Confluence

2015 London

Glimpses of Previous Confluence

2016 Mumbai

2016 New Delhi

Glimpses of Previous Confluence

2017 Kolkata

Glimpses of Previous Confluence

2018 Kolkata

The Universe

The all-controlling immortal wheel of the universe is revolving in infinite space.

The wisdom of God, united with energy manages the whole universe.

On this energy rest and depend all regions and planets.

In the very infinite are well placed, the mind, the vital breath and the name.

All these elements enjoy themselves.

At His very approach.

In the self-same Infinite are fully established.

The austerity, the grandeur, the vast universe and the Vedic

He is the Lord of all.

In Him all divine cosmic powers become one.

He is the Father of all hymns and praises.

Messenger of all Divines.

He purifieth all regions and watcheth all creatures.

In Him all deities become one and only one.

The sun, the eye of the universe is divinely placed.

The whole of the universe is stained in the omnipresent and omnipotent God, we see Him in various forms.

He brings to light, all these worlds pervading the vast sky.

Dr. H. P. Kanoria

- Based on the Holy Vedas

Media Coverage

Hon'ble President of India, Shri Pranab Mukherjee inaugurating the 9th World Confluence of Humanity, Power & Spirituality held in New Delhi, India.

Late Dr. A. P. J. Abdul Kalam, Former President of India, Lighting the lamp at the 4th World Confluence of Humanity, Power & Spirituality held in Kolkata, India.

Former President Pranab Mukherjee (C) receives a plaque at the 10th World Confluence of Humanity, Power and Spirituality as Kanoria Foundation chairman H P Kanoria (L) and Hemant Kanoria (R) look on

A conglomeration of Spiritual Gurus, Dignitaries and great Humanitarians of the world!

Harmful Effects of Alcohol

We all are aware that alcohol is bad for health and it has a negative effect on the body because it mixes in his blood and reaches all the vital parts of the body, having a damaging effect on them. Over 30% of Indian consumes Alcohol. India is the third largest consumer of liquor. Let us have a look at the harmful effects of drinking alcohol in detail.

... on the Brain

The worst effect of alcohol addiction is on the brain. As mentioned above, alcohol directly affects the central nervous system and slows down its function. The other effects include:

• Impaired behavior and judgment • Memory loss • Lack of concentration and coordination • Impaired vision and hearing • Slower motor skills and reactions • Mood swings • Slurred speech

... on the Liver

Alcohol slows down the process of metabolism in liver. If this continues for a longer time, it can result in permanent damage of the liver. Effects of alcohol on the liver include:

• Jaundice • Liver cirrhosis • Alcoholic hepatitis • Alcoholic fatty liver

• Liver cancer

... on Digestive System

Excess consumption of alcohol damages the internal lining of the GI tract. It indirectly affects the internal organs and glands of the digestive system. Alcohol side effects on digestive system include:

• Vomiting • Peptic ulcers • Throat cancer • Stomach cancer • Gastritis • Haemorrhage • Colon cancer

... on Reproductive System

One may not be aware but drinking alcohol indirectly affects the reproductive system in both men and women. In their pregnancy period, women are advised to stop alcohol consumption completely as it can lead to mental retardation in babies. The following are the other damaging effects of alcohol on the reproductive system:

• Infertility • Impotency • Breast cancer • Sterility (in men) • Atrophy of testis (in men)

Symptoms

• Demand more money • Waste more time in toilet • Late return in homes • Carelessness • Not attentive • Irritation • Short tempered • Physically Weak • No health discipline

Religious Commands

Christianity: "Wine is a mocker, beer is a brawler, and whoever staggers because of them is not wise" (Proverbs 20:1).

Islam: "O ye who believe! Intoxicants and Gambling, (Dedication of) stones, And (divination by) arrows, Are an Abomination – of Satan's handiwork; Eschew such (abomination), That ye may prosper." [Al-Qurân 5:90]

Sikhism: Drugs, Smoking and Alcohol are strictly forbidden for Sikhs

Buddhism: The Buddha encouraged his followers to refrain from consuming any kind of intoxicant. This included alcohol, cigarettes and drugs.

These substances are said to be inconsistent with Buddhist beliefs as they distort the mind. Buddhists regard the mind as precious; they work diligently, through meditation, to master it.

Hinduism: Any form of intoxication is forbidden in Hinduism; no alcohol or drugs.